ISLAMIC URBANISM IN HUMAN HISTORY

ISLAMIC URBANISM IN HUMAN HISTORY

POLITICAL POWER AND SOCIAL NETWORKS

Edited by SATO Tsugitaka

Routledge
Taylor & Francis Group
LONDON AND NEW YORK

First published in 1997 by
Kegan Paul International

This edition first published in 2009 by
Routledge
2 Park Square, Milton Park, Abingdon, Oxfordshire OX14 4RN

Simultaneously published in the USA and Canada
by Routledge
711 Third Avenue, New York, NY 10017
First issued in paperback 2014

Routledge is an imprint of the Taylor and Francis Group, an informa business

Transferred to Digital Printing 2009

British Library Cataloguing in Publication Data
A catalogue record for this book is available from the British Library

ISBN 978-0-7103-0560-2 (hbk)
ISBN 978-0-415-76014-0 (pbk)

Publisher's Note
The publisher has gone to great lengths to ensure the quality of this reprint but points out that some imperfections in the original copies may be apparent. The publisher has made every effort to contact original copyright holders and would welcome correspondence from those they have been unable to trace.

CONTENTS

PREFACE

Just before I left Japan for the United States at the end of March 1993, Professor Itagaki Yuzo suggested that I propose a round table to be held at the 18th International Congress of Historical Sciences in Montreal in 1995. I was on sabbatical that year, so after applying to the Congress Committee in Paris for the round table, I departed from Tokyo in search of new materials on the *iqṭā'* system of medieval Islam at libraries in the United States and the Middle Eastern countries.

In May 1993 while I was at Princeton, I received a letter from Tokyo, informing me that the committee had accepted my proposal to hold a round table on *Islamic Urbanism in Human History: Political Power and Social Networks.* I answered to the Committee and continued my research trip from Princeton University to Harvard University, Suleymaniye Library in Istanbul, Asad Library in Damascus, and the Egyptian National Library in Cairo.

In Damascus I met Dr. James A. Reilly, who was also on sabbatical there. He became the first specialist in Syrian cities under the Ottoman rule to consent to participate in the round table.

When the Japan-USA Area Studies Conference was held in Tokyo in early March 1995, Dr. Ann M. Lesch and Dr. Anne H. Betteridge (both from Middle East Studies Association of North America) kindly introduced me to Dr. Diane Singerman who studies informal network formed in contemporary Cairo. Dr. Abdul-Karim Rafeq and Dr. Iik A. Mansurnoor have been our friends since the International Conference on *Urbanism in Islam* held in Tokyo in 1989, while Dr. Mohamed Mezzine joined us through an introduction by Professor Miura Toru and Dr. Haneda Masashi who met him during their field work in the Maghreb countries in 1994.

All these members assembled on the morning of 29 August

1995 in Montreal. The papers submitted were empirically oriented studies in their fields, but the time was too limited to discuss the subject matter sufficiently. Luckily, we are given opportunity to continue the discussion by Kegan Paul International Ltd., who kindly consented to publish the proceedings submitted to the round table, thus opening the exchange of views on the subject of Islamic urbanism in human history to a much wider audience. I would like to express my gratitude also to the Tokyo Club for its funding of the original round table and the compilation of the book.

Finally, the compilation of this book was accomplished with the gracious help provided by Mr. Horii Yutaka (Post Graduate Student, The University of Tokyo), Mr. Morimoto Kazuo (Research Associate, The University of Tokyo), Mr. Nakamachi Nobutaka and Miss Watabe Ryoko (both Post Graduate Students, The University of Tokyo).

7 April 1996
SATO Tsugitaka
The University of Tokyo

INTRODUCTION

SATO Tsugitaka

The research project, *Urbanism in Islam*, was carried out during the years 1988–1991 in Japan, as a program of Scientific Research on Priority Areas under the aegis of the Ministry of Education, Science and Culture. It aimed at studying the various aspects of urbanism in Islam in comparative perspective. Nearly 200 historians, sociologists, anthropologists, economists, political scientists, urban architects and planners, including 70 scholars from abroad, participated in the program to conduct synchronical and diachronical comparative research, in an attempt to disclose cross-sectional dimensions of urban phenomena with special reference to Islamic urbanism.

At the First International Conference on *Urbanism in Islam*, which was held at the Middle Eastern Culture Center in Japan, Tokyo, in 1989, over 80 papers were submitted to such research sections as "Methodology in Urban Studies," "The City's External Network," "Urban Images of Muslim Intellectuals," "City Planning and the Structure of Urban Society," "Cities and Political Power," and "Intra-City Networks and Popular Movements." An important achievement of the conference was the discussion of Islamic urbanism comparing it with, for example, Chinese, Indian, African and European urban societies. The proceedings were published in five volumes under the title *Urbanism in Islam* (Tokyo, 1989).[1]

The second International Conference on *Urbanism in Islam* was held also in Tokyo the following year. The conference was

---

[1]T. Yukawa ed., *Urbanism in Islam: The Proceedings of the International Conference on Urbanism in Islam*, 5 vols., Tokyo, 1989 (*Urbanism in Islam I*).

composed of four workshops: (a) Change and Continuity in the Urban Settlement Patterns, (b) *Waqf* Institutions – Towards the Comparative Study of Public Goods, (c) A Challenge to the Notion of "Islamic Cities," and (d) Contemporary Cities and Islam. The proceedings were published in one volume under the same title ***Urbanism in Islam*** (Tokyo, 1994).[1]

Another important result of the research carried out on the subject over three years has been published in the book ***Islamic Urban Studies: Historical Review and Perspectives.***[2] The book surveys urban studies done since the 19th century concerning the five regions that came early under Islamic influence: al-Maghrib, al-Mashriq, Turkey, Iran and Central Asia. Through comparing academic works on the cities of those five regions, the co-authors attempted to show the present issues in Islamic urban studies and suggests new perspectives for future research. Concerning the Japanese studies done during the project of ***Urbanism in Islam,*** we may refer to an epitome by A. Goto in ***Historical Studies in Japan (VIII): 1988–1992*** compiled by The National Committee of Japanese Historians.[3]

At this Round Table 10, Islamic urbanism in human history will be reviewed based on the achievements of the Project. First

---

[1]T. Yukawa ed., ***Urbanism in Islam: The Proceedings of the 2nd International Conference on Urbanism in Islam,*** Tokyo, 1994 (***Urbanism in Islam II***).

[2]M. Haneda and T. Miura eds., ***Islamic Urban Studies: Historical Review and Perspectives,*** London, 1994. On the studies of Islamic and Middle Eastern History in general, see R. S. Humphreys, ***Islamic History: A Frame Work for Inquiry,*** Princeton, 1991.

[3]Goto Akira, "Urbanism in Islam," in The National Committee of Japanese Historians ed., ***Historical Studies in Japan (VIII): 1988–1992***, Tokyo, 1995. On Islamic and Middle Eastern studies in Japan since the beginning of Meiji Era, see ***Bibliography of Islamic and Middle Eastern Studies in Japan 1868–1988***, compiled and published by The Centre for East Asian Cultural Studies for Unesco, The Toyo Bunko, Tokyo, 1992.

of all, we must recall that city-states and urban life first appeared in history in ancient Mesopotamia. According to A. L. Oppenheim, urbanization occurred quite early in the third millennium B.C. in southern Mesopotamia. The typical Mesopotamian city consisted of three parts: the city proper, the outer city and the harbor section. Both the palace and temple operated basically as "internal-circulation organizations" centered in the person of the lord of the manor, deity or king.[1] Cities since the early Islamic period have inherited the traditions of Mesopotamian urban life, as well as that of the Mediterranean world under the Byzantine rule. People in the Middle East thus have been masters of urban life, being accustomed to the advanced urbanism in human history.

Certainly we have doubts about the notion of "Islamic city" or "Islamic urbanism" being uniformly applied to the regions from Central Asia to Morocco, as often indicated in the previous studies. However, we may cite some characteristics of urbanism in Islam as compared with urbanism in non-Islamic world. Here I would like to compare the Middle Eastern cities of medieval Islam with Japanese cities under the regime of the Tokugawa shogunate during the Edo period (1600–1868).

According to N. Yoshida,[2] the urban residential space of the Edo period city was divided up in a very ordered way according to social status: that is, between the *samurai* class (warrior vassals of *daimyo*, the feudal lords), *Shinto* priests and Buddhist monks, and the common townsfolk. The largest portion of the city's land area was occupied by the feudal lords, whose dwelling compound existed as a space completely isolated from the surrounding urban society. During the Edo period Buddhist institutions tended to

---

[1] A. L. Oppenheim, "Mesopotamia—Land of Many Cities," in I. M. Lapidus ed.,*Middle Eastern Cities: Ancient, Islamic, and Contemporary Middle Eastern Urbanism,* Berkeley and Los Angeles, 1969, pp.3-16.

[2] N. Yoshida, "The Spatial Configuration and Social Structure of the Great Pre-Modern City of Edo," in *Urbanism in Islam I*, vol.2, pp.37-73.

sprout up throughout the city in clusters, forming sections called *teramachi* or "temple towns." Yoshida states that a large part of the products consumed by *samurai* was supplied directly by petty merchants living in the backstreets of the city. They provided *samurai* and Buddhist monks with a corvée labor force as well as everyday necessities. In other words, the wealthy and powerful townsfolk were unavoidably dependent on the function of urban provision borne by these backstreet residents.

From the above viewpoint, let us now extract some points to be compared. First, as to the spatial structure of the city, we find isolated spaces of the citadel or palace for the rulers in such old Muslim cities as Baghdad, Damascus, Cairo and Samarqand.[1] However, the citadel's land mass was rather small, compared with the city of Edo, where two-thirds of the residential space was taken up by the *Shogun* and *samurai* residences. Secondly, for Muslim cities in medieval times, it seems difficult to identify any well-ordered division of residential space according to social status as seen in the city of Edo. These facts reflect the clear differences between the two societies with respect to the manner in which political power-holders ruled over the townsfolk.

Now, what about the formation of temple towns? In Islamic society the complex made up of mosque and markets (*sūq, bāzār*) formed the core of urban life. We find a common characteristic in that religious institutions were constructed and maintained by the donations received from wealthy patrons or merchants, but the market residents in Muslim cities were not obliged to offer corvée to the mosque managers or religious leaders. Different from the Muslim society, the temples of Edo and the common people living around them were closely tied in patron-client

---

[1] On the composition of the town/madina and the citadel or court-citadel, see J. L. Bacharach, "The Court-citadel: An Islamic Urban Symbol of Power," in *Urbanism in Islam I*, vol.3, pp.205-245.

relationships.

Another point concerns the relationship between the *samurai* class and the common people. Yoshida states, "Moreover, the maintenance of the [*samurai*] estates' buildings and facilities, not to mention keeping sufficient inventories of weapons on hand, could not have been accomplished without the artisans and tradepeople living close by."[1] I. M. Lapidus has related that during the Mamluk period the rulers governed cities not by administration, but by holding all of the vital social networks in their hands. They established direct ties to the *'ulamā'*, high and low, to merchants, to the common people of the quarters and markets, and finally to the lumpenproletariat of the city. He asserts that these political ties took the form of patronage-clientage relations, relations between two people such that one protected and sustained the other, who in turn provided his patron with certain resources or services.[2]

Although Yoshida does not say that the *samurai* protected the common people, the Tokugawa shogunate did provide maintenance for the public safety of Edo by appointing guards in the streets and quarters of the city. Accordingly, we may find that patron-client relations in both societies were in principle reciprocal. This leads us to the conclusion that social networks as described by Lapidus were not unique to Islamic society in the Middle East.

Lapidus has himself attempted comparison between Chinese and Islamic society in an article entitled "Hierarchies and Networks."[3] In this article Lapidus characterizes Chinese society

---

[1]Yoshida, "The Spatial Configuration," p.58.

[2]I. M. Lapidus, *Muslim Cities in the Late Middle Ages*, Cambridge, Mass., 1967, pp.185-191.

[3]I. M. Lapidus, "Hierarchies and Social Networks: A Comparison of Chinese and Islamic Societies," in F. J. Wakemann ed., *Conflict and Control in Late Imperial China*, Berkeley, 1975, pp.26-42.

as lineage, gentry, bureaucracy, emperor, and world order forming a hierarchy of levels, the architectural backbone of the Chinese order. In contrast, Islamic societies did not possess the integral unity of Chinese society. Instead of ramified lineages, one finds a vast mosaic of small groups with little unity or even similarity of type. In this sense the network model fits the actualities of Islamic society and enables us to comprehend a society which has a coherent overall order without formal structure.

During the Edo period we find features similar to Chinese society. That is to say, a solid class structure composed of *samurai,* cultivators, artisans and merchants, each one of them educated in the Confucianist tradition of respecting parents, lord or elders. However, the reciprocal patronage relationships also appeared between the ruling class and the common people in the city of Edo, resembling social networks in Islamic society. And in that sense, even Chinese society probably remains to be understood fully by the network model, which has been considered to be unique to Islamic society.

What perplexes me in the discussions of the network model by Lapidus is his statement that networks of overlapping and crisscrossing relationships were typical of "urban life" in general.[1] But he later expands the network model to "all Islam societies" as seen in the article "Hierarchies and Networks." However, if we consider Islamic state and society in total, we should certainly consider peasants and nomads other than townsfolk. Lapidus states in his first work *Muslim Cities in the Later Middle Ages* that the basic resources in urban livelihood depended on control of the land, and that mastery of the countryside was converted into "direct political control" by the Mamluks, who were city dwellers.[2] Here Lapidus carefully excludes the control of countryside from

[1]Lapidus, *Muslim Cities*, p.187.
[2]Lapidus, *Muslim Cities*, p.188.

the patronage networks found in urban societies, showing that the network model does not work to explain the relationship between the political powers and peasants or nomads in Islamic society.

Furthermore, as R. S. Humphreys states, Lapidus' functionalist approach is ill-suited to dealing with change and development; that is, in his presentation, patterns of political action appear to remain much the same throughout a 250-year period.[1] Needless to say, urban studies should contribute to furthering our comprehension of state and society in total. In this sense, the most important and urgent task is to search for ways of understanding Islamic state and society in a history that considers both urban and rural populaces. I have tried to describe the relationship between political power-holders and urban-rural society during the Mamluk period, by taking the example of the Memorandum to Amir Kitbughā issued in 1281.[2]

On 23 March 1281 Sultan al-Malik al-Manṣūr Qalāwūn (reigned 1279–90) set out from Cairo to conquer the Hospitallers stationed at al-Marqab. At that time he issued a memorandum (*tadhkira*) to Amir Kitbughā, vice-sultan (*nā'ib al-salṭana*), indicating how to manage and control state affairs in Egypt during his absence. This is what is called "A Memorandum to Amir Kitbughā." The full text is quoted by Ibn al-Furāt (d. 1405) in his *Ta'rīkh*, and a portion of it by al-Qalqashandī (d. 1418) in

---

[1]Humphreys, *Islamic History*, p.246.

[2]On the Memorandum to Amir Kitbughā, see T. Sato, *State and Rural Society in Medieval Islam: Sultans, Muqta's and Fallāhūn* (forthcoming), Chapter 5. Amir Kitbughā al-Manṣūrī who hailed from among the Oirates was appointed *nā'ib al-salṭana* in 679/1280-1 and proclaimed himself Sultan al-Malik al-'Ādil when al-Malik al-Nāṣir resigned the sultanate to go to al-Karak in 694/1294. However, his rule ended a short time later due to challenges from influential amirs.

Ṣubḥ al-A'shā.[1] We may extract from it several important points related to our present subject, because it deals with the maintenance of public safety in Cairo and Fustat, as well as the management and control of rural society, including the Bedouins, under the *iqṭā'* system[2] in Mamluk Egypt.

The "Memorandum" is composed of twenty eight articles. Articles (4) – (11) are all concerned with urban life in Cairo and Fustat. Let me take some examples.

> (5) At night no one should walk needlessly or loiter around Cairo and its suburbs of al-Ḥusaynīya and al-Aḥkār, or leave house except for urgent necessity. Women especially should not be allowed to conduct themselves as they please, and not wander around at night.
> (7) A group of soldiers is to be appointed to patrol the city of Cairo and investigate lanes and narrow alleys. They are to inspect the night watchmen of the streets (*aṣḥāb al-arbā'*), and those who are absent from their posts are to be punished.
> (11) On Thursday nights, people, especially women, are not to assemble at the two Qarāfas.

During the Ayyubid and Mamluk periods, the Cairene people had the custom of strolling around the sacred mausolea in the Great and Small Qarāfas south of Cairo with their children every Thursday night. According to al-Yāqūt (d. 1229), al-Qarāfa was a graveyard with big buildings and markets, which was used by the people of Cairo and Fustat as a place of amusement and excursions.[3] Al-Maqrīzī (d. 1442) also says, "The notables (*ru'asā'*) customarily sit in the court of the mosques at al-Qarāfa enjoying the moon in the summer night and sleep at the pulpits

---

[1]*Ta'rīkh Ibn al-Furāt*, VII, 196-200; al-Qalqashandī, *Ṣubḥ al-A'shā*, XIII, 91-98.
[2]*Iqṭā'* means the land or, rarely, taxes allocated by the sultan to soldiers in return for military service.
[3]al-Yāqūt, *Mu'jam al-Buldān*, IV, 317.

(*minbar*) in winter.[1] As indicated in Memorandum articles (5) and (11) above, the Mamluk government intended to prohibit such meetings both for religious activities and amusement, in order to maintain public safety and morality in the city of Cairo. The prohibition order must have been issued according to appeals from the scholars (*'ulamā'*), who had been disgusted with these night meetings involving both men and women. In this we can see the formation process of a social order under the leadership of political power-holders.

Next, we will take up the management and control of rural society by the Mamluks. Here are some examples from the "Memorandum."

> (15) Concerning irrigation works, the government orders should be obeyed and also executed without any exception. Harrows (*jarrāfa*) and large ploughs (*muqalqila*) are to be furnished according to these orders. However, everyone will do his duty not according to authority (*jāh*), but to custom (*'āda*), as in the days of al-Malik al-Ṣāliḥ (1240-49). He [Kitbughā] is to assure that governors (*wālī*) act themselves, not entrusting work to representatives (*mushidd*).
> (20) The income of the amirs, the Baḥrī Mamluks, the *ḥalqa* cavalrymen, and the soldiers. Their shares are to be entrusted to their representatives (*nā'ib*) and managers (*wakīl*). These representatives or managers are to collect cash and crops, about which certification (*shahāda*) is to be delivered to quell any dissatisfaction.
> (23) It is said that managers (*wakīl*) have managed the *muqṭa*'s' estates freely just like landowners (*mālik*) freely dispose of their privately owned lands. He (*wālī*), thereby, shall investigate every *wakīl* managing his master's estates and compose documents for delivery to the central government.

Article (15) shows that irrigation works were to be carried out not according to authority, but to custom (*'āda*), as in the days of the Ayyubid sultan, al-Malik al-Ṣāliḥ. We know the

[1] al-Maqrīzī, *Khiṭaṭ*, II, 444.

importance of *'āda* regulating rural life in Egypt, as seen in the breaking of irrigation dikes, the opening of large and small canals, and the distribution of water among villages. Those who were responsible in maintaining such rural customs were village *shaykh*s and local officials called *khawlī* (overseer of agricultural production).[1] According to articles (20) and (23), the *muqṭa'*s (*iqṭā'* holders)—i.e. amirs, the Baḥrī Mamluks and the *ḥalqa* cavalrymen—commissioned representatives and managers to collect their income from *iqṭā'*s. And these managers' rule over rural society was based on such village notables as *shaykh*s and *khawlī*s, who were responsible for maintaining rural customs. Furthermore, even during the Mamluk period many representatives or managers were chosen from among the Copts or Coptic converts to Islam, who had inherited the knowledge and techniques of accounting (*kitāba*) in provincial administration.[2]

Ibn Mammātī (d. 1209) says, "Village community dikes (*al-jusūr al-baladiyya*): This is for the benefit of the individual village, managed by *muqṭa'* and *fallāḥūn* (peasants)."[3] The *muqṭa'*s were obliged to manage and control the irrigation system using corvée labor levied on their peasants, in return for taking their *iqṭā'* revenue. This was for enhancing public welfare (*maṣlaḥa*). The legitimacy to rule over rural society by *muqṭa'*s originated from the expectation that they would maintain "social order" in local provinces, in conformity with village customs.

The activities of the Bedouins (*'Urbān*) were also closely related to social order. The Memorandum reads as follows:

---

[1]Sato, *State and Rural Society*, Chapter 6.

[2]D.P. Little, "Coptic Converts to Islam during the Baḥrī Mamluk Period," in M. Gervers and R. J. Bikhazi eds., *Conversion and Continuity*, Toronto, 1990, pp.263-288.

[3]Ibn Mammātī, *Qawānīn al-Dawāwīn*, 232.

(22) *'Urbān* in the local provinces. Their sustenance is to be cut off, hostages *(rahā'in)* taken from them, and a close watch be kept on them. He (Kitbughā) is to write a letter to the *nā'ibs* or *wālīs* in the provinces ordering that they notify the *'Urbān* not to carry swords, spears and weapons of any other kind. They are to be prohibited from purchasing them in Cairo.

The article shows the government's oppressive measures taken against the *'Urbān* in Egypt. Since the *'Urbān* often rose and incited peasants to rebellion, the sultans during the Ayyubid and Mamluk periods took measures to include them in the regime by grants of cash, provisions, *iqṭā'*, and even the rank of amir. Baybars al-Manṣūrī (d. 1325) states that Sultan Baybars (1260–77) imposed on the Syrian *'Urbān* the duties of the provincial guards and the maintenance of the roads leading to border of Iraq, while he assigned the leadership of all the *'Urbān* to Amir Sharaf al-Dīn 'Īsā b. Muhannā.[1] Then he ordered the Egyptian and Syrian *'Urbān* to provide horses for the postal institution *(barīd)*, a very effective move towards the establishment of a centralized political system.[2]

Incidentally, we find a well-organized local province, a small network society, in Upper Egypt as described in *Ta'rīkh al-Fayyūm* by 'Uthmān al-Nābulusī (d. 1261), an Arab official of the late Ayyubid sultan, al-Malik al-Ṣāliḥ. He investigated the town of al-Fayyūm and its countryside in detail for two years between 1243 and 1244, searching the ways for restoration. We may find a clue in his description to better our understanding of the *muqṭa'*s'

---

[1]Baybars al-Manṣūrī, *Zubdat al-Fikra*, fol.51r.

[2]On the reformation of the barīd system by Sultan Baybars, see the following studies: J. Sauvaget, *La poste aux chevaux dans l'empire des Mamelouks*, Paris, 1941; S. F. Sadeque, "Development of al-Barīd or Mail-post during the Reign of Baybars I of Egypt (A.D. 1260–1276)," *JASP*, 14(1969), pp.167-183; A. A. Khoweiter, *Baibars The First*, London, 1978, pp.42-43; Sato, *State and Rural Society*, Chapter 4.

rule over Egyptian provinces through local towns under the *iqṭā'* system. His elaborate account shows that the local society of al-Fayyūm was a unity composed of the townsfolk, peasants and *'Urbān*. The *'Urbān* farmed out their duties as guards of the countryside, and the peasants living off a hundred villages were closely connected to the town of al-Fayyūm through their economic and religio-cultural activities. Local notables, like judges (*qāḍī*), notaries public (*'ādil*), teachers (*mudarris*), the representative of the state treasury (*wakīl bayt al-māl*), doctors (*ṭabīb*), and owners of orchard and farm seed lived in the town (*al-madīna*), where five schools (*madrasa*) had been constructed for the higher education of youth both from the town of al-Fayyūm and its surrounding countryside.[1]

The above-mentioned local notables were key-persons for introducing political rule in the countryside by the government or *muqṭa'*s. In other words, the holders of political power sent their representatives to *iqṭā'*s and controlled rural society via those notables living in local towns. As I mentioned above, rural society was organized through networks centered in the town; but this kind of rule over rural society by the *muqṭa'*s does not fit to the network model which exclusively focuses on urban society.

To summarize the above discussion, the social network model is still useful for understanding the internal structure of urban and rural societies; but it does not explain state and society in total, including the relationship between political power-holders

---

[1]al-Nābulusī, *Ta'rīkh al-Fayyūm*, 26-31. For the study of *Ta'rīkh al-Fayyūm*, see Cl. Cahen, "Le régime des impôts dans le Fayyūm ayyūbide," *Arabica*, 3(1956), 8-30. The description of al-Nābulusī shows that hundred villages around the town of al-Fayyūm were all located within a half day journey on donkeys: that is, the villagers went to and came back from the town for selling crops and buying the necessities in one day. Among five *madrasas* in the town, three were the Shāfi'ite, and the remaining two the Mālikite ones.

and rural society in medieval Islam. Rural society under the *iqṭā'* system was ruled, not by networks, but by administrative institutions.

CHAPTER ONE

POLITICAL POWER AND SOCIAL NETWORKS:
Popular Coexistence and State Oppression in Ottoman Syria

Abdul-Karim RAFEQ

Introduction

Four-hundred years of Ottoman rule in Syria (1516–1918) brought about profound changes in the relationship between the state and the people. The ruling institution, that is, the *'askeri* class which included the governor, the military forces, the tax farmers and the judicial officials governed the subject people, the *ra'iyya,* who are usually divided into urbans and rurals. Each party had its own networks through which it defended its own interests.

Through a historical process, the people developed their own social networks, established their economic institutions and maintained their internal coexistence within a common Arabic culture to which they all subscribed and contributed across time. Despite certain political and social limitations rigidly enforced on minorities under alien rule, as happened under the Mamluk Sultanate which encouraged conversion to Islam, Syrian Arab society has been able to transcend these limitations throughout its history.

Ottoman rule is noteworthy for its organizational capacity on the levels of both the administration and the popular institutions. The two most important social institutions which promoted integration among the people are the guilds and the residential quarters. The guilds referred to in the religious court records as *ṭawā'if* (sing. *ṭā'ifa*), constituted the backbone of traditional society and economy in Ottoman Syria. Through work ethic, these organizations reflected the communal coexistence which was predominant among the various religious and ethnic groups in Arab-Islamic society. The residential quarters, on their part, reflected the integrative aspect of society. Through the quarters, an almost unique culture of neighborliness developed among the residents.

State oppression, on the other hand, focused basically on the economic exploitation of the people. Oppression was practiced primarily by governors, holders of land grants, known as *Sipahi*s and *Timariot*s, Janissaries, mercenary troops, tax farmers as well as notables allied with the government. The populace, whether urban or rural, reacted to oppression in a variety of ways. The continuing struggle between the people and the political authority eventually created a legacy of mistrust between the parties.

The Guilds and Communal Integration

The establishment of guilds in Syria in the Ottoman period institutionalized business and labor in ways which were not known before. Under earlier Arab-Islamic rule there were crafts and craftsmen but no craft organizations with corporate bodies and autonomy. Islamic and customary law then regulated the affairs of the crafts. Under the Ottomans, however, the guilds were allowed to function as autonomous bodies. They established their own rules, defended their own interests, organized and supervised their products and set prices for them. Like modern business and industry, the guilds maintained a strict division of labor and promoted specialization in business.[1]

---

[1]For details about the organization of the guilds in Ottoman Syria and the economic and social role they played, see my: "Craft organization, work ethics, and the strains of change in Ottoman Syria," *Journal of the American*

The major aspect of the guilds which promoted the coexistence of the religious communities is work ethic. The guilds emphasized expertise over religious belonging. Good behavior, correctness and trustworthiness in the profession were the basic criteria for promotion from one professional rank to a higher one and for election to administrative positions within the guild. The same qualities also determined the selection of the head of the guild, the *shaykh,* by the guild members. The failure of the *shaykh* to maintain these qualities during his tenure in office usually caused his deposition.

The integration of the religious communities in the guild system reflected their integration and coexistence in society at large. This explains why no socio-economic and religious riots of the type that had occurred later on in the mid-19th century ever took place in Syria in the three preceding centuries. Mercantilist Europe prior to the 19th century coexisted with the traditional economy and society of the Middle East. This was not the case with capitalist and revolutionary Europe in the 19th century which destabilized local society and economy and contributed to the occurrence of the local riots which were exploited religiously.

The guilds mirrored the socio-religious structure of society at large. Since the majority of the people were Muslim, the majority of the guilds' members had to be Muslim. The tendency among craftsmen to teach their children their own profession contributed to the continuing presence of the same communities in the same guilds. Thus, in the guilds whose membership was limited to either Jews, Christians or Muslims, the one-community monopoly over the guild was maintained. In such cases, the hereditary aspect of the craft is based on the monopoly by a few families from the same community of a certain craft which they were reluctant to

Oriental Society, 111.3 (1991), 495-511.

share with others. However, due to shared expertise and cultural mixing among the communities in certain crafts, there also existed many guilds with mixed religious membership. Thus, the guild of butchers (*ṭā'ifat al-qaṣṣābīn*) was shared by the Muslims and the Jews who, unlike the Christians, were bound by their religious practices to observe the lawful slaughter of animals. Likewise, Muslims and Jews monopolized the guild of druggists (*ṭā'ifat al-'aṭṭārīn*) because of the interest and the expertise they shared in preparing and selling drugs and perfumes. The Jews on their own monopolized the guild of smelters of silver and gold (*ṭā'ifat murawbiṣṣī al-fiḍḍa wa'l-dhahab*) in Aleppo in 1590 and had the *shaykh* of this guild installed from among their ranks. Christians, on the other hand, monopolized, for example, the guild of sculptors in Damascus (*ṭā'ifat al-naḥḥātīn*) which had twenty-seven members in 1689. The three communities figure together in several guilds, such as those of tailors, bakers and builders. They also share the membership of several guilds involved in the textile industry.

In the guilds which had mixed membership no restrictions were imposed on any member on account of his religion. All guild members shared on equal footing in the responsibilities of the guild. The elderly members (*ikhtiyāriyya*) represented the guild before the *Sharī'a* court in matters relating to the guild as a whole. The court records of Ottoman Syria abound with information about the names, the religious affiliations and the titles of the members representing the mixed guilds on the delegations. The number of delegates belonging to the various communities reflects the religious structure of the guild.

The delegation representing the guild of druggists before the court in Aleppo in 1633 consisted of twelve members, seven of whom were Muslim (58.33 per cent) and five Jewish (41.67

per cent).[1] Twenty-five years later, another delegation of Aleppine druggists consisted of nine members, six of whom were Muslim (66.67 per cent) and three Jewish (33.33 per cent).[2] Two years later, another delegation of Aleppine druggists consisted of seventeen members who included nine Muslims (52.94 per cent) and eight Jews (47.06 per cent).[3] Thus, within a period of twenty-seven years, between 1633 and 1660, three delegations representing the druggists in the court consisted of a total of thirty-eight members who break down into twenty-two Muslims (57.89 per cent) and sixteen Jews (42.11 per cent). Among the druggists' delegates in 1633 two of the seven Muslim members carried the title of *ḥājj* (indicating that they had performed the Muslim pilgrimage), one was a *shaykh* (religious scholar), one was a *chelebi* (a sage man of letters), and two had no titles. In the delegation of 1658, all six Muslim members carried the title of *ḥājj*. In the third delegation of 1660, six of the nine Muslim members held the title of *ḥājj*, one was a *chelebi* and two had no titles. Thus, the dignified Muslim members together with their Jewish fellow craftsmen appeared before the Islamic court as representatives of the guild of druggists in matters affecting the interests of the guild as a whole.

The guilds composed of Muslim and Christian members likewise had both communities represented on their delegations. The delegation representing the guild of furriers (*ṭā'ifat al-farrāyīn*) in Aleppo in 1658, for example, consisted of eleven members eight of whom were Muslim (72.73 per cent) and three were Christian (27.27 per cent).[4] The delegation representing the

---

[1]Law Court Records (LCR), Aleppo, vol. 15, p.288, case dated 4 *Rabī'* II 1043/(8 October 1633).

[2]LCR, Aleppo, vol. 27, p.71, 7 *Jumādā* II 1086/(14 March 1658).

[3]LCR, Aleppo, vol. 27, p.207, 26 *Jumādā* I 1070/(8 February 1660).

[4]LCR, Aleppo, vol. 27, p.110, 21 *Dhu'l-Ḥijja* 1068/(19 September 1658). For more details on mixed memberships in the guilds, see my: "Craft

Aleppine guild of sellers of satin (*ṭā'ifat al-aṭlasjiyya*) in 1659 had twenty members on its delegation to the court. Thirteen of them were Muslim (65.00 per cent), the remaining seven were Christian (35.00 per cent).[1] Three years later, a delegation from the same guild was composed of eleven members seven of whom were Muslim (63.64 per cent) and three were Christian (36.36 per cent).[2] The ratio of the members of the two communities on both delegations is close. A delegation from the Aleppine guild of tailors (*ṭā'ifat al-khayyāṭīn*) in 1658 consisted of twenty-one members, thirteen of whom were Muslim (61.90 per cent) and eight were Jewish (38.10 per cent).[3] The professional surname of tailor (*khayyāṭ*), like that of blacksmith (*ḥaddād*), in fact occurs among all three religious communities. The delegation representing the Aleppine guild of bakers of pastry (*ṭā'ifat khabbāzī al-ma'rūk*) consisted in 1657 of sixteen members, thirteen of whom were Muslim (81.25 per cent), one was Christian (6.25 per cent) and two were Jewish (12.50 per cent).[4]

Religious tolerance within the guilds was also evident in the ceremonies marking the promotion of a member from one professional rank to a higher one. When a Muslim member was promoted, the *Fātiḥa* (the Opener, that is the first *sūra* in the Holy Qur'ān) was recited. For a Christian, the Lord's Prayer was recited, and for a Jew, the Ten Commandments were read.[5]

---

organizations and religious communities in Syria (XVI-XIX Centuries)," *La Shī'a Nell'Impero Ottomano*, Accademia Nazionale Dei Lincei, Fondazione Leone Caetani, Roma, 1993, 25-56.

[1]LCR, Aleppo, vol. 27, p.173, 8 *Muḥarram* 1070/(26 September 1659).

[2]LCR, Aleppo, vol. 28, p.371, end of *Dhu'l-Qa'da* 1072/(17 July 1662).

[3]LCR, Aleppo, vol. 27, p.65, 20 *Jumādā* I 1068/(23 February 1658).

[4]LCR, Aleppo, vol. 27, p.18, 26 *Shawwāl* 1067/(7 August 1657).

[5]Ilyās 'Abduh Bek Qudsī, "Nubdha tārīkhiyya fi'l-ḥiraf al-Dimashqiyya," *Actes du VIe congrès des orientalistes*, tome 2, Leiden, 1885, 15-30.

Residential Quarters and Religious Coexistence

Religious coexistence in Syrian society is also amply evident in the residential space. Many residential quarters, it is true, were limited to one community. This was not dictated by a determined policy on the part of the population or the state as it was the result of patriarchal policy, family structure, common geographical origins of the population of the quarter, the persistence of social customs, and occasionally political factionalism. Also, lack of security necessitated that communities close ranks and live near each other for defence purposes.

Christians and Jews usually predominate in separate quarters, not because they want to live in a ghetto-like situation but to be close to their relatives and to their places of worship which were very often located in their midst. These quarters are usually designated by religious names, such as *ḥārat al-Naṣārā* (Christian quarter) and *ḥārat al-Yahūd* (Jewish quarter). But these quarters were not exclusively limited to Christians and Jews. Muslims also, albeit in small numbers, used to live in these quarters.

The mixing of the communities in the residential quarters is quite evident in the court records, especially when residential real estate was put on sale. The boundaries of the property would be given by way of identification. Thus, for every house put on sale, its four boundaries were given in the act of sale which was registered in the court records. The names, titles, religious identity and very often the ethnic background of the owners of the houses bordering the sold property are usually given. The mixing of inhabitants in any one quarter thus becomes apparent. A Maghribī may be living next to a Turkomānī, a Druze next to a Ḥawrānī Sunnī Muslim, a Christian next to a Muslim, or a Muslim next to a Jew.

The mixing of inhabitants is amply evident in the suburban Mīdān quarter of Damascus. The Mīdān forms a residential and a commercial neighborhood which extends along the pilgrimage route to the Hijaz. Most of the inhabitants of this neighborhood were relatively newcomers from the Hawran, Mount Lebanon, and even from as far away as the Maghrib (Arab North Africa), notably after the occupation of Algeria by the French in 1830. The inhabitants of the Mīdān included Muslims, Christians and Druzes. The Muslims were mostly Sunnīs and Shāfi'ī school (*madhhab*). The Maghāriba were Sunnīs of the Mālikī school. The Christians included Greek Orthodox and Greek Catholics. The Druzes came from the Hawran and from Wādī al-Taym in Mount Lebanon and belonged to the Qaysī and Yamanī factions who were always at loggerheads.

Despite the diversity of the inhabitants of the Mīdān and the large percentage of Christians living there, the Christians were not molested during the religious riots in Damascus in 1860 which devastated the dominantly Christian quarter of Bāb Tūmā inside the walls of the city. Mostly wealthy Christian families lived in Bāb Tūmā. The disparity in wealth between the impoverished craftsmen, especially those in the textile industry, who suffered the most from the competition of European textiles, and the *nouveaux-riches* Christians who resided in Bāb Tūmā and acted as agents and middlemen for European merchants was one of the main causes for the riots. Another cause was the complicity of Ottoman officials, including the governor of Damascus, who were later on executed by the Ottoman Commission of Inquiry for their role in fomenting and not stopping the riots. Thus some state officials had an interest in conspiring against the solidarity of the people. Religious fanaticism was used as a catalyst to whip up the emotions of the poor. Religion, however, was not the basic issue; economy was.[1] This explains

[1]See my: "New light on the 1860 riots in Ottoman Damascus," *Die Welt des Islams*, 55/56(1990), 180-196 (Festschrift in honor of Fritz Steppat, eds. Axel

why the Christians of the Mīdān neighborhood were spared the massacres because they shared poverty with the Muslim poor. The Jews were also spared the massacres because their majority were likewise poor. In addition to poverty, the mixed residences in the Mīdān, the common rural origins of its inhabitants, mostly catering for the needs of the peasantry and the pilgrims, strengthened their solidarity of their neighborliness and promoted cordial relations among the inhabitants.[1]

In the 1850 riots in Aleppo, the wealthy suburban Christian quarter of Judayda, outside the walls of the city, where the *nouveaux-riches* Greek Catholic community lived, was the primary target of the attackers. The poor Christian quarters in Aleppo, like those in Damascus, were not affected which again indicates that the riots were motivated by economic factors under the impact of capitalist Europe rather than by religious fanaticism.[2] This is also ascertained by the fact that in the preceding three-hundred years, no such riots had ever taken place.[3] Traditional society and economy then were fully integrated and Mercantilist Europe coexisted with them.

Havemann and Baber Johansen).

[1]For a detailed study of why the Bāb al-Muṣallā neighborhood in the Mīdān in Damascus was not affected by the riots in 1860, see my: "The Social and economic structure of Bāb al-Muṣallā (al-Mīdān), Damascus, 1825–1875," *Arab Civilization, Challenges and Responses: Studies in honor of Constantine K. Zurayk*, eds. George N. Atiyeh and Ibrahim M. Oweiss, State University of New York Press, 1988, 272-311.

[2]See the important study on the Aleppo riots by: Bruce Masters, "The 1850 events in Aleppo: an aftershock of Syria's incorporation into the capitalist world system," *International Journal of Middle East Studies*, 22 (1990), 3-20.

[3]On the impact of industrial Europe on nineteenth-century Syria, see my: "The impact of industrial Europe on a traditional economy: the case of Damascus, 1840–1870," *Economie et sociétés dans l'Empire Ottoman (fin du XVIIIe-début du XXe siècle)*, eds. Jean-Louis Bacqué-Grammont et Paul Dumont, CNRS, Paris, 1983, 419-432.

In the Kisrawān region of Mount Lebanon, a Maronite peasant movement under the leadership of blacksmith Ṭāniyūs Shāhīn rose in rebellion in the late 1850s seeking emancipation from the feudal rule of the Maronite Khāzin family. The revolt spread into the southern Shūf district where the peasants consisted of Druzes and Maronites whereas the feudal lords were Druzes. The revolt in the Shūf was exploited religiously and it turned into an ugly sectarian war which engulfed the whole mountain.[1]

The seaport of Jidda also witnessed in June 1858 massacres perpetrated by natives against foreign merchants and foreign protégés. Religious resentment there was intensified by political and economic rivalry.[2]

The Ottomans acted promptly to diffuse the bloody situation in Mount Lebanon and Syria. They succeeded in preventing the European powers from exploiting the situation. The French Emperor Napoleon III was actively seeking intervention abroad to divert attention from his authoritative rule inside France. French troops were sent to Lebanon only to leave shortly afterwards under European and Ottoman pressure.

The people soon put the events behind them and resumed their traditional tolerance and coexistence. The emerging Syrian proto-bourgeoisie soon reconciled its interests with Industrial Europe. Syrian manufacturers imported European machinery such as the mechanical Jacquard loom which produces a fabric with a figured weave. They also began to imitate European fashions which were spreading locally. More importantly, they pooled

---

[1]For the events in Mount Lebanon, see Leila Fawaz, *An Occasion for War, Civil Conflict in Lebanon and Damascus in 1860,* California University Press, 1994.

[2]William Ochsenwald, "The Jidda massacres of 1858," *Middle East Studies*, 1(1977), 314-326; *Religion, Society and the State in Arabia: the Hijaz under Ottoman Control, 1840–1908,* Ohio State University Press, Columbus, 1984, 144-151.

resources and introduced partnerships cutting across religious barriers in a bid to restore cooperation among the communities and measure up to the European challenge.[1]

Arabism and Communal Integration

The emergence of a proto-bourgeoisie class in Syria in the 19th century promoted the spread of Arab national consciousness which basically called for communal coexistence through modernization. This was an attempt to recreate the traditional coexistence which historically characterized the Arabic culture of Syria. Buṭrus Bustānī's use in 1860 of the ḥadīth (saying) attributed to the Prophet Muḥammad which says "Love of the Fatherland is an act of Faith" (*ḥubb al-waṭan min al-īmān*) as the motto for his newspaper Nafīr Sūriyya (The Clarion of Syria) echoes earlier calls for coexistence made by the so-called Syrian Muslim traditional intellectuals. Those intellectuals of the preceding centuries had already advocated love of the *waṭan* and called for coexistence. The example of the Damascene Ḥanafī Muftī (jurist) and famous Ṣūfī Shaykh 'Abd al-Ghanī al-Nābulsī (1641–1731) stands high in this regard.

In a controversy between Nābulsī and a Rūmī (Turkish) *'ālim* (Muslim religious scholar) in which the latter adamantly maintained that Muslims are promised by God to go to Paradise and that non-Muslims are destined to go to Hell, Nābulsī faulted the Rūmī *'ālim* on the issue of non-Muslims. In a long treatise entitled: *Hādhā kitāb al-qawl al-sadīd fī jawāz khulf al-wa'īd wa'l-radd 'alā al-Rūmī al-jāhil al-'anīd* (Book of sound doctrine on the permissibility of opposing a threat in reply to the ignorant

[1] See my, "The impact of Europe," 429.

and obstinate Rūmī),[1] Nābulsī maintained that God has merely threatened the non-Muslims by Hell. Because of God's mercy and forgiveness, according to Nābulsī, God is capable of dropping his threat and allowing the non-Muslims to go to Paradise. After all, Nābulsī goes on to say, all people become Muslims in the Hereafter. In other variations of the title of this treatise as well as in its contents, Nābulsī defends the Arabs against the slights of the Rūmī who belittled the Arabs including Nābulsī's Sufi master Shaykh Muḥyī al-Dīn ibn 'Arabī. Nābulsī reminds the Rūmī of a *ḥadīth* attributed to the Prophet Muḥammad who says: "you should love the Arabs for three things: because I am an Arab, because the Qur'ān is written in Arabic and because the language of the people in Paradise is Arabic."

Contemporary with Nābulsī, the Damascene Greek Orthodox priest Mikhā'īl Breik, who wrote a history of Damascus between 1720 and 1782, praised the governor of Damascus As'ad Pasha al-'Aẓm (1743–1757) for his tolerance towards the local Christian community in glaring contrast to the indifference of the other Ottoman governors. Breik prided himself on the rule of As'ad Pasha because of his Arab origin and his tolerance implying that tolerance is an integral part of Arabness. He went to the extent of considering the appointment of the first 'Aẓm governor in Syria in 1720 as one of three reasons which prompted him to begin his history in that year. The two other reasons were the spread of Greek Catholicism which affected the church of Breik and his becoming conscious of events around him.[2] Thus, the traditional intellectuals who were not exposed to the liberal thought of Europe were no less conscious of their Arab identity than the

---

[1]The copy used here is the one in the Staatsbibliothek in Berlin, MS. Mq. 1581.

[2]Mikhā'īl Breik, *Ta'rīkh al-Shām, 1720–1782*, ed. Qusṭānṭīn al-Bāshā, Ḥarīṣā, Lebanon, 1921, 2, 62.

Arab liberals of the 19th century.

State Oppression and Popular Reaction

While the people were living in harmony and restructuring their lives according to circumstances, the alien state from the Mamluk Sultanate through the Ottoman Sultanate was developing its means of exploitation and oppression. The aggrieved populace reacted to oppression and injustice through their own social networks. The guilds, for instance, paraded in the streets of 18th-century Damascus while carrying arms apparently to defend their own interests. The youths of the quarters under the leadership of their *shaykh al-ḥāra* (head of the quarter), also known as *shaykh al-shabāb* (head of the youths) opposed state oppression and defended their quarter, indeed their city, against external attacks. The thugs, the *zu'r* (*zu'rān*), of the quarters of Damascus in the late Mamluk and the early Ottoman periods defended the people against state oppression. They also fought among themselves. In the eighteenth century, the local Janissaries in Damascus, the *Yerliyya*, who had succeeded in penetrating the Janissary Corps in the city, defended the interests of the local people, especially the grain merchants who had joined the Corps to protect their interest against the state. In Aleppo, the people could not penetrate the Janissary Corps, but they figured in the *ashrāf* faction (claiming descent from the Prophet Muḥammad) which engaged in deadly warfare with the Janissaries. However, the indigenous group that was always there to defend the people against injustice were the *'ulamā'* (the religious scholars).

In the early years of Ottoman rule in Syria, a distinguished *'ālim* from Ḥamāh, Shaykh 'Alī ibn 'Alwān (d. 1530), better known as Shaykh 'Alwān, offered a series of advice (*naṣīḥa*) to Sultan Selim I the Grim (1512–1520), the conqueror of Syria, in which he urged him to implement the *Sharī'a* by word and deed, to prevent atrocities and obscenities, to stop the encroachment of governors and soldiers on civilians, and to spare the villages the payment of protection money.[1] The advice underlines the injustice and the oppression committed by the state as much as it highlights the role of the *'ulamā'* in defending the people.

Immediately after the Ottoman conquest of Syria, the *'ulamā'* protested vehemently against the imposition by the Chief Ottoman Ḥanafī Judge of fees on the drawing up of marriage contracts. The fees, known as *resm-i 'arūs* (bride's fees), were in violation of the established Arab-Islamic practice which encourages marriages by not imposing fixed fees. The *'ulamā'* of al-Azhar in Egypt went on strike to protest the fees.[2]

The major issue, however, which was strongly condemned by the Syrian *'ulamā'* deals with the injustices committed by the Ottoman feudal lords, the *Sipahi*s or *Timariot*s, against the peasantry. In a case brought before the Islamic court in Ḥamāh in 1586, a peasant complained that he was beaten by the *Sipahi* who chained him and imprisoned him in his private prison. Some villagers reacted to oppression by taking to banditry, intercepting caravans on the highways and challenging state authority. Others fled their villages to safer places, and many of them settled in the neighborhoods of towns as in the case of the Mīdān quarter of Damascus. The flight of the villagers caused a loss in revenue to the *Sipahi*s who were in charge of the villages. The *Sipahi*s, therefore, tried to prevail on the judges to order the villagers go back to their land. The *'ulamā'* came out strongly in support of the fleeing villagers. They condemned the Ottoman laws and the

---

[1]The treatise is entitled: *Naṣā'iḥ Sharīfa wa-Mawā'iẓ Ẓarīfa* (Noble advice and elegant sermons), MS. Asad Library, Damascus, no. 21580.

[2]See my: "The Syrian 'Ulamā', Ottoman Law and Islamic Sharī'a," *Turcica,* tome XXVI (1994), 9-32, see 10-13.

feudal practices which violated the *Sharī'a*. The *'ulamā'* quoted the example of the Prophet Muḥammad who fled Mecca to Medina to be spared injustice. They urged the peasants to rise in revolt against the unjust *Sipahi*s and not to fear punishment.[1]

The urban poor, many of whom were displaced peasants who had suffered from exploitation at the hands of the state officials in complicity with notables, expressed their dissatisfaction in a different way. In the early 17th century, for example, the poor in Damascus expressed their anger by supporting a dissenting *'ālim*, by the name of Yaḥyā al-Karakī, referred to as *zindīq* (free thinker), who was opposed by the religious establishment and was eventually executed.[2] When exasperated, the poor also rose in revolt as happened in 1725 when the Chief Ḥanafī Muftī of Damascus led them against the oppressive governor and his entourage.[3] When bread was rare and expensive, the poor crowded the bakeries, held the Ottoman Chief Ḥanafī Judge accountable for not implementing the *Sharī'a* and stopping the hoarding of grain by the notables, and stoned his court. They also shouted at the notables who allied themselves with the authorities and called them hypocrites (*munāfiqūn*).[4]

In the course of time, a tradition of insurgency developed among the people in the urban and the rural regions. In 1830, for example, the Damascenes rose in revolt against their Ottoman governor who tried to impose extra taxes on them and they killed him. The urban and the rural revolts in Syria at the time played

---

[1] *Ibid.*, 23-26.
[2] Muḥammad Amīn al-Muḥibbī, *Khulāṣat al-Āthār fī A'yān al-Qarn al-Ḥādī 'Ashar,* 4 vols., Cairo, 1284/1869 (reprinted Beirut, 1966), vol. 4, 487-480.
[3] See my: *The Province of Damascus, 1723–1783,* Beirut, Khayats, 2nd ed. paperback, 1970, 79, 81-84.
[4] Aḥmad al-Budayrī al-Ḥallāq, *Ḥawādith Dimashq al-Yawmiyya, 1154–1175/1741–1762,* ed. Aḥmad 'Izzat 'Abd al- Karīm, Cairo, 1959, 41, 63, 197.

into the hands of Muḥammad ʻAlī Pasha of Egypt and helped him in conquering Syria without encountering popular opposition. However, revolts in the countryside against Muḥammad ʻAlī's rule were soon to follow when he tried to disarm the people and to conscript them into the army.

The persistence of state oppression over a long period of time corrupted the people's sense of justice. The Damascenes were reported to have become aggressive against governor ʻAbd al-Ra'ūf Pasha (1827–1831) because of his excessive justice (*wa-min ʻadlihi al-zā'id ṭamiʻat fīhi ahl al-Shām*).[1]

The two patterns evidenced in Syrian society during the Ottoman period, namely, the coexistence of the local communities and the corruption and oppression of political power indicate the extent of the gap that separated the rulers, the *ʻaskeri* class, from their subjects, the *raʻiyya*. The reciprocal mistrust was almost institutionalized. Complex networks developed across time to serve the interests of the parties. The legacy of this relationship of mistrust continued for decades after the demise of the Ottoman Empire. Civil society, however, has proven its worth and has demonstrated that it can survive despite state oppression.

---

[1]Mikhā'īl al-Dimashqī, *Ta'rīkh Ḥawādith al-Shām wa-Lubnān, 1197–1257/1782–1842*, ed. Louis Maʻlūf, Beirut, 1912, 49.

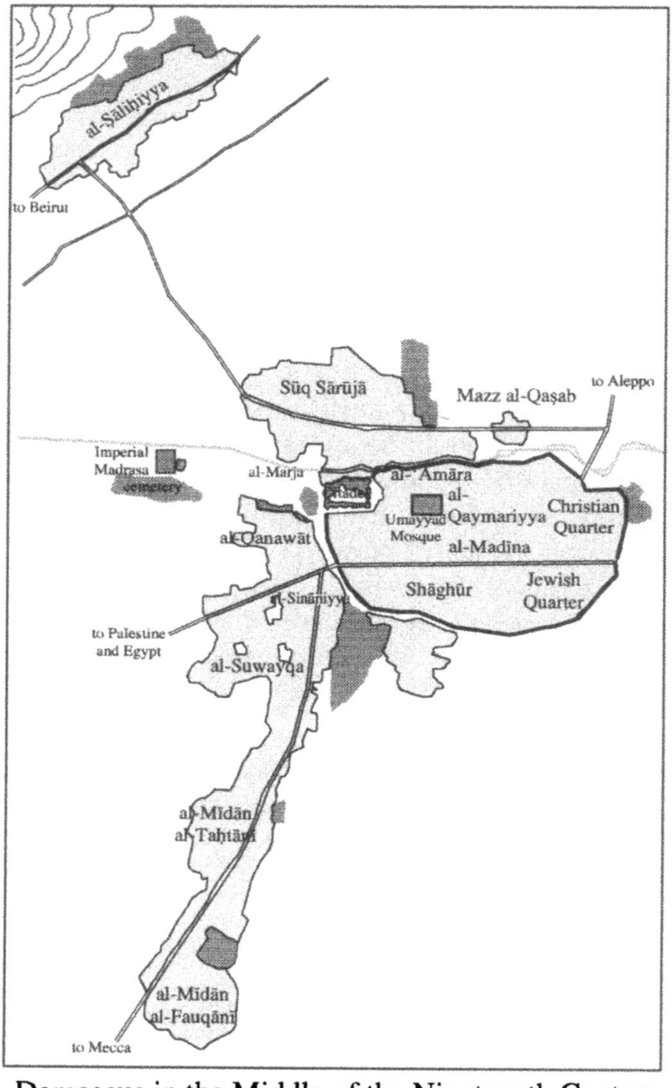

Damascus in the Middle of the Nineteenth Century
(Source: J. Sauvaget, "Esquisse d'une histoire de la ville de Damas,' *REI*, IV (1934).)

CHAPTER TWO

ADMINISTRATIVE NETWORKS IN THE MAMLŪK PERIOD: Taxation, Legal Execution, and Bribery

MIURA Toru

I *Networks as Method of Urban Studies*

The term of 'network' has become very popular in the fields of sociology, economics, politics, and anthropology as well as history, but its meaning varies slightly in each field. In the field of Middle East studies, I think I. M. Lapidus is the first to have used it positively as a method of urban research, although he initially used terms such as social relations, or social ties, and only intentionally adopted 'networks' as a term designating his method of Islamic study in general in his article of 1975 which was written from a comparative perspective. In this article, he used the word of 'network' on three levels: as an analytical tool, as a metaphor for "informal and unstructured interconnections" of Islamic societies, and as a metaphor for Islamic culture.[1] Today scholars are taking as their subjects social networks such as the *'ulamā'*, merchants, artisan, Sufi orders, the quarters, the family, outlaws, and patron-client relationships to shed positive light on cities and local societies at particular periods, whether they use

[1]Ira M. Lapidus, "Hierarchies and Networks: A Comparison of Chinese and Islamic Societies," F. J. Wakemann (ed.), *Conflict and Control in Late Imperial China*, Berkeley, 1975. His method and model on Islamic societies is discussed in: Masashi Haneda and Toru Miura (ed.), *Islamic Urban Studies: Historical Review and Perspectives*, London, 1994, pp.89-90, 116-117.

the word 'network' or not.

Outside of Middle East studies, most scholars also show increasing recourse to the word of 'network': Historians of Chinese societies present a new approach in regarding power as a nexus of formal and informal, physical and metaphysical, relations.[1] As early as the 1960s the Annales school of French history employed the word *sociabilité* to designate social relationship in clubs, fraternities, quarters and so on.[2] As for studies on Japanese cities, some scholars are drawing attention to networks of traveling artisans and merchants, and religious men, and their relations to the authority of the city. They are creating a new definition of the 'city' as, I dare to say, "asylum" for those people[3], challenging the commune model of West European cities which had long influenced Japanese urban studies.

The growing popularity and prevalence of the term 'network' increases our need to define properly its meaning and scope of its application in each field. Lapidus himself mentioned three principal institutions which formed Islamic urban societies: (1) parochial groups (*'aṣabiyya* ties) such as families and lineage, quarters or outlaws, (2) religious associations (law schools, Sufi orders, sects, etc.), and (3) imperial regimes (slave soldiers,

---

[1]Cf. Prasenjit Duara, *Culture, Power and the State: Rural North China, 1900–1942*, Stanford, 1988. Joseph W. Esherick and Mary Backus Rankin (ed.), *Chinese Local Elite and Patterns of Dominance*, Berkeley & Los Angeles, 1990.

[2]Maurice Agulhon, *La Sociabilité méridionale: Confréries et associations en Provence orientale dans la deuxième moitié du XVIIIe siècle*, Aix-en-Provence, 1966. Hiroyuki Ninomiya (ed.), *The Scope of Sociabilité*, Tokyo, 1995 (in Japanese).

[3]Yoshihiko Amino, *Muen, kugai, raku (Freedom and Peace in Medieval Japan)*, rev. ed., Tokyo, 1987; id., *Nihon chusei toshi no sekai (The World of Medieval Cities in Japan)*, Tokyo, 1996 (both in Japanese).

nomadic soldiers, the *iqṭāʿ* system).[1] His insistence that these institutions are not restricted to the cities, but extended to rural regions and served to link urban and rural areas, is characteristic of his network theory. A second feature is that he treats the state organization according to the same standard as other social groups. It suggests his 'network' theory includes all types of social, political and religious organizations and institutions, whether it be formal or informal, physical or metaphysical.

My own viewpoint of network theory in historical studies—not especially that of Lapidus—differs in three points from usual usage in analyzing social relations or social ties. Firstly, it suggests multi-directional relationships, just as the original meaning of network derives from the word 'net.' Secondly, it means flexibility, which is also implied by the word 'net.' A third feature is generality, as it could include any sort of relationship, and be applied to any type of organization. I concur with Lapidus's inclusion of state organizations as being one type of network, but I find unsatisfactory his overall reliance on preceding studies of administrative systems such as the *iqṭāʿ* system, finance and taxation, and legal e]xecution without having conducted his own examination.[2] This made the relation of the

[1]Lapidus, "The Evolution of Muslim Urban Society," *Comparative Studies in Society and History,* 15, 1973. This model is re-defined and re-examined in his later paper, "Muslim Cities as Plural Societies: The Politics of Intermediary Bodies," in *Urbanism in Islam: The Proceedings of the International Conference on Urbanism in Islam,* vol.1, Tokyo, 1989, pp.136-146.

[2]Studies on administrative systems have so far concentrated on those of the military, while studies on legal and financial administration are relatively lacking. David Ayalon has published very detailed work on the military system: "Studies on the Structure of the Mamluk Army," *BSOAS,* 15/2-3, 16/1, 1953–1954; "The System of Payment in Mamluk Military Society," *JESHO,* 1/1, 1/3, 1958. William Popper's *Systematic Notes to Ibn Taghrî Birdî's*

state organization to the other institutions of the people ambiguous, whether it stood against social networks, or was included in the networks, or operated through the networks.

In this paper I attempt to examine the administrative system in the Mamlūk State, focusing on the informal networks, rather than official systems, for the former assumed an important role of collecting revenue and executing administrative affairs in the declining period of the 15th century. One topic on which I shall dwell is that of bribery, which has been regarded as a sign of depravity of the Mamlūk State and as a reason for its decline. I intend to make clear that it was adopted as financial policy, and that the state administration was executed through a form of bribery network. Finally, I shall discuss the reason why such a system prevailed up to the Ottoman period.

II *Bribery*

1. Bribery in the Mamlūk Period

Bribery dates back to the dawn of human history as the Old Testament states that judges should not receive bribes, and that Jehova is so impartial in his justice as not to receive a bribe.[1] The *Qur'ān* also says: Consume not your goods between you in vanity; neither proffer it to the judges, that you may sinfully consume a portion of other men's goods, and that wittingly (*al-Qur'ān*, II:184-188). The Tradition of the Prophet Muḥammad (*ḥadīth*) tells that the Prophet Muḥammad cursed both one who bribed and one who took a bribe.[2] Aḥmad 'Abd al-Rāziq who

---

Chronicle of Egypt, 2 vols., Berkeley & Los Angeles, 1955–1957 gives a sketch of the Mamlūk State organization.

[1]*Deuteronomy*, 16:19; *Chronicles II*, 10:7.

[2]Aḥmad b. Ḥanbal, *al-Musnad*, al-Qāhira, 1951–1953, X, p.55, XII, p.53.

wrote a book on bribery entitled "Bribery in the Mamlūk Period" mentions that the first case of bribery in the Islamic history was that al-Mughīra b. Shu'ba who held the post of *'amal* al-Kūfa (tax-collector of Kufa City) in 42/662,[1] and he cites many examples of bribery in the Islamic history, although Islamic law prohibited it.[2]

The historians of the Mamlūk period stated in their chronicles that bribery was uncommon until the reign of Sultan al-Nāṣir (d. 741/1341), but after the reign of Sultan Barqūq (d. 801/1399) was pervasive[3] among the military officials, religious officials and the common peoples in the Mamlūk period as al-Maqrīzī wrote in 808/1405:

> The most fundamental reason for the calamity was that the land of the Sultan and the religious offices were assigned by bribery (*rishwa*). Nobody could obtain the offices of *wazīr*, judge (*qāḍī*), governors of province and district, and market inspector (*muḥtasib*) as well as all lands, without a great deal of money. Thus every kind of ignorant, vicious, unjust, and oppressive person was able to gain such [posts of governors of] important and immense provinces that could never have been offered to them, were it not for connections to close associates of the Sultan or for money promised to him for such favours.[4]

---

[1]Aḥmad 'Abd al-Rāziq Aḥmad, *al-Badhl wa al-Barṭala zamana salāṭīn al-mamālīk,* al-Qāhira, 1979, p.12. Here he examines in detail the system of bribery in the Mamlūk period by collecting many examples from various sources.

[2]al-Māwardī tells: It is prohibited to offer a gift (*badhl*) pertaining to the lawsuit, because it is a bribe (*rishwa*) to be prohibited. Both to bribe and to take a bribe should be punished. (al-Māwardī, *al-Aḥkām al-sulṭāniyya wa al-wilāyāt al-dīniyya,* Bayrūt, 1985, p.96). See also, Joseph Schacht, *An Introduction to Islamic Law,* Oxford, 1964, p.188.

[3]*Nujūm,* IX, p.175; *Sulūk*, III, p.617.

[4]*Ighātha,* pp.43-44.

As al-Maqrīzī suggested, bribery was regarded as a depravity and weakness of the administration which caused great calamity, such as famine and price inflation which frequently beset the people of Egypt since the beginning of the 15th century. Most scholars such as Aḥmad 'Abd al-Rāziq, adopt this view and hold the prevalence of bribery to be one of the main factors behind the decline of the Mamlūk dynasty.[1]

What is the reason why offering and receiving of bribes continued among the officials against strong criticism from the *'ulamā'* such as al-Maqrīzī? Why did the Sultan not abandon the receiving of bribes in exchange for official appointment? Why did he not forbid officials from offering and receiving bribes? It seems futile to criticize such bribery as shameless conduct, rather we should examine the reason why the Sultan, officials and common people, offered and received bribes despite knowing that they were committing a moral vice. Instead, there seems to be a socio-economic reason of the Mamlūk State facing the economic decline and financial problems. Here I would like to examine the system of bribery and its effect during the period from the reign of Sultan Barsbāy (825–841/1422–1438) until the end of the Mamlūk dynasty, based on historical sources.

2. *The System of Bribery*

Our survey of the above-cited period will be divided into three parts: The first is during the reign of Sultan Barsbāy when he adopted a policy of increasing state revenue, such as by imposing a monopoly on the spice trade between the Indian Ocean and the

---

[1] Aḥmad 'Abd al-Rāziq, *op. cit.*, pp.131-139. Most scholars on the Mamlūk period concur in the view that the depravity of the high officials caused the disorder of administration which led to the final decline of the State.

Mediterranean.[1] The second is from the reign of Sultan Jaqmaq to the eve of Sultan Qā'itbāy, that is, the period 841–872/1438–1468 when the state was in such grave and constant financial crisis that it was forced to stop distribution of the salaries of the Royal *Mamlūks*.[2] The third one is from the reign of Sultan Qā'itbāy to the disappearance of the Mamlūk dynasty as a result of conquest by the Ottoman Empire, 872–923/1468–1517, when Sultan Qā'itbāy adopted a new financial policy of taxing the properties of the citizen and of cities which had accumulated wealth during the preceding ages of prosperity, to compensate for decreasing income from *iqṭā'* and rural resources.[3]

a. *Terms*

The terms *rishwa*, *barṭala*, and *badhl* [4] which mean bribery, appear very rarely in narrative sources. Rather we are told simply that somebody obtained the office for the sum of 1,000 dinars, etc. We will afterwards discuss the reason why such a style of

---

[1]Cf. Aḥmad Darrag, *L'Égypte sous le règne de Barsbay 825–841/1422–1438*, Damas, 1961.

[2]Sultan Jaqmaq wasted a great amount of money, three millions dinars, which the former Sultan Barsbāy left at his death, and nothing remained in the Royal Treasury when Jaqmaq's son 'Uthmān ascended to the throne in 857/1453 (*Ḥawādith*, pp.175-176; *Nujūm*, XV, pp.457-458, XVI, p.64). Stopping the distribution of meat to the Royal *Mamlūks*: *Ḥawādith*, p.225, 253, 270.

[3]*Ḥawādith*, pp.635-637, 689-693; *Inbā'*, pp.33-37; *Badā'i'*, III, pp.13-15, 20-23.

[4]*Rishwa* originally meant a young bird stretching forth its head to its mother to receive food into its beak (*Lisān*, XIX, p.37), while *barṭala* meant to place a long stone in the fore part of one's watering-trough (*Lisān*, XIII, pp.53-54). Both are used to designate bribery. *Badhl* means a gift and is similarly used to designate bribery.

expression was popular.

b. *Purpose*

Our sources give the accounts of bribery in each period: 61 cases in the first era, 75 cases in the second, and 94 cases in the third era.[1] Most of them refer to bribery offered to obtain appointment to state office. The administrative offices were assumed by two major classes of *mamlūks* (slave soldiers, military elite in the dynasty) and *'ulamā'* (religious and legal elites) in the Mamlūk period. Civil officials occupied about 70-80% of all the bribed offices in the first and third period, whereas they occupied less than 30% in the second period (see Table 1). It shows that offering a bribe to take a state office was a common habit not only for military officials of *mamlūks* but also for civil officials of *'ulamā'*.

c. *Bribe takers*

The sources did not usually refer to the bribe takers, but we can safely assume that the dispenser of office must have taken it in cases of appointment, which for state officials, would mean the Sultan. We can also assume in some cases that the bribes were offered to the Treasury (*khizāna*) of the Sultan.[2]

d. *The Amount of Bribes*

Table 2 Amounts taken as Bribes was compiled from our sources. The total amounts of bribes as well as their average are both bigger in the first period than in the second one.

There was a standard bribe amount to obtain some high offices. To offer some examples, 10,000 dinars was usually offered

---

[1] Sources are: *Sulūk, Nujūm,* and *Ḥawādith* for the first and second period. *Badā'i', Mufākaha* and *Inbā'* for the third period.

[2] *Ḥawādith*, p.46, 482, 560.

to obtain an office of Chief Secretary (*kātib al-sirr*) of the Sultanate in the first period, and 3,000 dinars to obtain a office of chief *qāḍī* (*qāḍī al-quḍāt*) of Cairo in the third period.[1] In 869/1464 Grand Chamberlain (*ḥājib al-ḥujjāb*) paid 12,000 dinars to assume the office of Governor of Karak, and at the same time another four persons who assumed the offices of Grand Chamberlain, Chamberlain of Damascus, *Atabeg* of Tripoli, Commander of the Thousand (*amīr muqaddam alf*) in turn which became vacant in turn owing to the promotion of the former office holders, all paid bribes of 10,000 dinars, 10,000 dinars, 3,000 dinars, and 1,500 dinars to the Treasury.[2] This shows that bribes were not offered just by greedy applicants but was regarded as standard payment required of all candidates to become state officials.

The average amount of bribe exceeds 20,000 dinars in the first period, and 12,000 dinars in the second period, while it decreases to less than 10,000 dinars in the third period. The changes of high officials were very frequent in the Mamlūk State because it had a hierarchical organization of military and civil officials in which every official vied for promotion from a lower to a higher office in the hope of eventually assuming the rank of Provincial Governor (*nā'ib*, *wālī*) or chief *qāḍī*, etc.

Considering the routine nature of appointments, bribes must have been a great source of income to the Treasury which was in a state of constant financial crisis. The Sultan paid 18,000 dinars to Royal *Mamlūks* per month as their cash salary (*jāmakiyya*) and it rose to 46,000 dinars in 873/1468. When dispatching a military expedition, the Sultan used to provide each Royal

---

[1]Chief Secretary: *Sulūk*, IV, p.685; *Nujūm*, XV, p.273, p.360, *Sulūk* IV, p.870. Chief *qāḍī: Badā'i'*, IV, p.91, 171, 280, 469, 477; *Mufākaha*, I, p.30. In 919/1514 the Sultan appointed four chief *qaḍīs* concurrently without taking ordinary bribes which should bring him 12,000 dinars (*Badā'i'*, IV, p.351).

[2]*ibid.*, p.482.

Mamlūks with an extra fee (*nafaqa*) of 100 dinars, which amounted to about 400,000 dinars for a whole army.[1] In contrast to such budgetary outlays, income from bribes would have been a constant source of income to the Treasury to cover the shortfall from ordinary tax revenue.

The third question to be addressed is the financial significance of the bribe to the bribe-giver. We may firstly compare it to the salary of state officials, because it was to attain such office. Data on the salary of state officials in the Mamlūk period is regrettably very scarce, however, although al-Maqrīzī mentioned the monthly salary of *qāḍī* as being 50 dinars, and that of *wazīr* 250 dinars plus provisions of equal value (500 dinars in total).[2] As for civil officials, we now have more accurate data on the salaries of officials serving religious institutions founded by *waqf* endowment such as *jāmi'*, *madrasa*, and Sufi convents using *waqf* documents. They were mostly denominated in dirhams (silver coin), but can be estimated as having been less than 10 dinars (gold coin) per month.[3] To military officials were bestowed *iqṭā'* (tax income from the land) as their salary. The higher ranked officer, the Commanders (*amīr*s) of the Hundred, Forty, and Ten got *iqṭā'* which brought him annual revenue ranging from about 10,000 to 100,000 dinars according to the land survey of Sultan al-Nāṣir in

---

[1]46,000 dinars of *jāmakīya*: *Ḥawādith*, p.689. 400,000 dinars of *nafaqa* for the expedition to Suwār in Elbistan in 873/1468: *Badā'i'*, III, p.27, 29.

[2]*Khiṭaṭ*, II, p.224.

[3]Staff of madrasa such as professor were paid salaries of between 60 to 120 dirhams in Syria between 8th–9th/14–15th centuries, which deserved 5 to 10 dinars in gold coin. In 9th/15th century Egypt the salaries suddenly rose to over 1,000 dirhams which deserved about 5 dinars according to the exchange rate of Egypt (1:200 at the beginning of the 9th/15th century). Cf. E. Ashtor (Strauss), "Prix de salaires à l'époque mamlouke," *REI*, 1949.

715/1315-16.[1]

Assuming a 3,000 dinars bribe needed for appointment of chief *qāḍī*, it would be equivalent to have five years salary if we assume his monthly salary as having been fifty dinars. The bribe of 10,000 dinars for Chief Secretary would have equalled 1.7 years salary, if we assume his monthly salary to have been equal to that of *wazīr*. It is clear that the bribe amount was very high, though our calculations depend on inadequate sources. Comparing it to the price of daily foods such as one *ardabb* (90 liters) of wheat ranging between one and three dinars in the second period, and one *raṭl* (450 grams) of meat ranging between six and ten dirhams[2], a bribe of 3,000 dinars was far beyond the range of common people.

e. *The Manner of Paying Bribes and their Reward*

Appointees often paid their bribes in installments during their tenure of office, as the amount was too onerous for a single payment.[3] In some cases the remaining due portion of the bribe was treated as a personal debt.[4] The appointee would endeavor to pay his debt from money collected from bribes he in turn received, by levying heavy taxes or by extorting protection fees

[1]Tsugitaka Sato, *State and Society in Medieval Islam: Studies on the Iqṭā' System in Arabic Society*, Tokyo, 1985, p.240 (in Japanese). Revised English edition will soon be published.

[2]Based on the data collected from *Ḥawādith*. Cf. Eliyahu Ashtor, *Histoire des prix et des salaires dans l'Orient médiéval*, Paris, 1969, pp.290-292, 311-312.

[3]An *amīr* was appointed *shurṭa* (police) of Cairo in 922/1516 after promising to pay a bribe of 41,000 dinars, and he paid 20,000 dinars in advance (*Badā'i'*, V, p.26). Other examples: *Sulūk*, IV, p.1204; *Mufākaha*, I, p.87.

[4]Sultan arrested Shāfi'ī chief *qāḍī* Ibn al-Naqīb to pay the remainder of his bribe to assume the office in 916/1510 (*Badā'i'*, IV, p.189). Other examples: *Nujūm*, XV, p.259.

(*ḥimāya*) through wielding their authority as state officials.[1] When we observe this manner of payment, it becomes clear that the bribe sum should be regarded as a bidding price, which was not necessary to pay at the time of appointment, but during the tenure of office. Applicants thus tended to raise the "bidding" price when many rivals were competing for the same office.[2]

What kind of return was expected from bribing? The amount of bribes seems excessive compared to the average brevity of office tenure: the term of chief *qāḍī* in Cairo averaged 2.1 years and that of Damascus was 3.8 years in the third period. That of Chief Secretary of Cairo was 1.13 years in the first period.[3] It shows that the bribe-giver could not recover the cost of being a state official from his normal salary during his tenure. Thus the bribe-giver, receiving his appointment as a state official strove to maximize private profit from his work by means of taking bribes,

---

[1]al-Maqrīzī reports all manner of injustice by State officials in the account of 820/1417: *Muḥtasib* collected taxes from the merchants to pay the bribes for their appointment. *Qāḍī*s and their deputy-judges were not ashamed to receive bribes at a trial. *Ḥājib*s and their subordinates assumed their offices to take bribes from both plaintiffs and defendants whether or not they had their proper legal right. *Wālī*s (city police) and their subordinates deprived citizens of their property, even demanding a great deal of money from both plaintiffs and defendants in unjust lawsuit, just to pay their bribes to the Sultan (*Sulūk*, IV, pp.388-394).

[2]In 871/1466 two candidates competed for the office of *ḥājib* of Tripoli, while their offer of bribes was raised from 45,000 dinars to 75,000 (*Ḥawādith*, p.528). Other examples: *Mufākaha*, I, p.130; *Quḍāt*, pp.231-232.

[3]The average term of chief *qāḍī* in Cairo during the reign of Sultan al-Ghawrī (907–922/1502–1516) based on *Badā'i'*, V, p.92: Shāfi'ī 0.92 years, Ḥanafī and Mālikī 3.7 years, Ḥanbalī 4.9 years. Chief *qāḍī* in Damascus during the third period based on *Mufākaha*, *Badā'i'* and *Quḍāt*: Shāfi'ī 5.00 years, Ḥanafī 2.78 years, Mālikī 3.13 years, Ḥanbalī 5.57 years. As for Chief Secretary, see Bernadette Martel-Thoumian, *Les civils et l'adminstration dans l'État militaire mamlūk (IXe/XVe siècle)*, Damas, 1992, Annex C.II.

fees, heavy taxes, gifts and so on. An official allegedly exclaimed that he would pay his bribe by earning (or eating) ribs of Muslims when he was appointed.[1]

Bribery should be viewed as a financial policy for the Mamlūk State to cover its constant lack of income. For officials, paying bribes was an unavoidable expenditure. We might think of it a system of *vénalité* as institutionalized in the *Ancien Régime* of France. Such a system of appointment led to two basic changes in the administrative system. Firstly, expensive bribes became a prerequisite to assuming high office, and personal wealth was all that was needed to attain it as long as no special ability was required, as for instance knowledge of literary arts or legal affairs. In essence, it changed the necessary condition of becoming an official. Secondly, it affected the working of administration, because high officials were eagerly reaping private profits, and bribery pervaded not only all officialdom, from the most senior ranks to the lowest, but also reached down to the common people. These changes in administration will be discussed in detail in the 4th and 5th chapters.

III *Confiscation of Property*

There was another method of collecting from the property of officials. It was called *muṣādara* in which the state forcibly confiscated the property of dismissed officials by such means as imprisonment and torture, but it should be noted that after payment of the demanded, the victim was released without any criminal record and could return to the same position. This signifies that *muṣādara* was executed for the purpose of confiscating wealth,

[1] *Nujūm*, XIV, p.259. Similar expression is found in *Badā'i'*, V, p.27.

not as a means of punishment.

a. *Officials*

As Table 3 Officials subject to Confiscation shows, most of the victims were civil officials: They occupied 70% of all in the second period and 75% in the third period. Financial officials such as *ustādār* and *wazīr* were so conspicuous in all the three periods accounting for seven (78% of the total) in the first period, 23 (49% of the total) in the second period, and 21 (20% of the total) in the third period.

b. *Amount*

As for the amounts confiscated, the total for the second period increased to about ten times as much as that of the first period, and then the total for the third period increased to twice as much as that of the second period. The total amount confiscated per year had risen from 8,824 dinars in the first period to 43,794 dinars in the second period, and then to 61,350 dinars in the third period. The average amount of each case also increased from 25,000 dinars in the first period to 36,879 dinars in the second period, and finally to 61,350 dinars in the third period. From the frequency of confiscation and raising of the amount we can see that the Mamlūk State began to adopt a deliberate policy of increasing its income by means of confiscation. Indeed 915/1514 the State ordered the confiscation from administrative officials the amount of which was so huge as 600,000 dinars. [1]

c. *Method of Confiscation*

When confiscation had been decided upon, the subject officials were detained in the prison of the Citadel or in one of

---

[1] *Badā'i'*, IV, p.169. In 917/1511, 400,000 dinars was imposed on the financial officials (*Badā'i'*, IV, p.235).

the private houses of high officials (*ustādār*, *wālī*, *wazīr*, etc.) who were responsible for securing the confiscation by torture and other means.[1] The sum was assessed and when it was too much to pay, it was sometimes lowered, or paid in installments. The official was forced to sell his property, such as horses, slaves, clothes, furniture, and his house when the assessed amount was high. There were some cases in which *waqf* property (charitable endowment) and rights of taxation were sold.[2] His family and subordinates were also forced to pay according to circumstances.[3] The growing scale of such confiscation drew public attention, as we note from detailed accounts which appear in the chronicles of the time. In some cases other high officials interceded on behalf of the accused official to end his detention and confiscation of property, perhaps by guaranteeing payment of the assessed amount.[4]

---

[1]The *muḥtasib* of Cairo and the *wālī* of Cairo were ordered to detain some officials for confiscation of the assigned amounts of money from them in 916/1510 (*Badā'i'*, IV, p.190). Other examples: *ibid.*, IV, p.235, V, p.91; *Ḥawādith*, p.407.

[2]Pay in installments: *Badā'i'*, IV, p.282; *Ḥawādith*, p.514, 516. Selling the property: *Sulūk*, IV, p.693, 1146. In 857/1453 *ustādār* Zayn al-Dīn Yaḥyā was tortured to pay 300,000 dinars. His property was sold in the market every day and finally the *waqf* property which he endowed for religious institutions was sold after their legal status as *waqf* property was canceled by the Mālikī judge (*Ḥawādith*, pp.165-167). Selling of taxation rights (*ta'allqāt*): *Ḥawādith*, p.407, 750.

[3]*Sulūk*, IV, p.1146; *Badā'i'*, IV, p.377, 381, 387.

[4]*Ustādār* Karīm al-Dīn was arrested and tortured in 838/1434. The *wālī* of Cairo was charged with to extracting payment from Karīm al-Dīn, who was taken for this purpose to the house of the *wālī*. Karīm al-Dīn paid 20,000 dinars by selling his property and the notables guaranteed (*ḍamina*) to pay the rest (*Sulūk*, IV, pp.933-934). Other examples of guarantee: *Badā'i'*, IV, p.39; *Mufākaha*, I, p.382.

d. *Reason for Confiscation*

It has not been clear why the Government could confiscate the property of the dismissed officials. The following descriptions are suggestive of the process by which confiscation was performed and the reason behind it. In 843/1439 Majordomo (*ustādār*) Jānībek was forced to pay 10,000 dinars as his assessed share of administrative authority (*jiha*) bestowed upon him by *Dīwān al-Mufrad* (Sultan's Special Bureau), but another imposition of 1,300,000 dirhams was withdrawn because it was not included in his authority.[1] The second account we have is of 869/1464 when *ustādār* al-Zaynī was forced to pay 20,000 dinars which was his debt (*dhimma*) owed to *Dīwān al-Mufrad*, because it was not recognized as his own right (*jiha*) under Islamic law.[2]

The *ustādār* and *Dīwān al-Mufrad* were charged with collecting revenue for the Sultan and providing the Royal *Mamlūks* with a monthly cash salary (*jāmakiyya*).[3] These accounts show clearly that confiscation was carried out on the basis of fair assessment and that the retired official should return the sum belonging to the State from what he had collected as revenue of the State. Indeed, at the confiscation of financial officials in 917/1511, they were requested to sign the documents, if they approved the demand as lawful (*ṣaḥīḥ*).[4] In this light, confiscation seems to suit its original meaning "an agreement with someone over the payment of taxation due," according to al-Khwārazmī, more properly than its definition by *Encyclopaedia of Islam* "Mulcting of an official of his ill-gotten gains or spoils of office,"[5]

---

[1] *Sulūk*, IV, pp.1156-1157.
[2] *Ḥawādith*, pp.481-482.
[3] *Ṣubḥ*, III, p.453.
[4] *Badā'i'*, IV, pp.235-236.
[5] *Encyclopaedia of Islam*, new ed., VII, s.v. MUṢĀDARA. *Lisān* also explains the usage of *ṣādara* in secretary work: An official was forced to bring the

although we cannot deny the possibility that the Sultan may have confiscated property in excess of a 'fair assessment' in cases where his officials had 'ill-gotten gains.' In conclusion, confiscation was not simply considered an arbitrary imposition, but the return of state revenue on a legal basis. It became more frequent and indispensable when the State fell into financial crisis as seen in the third period, for the State gave officials full authority to collect state revenue and thus needed to have that proportion returned which was in the hands of financial officials.

IV *Legal Administration*

Both the bribery to obtain official appointment and the confiscation of their property after their dismissal affected the quality of state officials, because plenty of money was needed not only upon appointment but also after resignation. State officials needed to be from wealthy strata or to possess special economic talent. This change in the quality of state officials was inevitably accompanied by a change in the character of the administration. In this chapter we scrutinize the change of legal administration.[1] Changes in financial administration will be addressed in the next chapter.

In the Mamlūk period after the reform of Sultan Baybars, four chief *qāḍī*s were appointed to each four major law schools

---

money or to promise the money (*Lisān,* IV, p.116).

[1]As for legal administration in the Mamlūk period, see: Emile Tyan, *Histoire de l'organisation judiciaire en pays d'Islam*, Leiden, 1960. Carl F. Petry, *The Civilian Elite of Cairo in the Later Middle Ages*, Princeton, 1981. Joseph H. Escovitz, *The Office of Qâḍî al-Quḍât in Cairo under the Baḥrî Mamlûks*, Berlin, 1984. Jorgen S. Nielsen, *Secular Justice in an Islamic State: Maẓālim under the Baḥrī Mamlūks 662/1264–789/1387*, Istanbul, 1985.

at capitals such as Cairo, Damascus, Aleppo, etc. Chief *qāḍī* enjoyed immense authority, not only as judges at *sharī'a* law courts and official executioners of sentences, but also through right of appointment and dismissal of legal officials, supervision over *waqf* institutions and *waqf* properties.[1]

He appointed various legal subordinate officials (*a'wān*) to execute his judgements: *Nā'ib* was deputized as judge on his behalf. *Nā'ib*s used to sit in judgement at their residences where they would take bribes from litigants.[2] The second is *shāhid* or *'ādil* (witness) who acted as witness to any legal affairs such as marriage, buying and selling etc. and received fees for notarizing documents. They performed their work at *madrasa*s and mosques and had shops (*ḥānāt*, *dukkān*, *maktab*) in the city center.[3] The third type were executors called *naqīb* and *rasūl* who executed sentences of judges, especially collection of debts on behalf of creditors.[4] The fourth one is *wakīl* (agent) who mediated between clients and judges and played a role of negotiator.[5]

These subordinates officials in turn profited by receiving

---

[1]*Ṣubḥ*, IV, pp.34-36, 192.

[2]Judgement: *Furāt*, IX, pp.298-299; *Inbā'*, p.341, 375, 439. Bribes: *Buṣrawī*, p.190; *Inbā'*, p.493; *Mufākaha*, I, p.311.

[3]Notarizing documents: *Mufākaha*, II, pp.29-30, 41. Shops: *Inbā'*, p.306; *Badā'i'*, IV, p.347 (in Cairo); *Kawākib*, I, p.118, 271; *Mufākaha*, I, p.345; *Buṣrawī*, p.128, 231 (in Damascus).

[4]It was prohibited for *rasūl* and *wakīl* to collect too much from both sides of the lawsuit in 919/1513 and to go to the execution without being accompanied by the plaintiff in 918/1513 (*Badā'i'*, IV, p.302, 312, 320). This shows they might profit by the execution of their legal duties.

[5]*Inbā'*, pp.224, 408-411; *Buṣrawī*, p.104. al-Shayzarī (d 589/1093) narrates that the *wakīl* under the *qāḍī* have great influence on the judgement receiving gifts from both parties of the lawsuit, and therefore the right (*ḥaqq*) has disappeard before them (id., *Kitāb Nihāyat al-rutuba fī ṭalab al-ḥisba*, al-Sayyid al-Bāz al-'Arīnī ed., 2nd ed., Bayrūt, 1981, p.110).

fees and bribes in executing legal affairs. We have no information whether they received regular wages from the State or chief *qāḍī*, but it is assumed that their work was self-supporting. In order to do their work, it is not necessary for them to have had knowledge of Islamic scholarship; more important was to have had practical experience of legal affairs. We can find a *shāhid* who was formerly a peasant or a weaver.[1] They started their legal careers from easier work as *shāhid* and *rasūl*, and could be promoted to higher position such as *nā'ib* through accumulating expertise. Such talent ensured great wealth, to the point where a *wakīl* built a grand house, bought slaves and became so influential that chief *qāḍī* himself visited a mere *wakīl*.[2]

Subordinates officials might be dismissed when the chief *qāḍī* retired as al-Māwardī (d. 450/1058) states in his book *al-Aḥkām al-Sulṭāniyya*.[3] Severe rivalry existed among the influential *'ulamā'* seeking the post of chief *qāḍī*, and as was shown in the previous chapter, the subordinate had a tight connection with his master, the chief *qāḍī* and vice versa. They formed an organization called *jamā'a* (faction) or *bāb* (household) under the leadership of chief *qāḍī*.[4] This body was composed of two groups: The first were the above-mentioned legal officials. The other were subordinates called *ustādār* and *dawādār* (Executive Secretary) who were charged with the affairs of the household. To take one

---

[1]A weaver obtained a job of *bawwāb* (gatekeeper) at a madrasa in Damascus, then worked as *shāhid* of Ḥanafī chief *qāḍī*, and was finally promoted to the *nā'ib* of Shāfi'ī chief *qāḍī* by offering a bribe (*Mufākaha*, I, p.50, *Buṣrawī*, p.107, 190, 221, *Kawākib*, I, p.260). A *fallāḥ* (peasant) became *rasūl*, then *ballāṣī* (tax-collector), and finally *shāhid* of the mamlūk (*Mufākaha*, I, p.344).
[2]*Inbā'*, pp.408-411.
[3]al-Māwardī, *op. cit.*, p.96.
[4]*Jamā'a*: *Mufākaha*, I, p.77, 103, 300 etc. *Bāb*: *Inbā'*, p.409, 450; *Buṣrawī*, p.106, 215.

example, Shihāb al-Dīn Ibn al-Furfūr and his son Walī al-Dīn possessed the post of Shāfi'ī chief *qāḍī* of Damascus during about 35 years from 886/1481 and formed a strong *jamā'a*. In 894/1489 a lampoon was thrown into the Governor's Office criticizing the injustice (*ẓulm*) and forcible collecting (*balṣ*) of his *nā'ib*. *Nā'ib*s, *shāhid*s, *dawādār* and *naqīb*s of his *jamā'a* were ordered to Cairo in 895/1490. These two events suggest his *jamā'a* must have committed at least some acts of injustice, if not habitually.[1]

It was the *jamā'a* who executed legal affairs in the later Mamlūk period. They were connected by personal networks among the chief *qāḍī* and subordinates. They could gain personal profit through their work, whether it was carried out in a fair or unfair manner. A further question arise as to why such profitable gain was possible, and whether persons were willing to pay such bribes or fees.

We should first note the increase of lawsuits in the 15th century. In 839/1435 the Sultan decided to free some prisoners due to the shortage of prison food arising from price inflation. Creditors were ordered either to pay for the cost of food or to free the imprisoned debtors and permit them to pay off their debts in installments.[2] This narration shows that there must have been a great many imprisoned on account of debts claimed by creditors, and we can easily imagine that such creditors would willingly pay fees and bribes to officers of the law if such debts were paid. Moreover in 914/1508-1509 a curious order was issued that one must not bring a suit against anybody without just cause (*ḥaqq*) and that the accused must not be deprived of anything by

---

[1]*Mufākaha*, I, p.133, 143; *Buṣrawī*, pp.143-144.
[2]*Sulūk*, IV, pp.966-967, 970. In Islamic law the debtor should be detained in prison until he pays his debt (cf. Schacht, *op.cit.* p.197).

such an unjust lawsuit, and that the lawsuit would not be accepted unless the accused agreed to stand trial.[1] There must have been illegal lawsuits by creditors who intended thereby to gain more than their proper deserts by bribing judges and executors. The *jamāʿa* of legal administration could not profit without these people who wanted to realize their right through legal process.

V *Financial Administration*

We unfortunately lack sufficient information on the financial system of the Mamlūk State, and so I should like to discuss it by focusing on the Treasury of the Sultan.[2] Its chief resources had been *iqṭāʿ* of the Sultan, which comprised 10/24 of all the land of Egypt after the land survey of Sultan al-Nāṣir in 715/1315-6. Two departments played an important role in providing salaries to the Royal *Mamlūks* whose number was estimated between 2,000 and 5,000. *Dīwān al-Mufrad* was responsible for distributing their monthly cash salary (*jāmakiyya*), clothes, and fodder, while the Department of *wazīr* was responsible for distributing meat and other food to them. The chief of the former was *ustādār* who was appointed from the rank of military officials, and head of

---

[1] *Badāʾiʿ*, IV, p.134; *Iʿlām*, p.214.

[2] Studies on financial and secretarial administration are now increasing. The review of the studies in this field is: R. Stephen Humphreys, "The Fiscal Administration of the Mamluk Empire," in id., *Islamic History: A Framework for Inquiry*, Princeton, 1991. See also, Hassanain Rabie, *The Financial System of Egypt A.H. 564–741/A.D.1169–1341*, London, 1972. B. Martel-Thoumian, *op. cit.* Petry, *op. cit.* J.H. Escovitz, "Vocational Patterns of the Scribes of the Mamlūk Chancery," *Arabica*, 23, 1976. Richard T. Mortel, "The Decline of Mamlūk Civil Bureaucracy in the Fifteenth Century: The Career of Abū l-Khayr al-Naḥḥās," *Journal of Islamic Studies*, 6/2, 1995.

the latter was *wazīr* of civilian origin.[1]

The Sultanate was faced with incessant financial crisis from the beginning of the 15th century, because of the decrease of revenue from *iqṭā'* land devastated by continuous epidemics and the disorder of the local administration. al-Maqrīzī mentioned in 837 /1434 the decrease of Egyptian villages from 10,000 to 2170.[2]

Treasury expenditure swelled while state revenue shrank. The cash salary of Royal *Mamlūks* was expanding: 10,000 dinars per month during the reign of Sultan Mu'ayyad Shaykh (815–824/1412–1421), 18,000 dinars during the reign of Sultan Barsbāy(1422–1438), 28,000 dinars during the reign of Sultan Jaqmaq (842–857/1438–1453) and finally at the beginning of the reign of Sultan Qā'itbāy in 873/1468 it reached 46,000 dinars, which was more than four times as much as that of Sultan Mu'ayyad Shaykh's reign. Such constant increase was caused by the new enrollment of beneficiaries other than the Royal *Mamlūks*, that is, *'ulamā'*, merchants, Christians, and common people.[3]

As for the revenue of *Dīwān al-Mufrad,* it did not exceed 120,000 dinars as ordinary revenue plus some illegal taxation in 828/1424, but in 832/1432 the ordinary revenue of *kharāj* (land tax), rents (*ujra*) and commercial tax decreased to 60,000 dinars. In response, the Sultan planned to increase his income, by 30,000 dinars from imposing a monopoly on trade of spices, sugar, cereals, etc., and by another 30,000 dinars from granting to the *ustādār* rights on local governors.[4] The latter plan was rejected. It must have meant bestowing on the *ustādār* the right of appointing local governors in order that the *ustādār* could obtain bribes by

---

[1]*Ṣubḥ,* III, p.453, 478-479. Cf. Ayalon, "The Structure of the Mamluk Army" "The System of Payment."

[2]*Sulūk*, IV, p.912.

[3]*Ḥawādith*, p.689, 691; *Inbā'*, p.34, 36.

[4]The account of 828 A.H.: *Sulūk,* IV, p.688. Of 832 A.H.: *ibid*., IV, p.796.

appointing these officials to cover the lack of ordinary income. The Sultan had already conferred on him the right of appointing local governors (*wālīs*) to supplement ordinary income of *Dīwān al-Mufrad* by bribe (*barṭala*) in 824/1421.[1] Indeed Sultan Barsbāy took various measures to increase state income such as imposing a monopoly on trade, compelling merchants to buy goods from the Sultan at high price (*tarḥ*), and a trade tax (*'ushr, maks*).[2] In addition, in 829-830/1426 he forbade the *ḥimāya* (protection fee) of *amīrs* (military commanders) levied on shops, factories, mills, etc., which can be interpreted as his intention to directly impose taxes on these economic facilities instead of *amīrs*.[3]

As for the Department of *wazīr*, we have data on its management in the second period when the *wazīr* could not provide the Royal *Mamlūks* with their meat regularly and they often revolted because of the shortage.[4] In 860/1456 the *wazīr* Faraj reappeared after fleeing from fear of an attack from the Royal *Mamlūks* and the Sultan bestowed upon him the *khil'a* (robe of honor) in recognition of his loyalty in staying in office. However he also decided to increase the revenue from the Treasury to 40,000 dirhams per day, but the *wazīr* declared he was not able to perform his duty by collecting the ordinary state revenue of *iqṭā'* and *maks* (commercial tax), or even by adding to it the illegal income (*ẓulm*).[5] As this narration indicates, the Sultan had to increase the resources for distribution of meat when he appointed

---

[1] *ibid.*, IV, p.574.

[2] Monopoly of spice trade in 832/1428: *Sulūk,* IV, p.791; that of pepper trade in 833/1430, *ibid.*, IV, p.823; that of sugar in 831/1428, *ibid.*, IV, p.766. Compulsory purchase of beans in 838/1434: *ibid.*, IV, pp.933-934. Trade tax in 829/1425: *ibid.*, IV, p.707; in 838/1434, *ibid.*, p.929.

[3] *ibid.*, IV, p.729, 735.

[4] Stop of the provision and the revolt of *Mamlūks*: *Ḥawādith,* p.225, 330.

[5] *ibid.*, p.251.

the *wazīr*, because the *wazīr* was reluctant to assume this obligation as he knew the difficulty it would entail. In 860/1456 the Sultan increased revenue to 75,000 dirhams per day with the addition of 35,000 dirhams from various taxation rights of *amīr*s of *iqṭā'* and *maks* etc.[1] Here we find that the Sultan tried to deprive the *amīr*s of their taxation rights. In 867/1463 the *wazīr* was offered the revenue of 65,000 dirhams per day from the Treasury with the addition of 100 dinars, which all amounted to 95,000 dirhams from various taxation rights (*jiha*) of the Sultan, other than taxation right (*iqṭā'* and *ta'allqāt*) of the *wazir*.[2]

We should take note of a slight but nevertheless important change in financial policies from the first to the third period. In the first period, the Sultan adopted various measures to increase revenue besides his well-known policy of establishing a personal monopoly on trade. In contrast, later Sultans surrendered direct control over taxation and trade, preferring to bestow rights on the *ustādār* and the *wazīr*. Following the failure to ameliorate the financial crisis, the Sultan Qā'itbāy embarked on a new policy of cutting the salary of the Royal *Mamlūk*s and imposing a tax on the *waqf* endowment and private property of the citizen soon after he ascended to the throne, both of which met with strong objection from the Royal *Mamlūk*s and *'ulamā'*. This policy is significant because the Sultan tried to invade the sanctuaries of the Royal *Mamlūk*s and the *'ulamā'*, the former of which were living on the salary from the Sultan, while the latter had been able to accumulate their properties in the form of *waqf* (religious foundation) and *milk* (private ownership) evading heavy taxation

[1] *ibid.*, p.253.

[2] *ibid.*, p.764; *Nujūm*, XVI, p.277. During the absence of the *wazīr* in 839–840/1436, *nāẓir al-jaysh* 'Abd al-Bāsiṭ accomplished the task by conferring taxation rights on the beneficiaries (*Sulūk*, I, p.997).

according to the regulations of Islamic law.[1]

Whether it was transfer of existing taxation rights or introduction of new taxation, the Sultan could only assign their implementation to financial officials to fill the shortfall in ordinary revenue. The effectiveness of these measures depended on the ability of the financial officials.

Here we shall examine the career of the *ustādārs* and *wazīrs* during forty-eight years of the first and second periods.[2] There appeared 44 appointments to *ustādār* during this period (including re-appointments of the same persons: it become 17 if we deduct persons who were reappointed). The average tenure of office is 1.09 years per appointment and 2.82 years per person. The frequency of changes and reappointments to this post itself suggests the difficult task it involved. Eight appointee were from the military, but most had a financial background in the bureaux of influential *amīrs*. Nine were civil officials, of whom eight were secretaries, and three were of Coptic origin and one was Armenian.[3] As for the *wazīr*, there were 37 cases of appointment

---

[1]*Ḥawādith*, pp.635-637, 689-693; *Inbā'*, pp.33-37; *Badā'i'*, III, pp.13-15, 20-23. Qā'itbāy was forced to withdraw his new tax, but enforced a policy to cut the salary of the *Mamlūks*. Thereafter he succeeded in taxing *milk* and waqf for the foreign expedition in 894/1489 , 896/1491, 907/1501 (*ibid.*, III, pp.260-261, 278-280, IV, pp.14-17, 20). The Sultan collected some of the monthly rents due to *milk* or *waqf* properties such as houses, shops, caravansaries, etc., while their owners collected rents in advance from tenants in order to pay the Sultan's tax. Such temporal taxation on *milk* and *waqf* property was performed during the expedition against the Mongols in 700/1300 and against the Timurs in 803/1401 (*Bidāya*, XIV, p.14; *Sulūk*, I, pp.906-907, III, pp.1052-1053; cf. Rabie, *op. cit.*, pp.107-108).

[2]The career of both officials is examined according to the sources of *Sulūk*, *Nujūm* and *Ḥawādith*.

[3]Financial experience of the military: Arghūn Shāh (*Ḍaw'*, II, p.267); Jānībek (*Ḍaw'*, III, p.56; *Sulūk*, IV, p.914). Coptic origin: *Nujūm*, XIV, p.353, XVI,

and reappointment as *wazīr* by 20 different persons. The average tenure is 1.3 years per appointment and 2.4 years per person. Eight came from the military, ten had been civil officials, two were former merchants. Among those of military background, most had been engaged in the affairs of the military household. The ten civil officials were all secretaries, six of which were of Coptic origin.[1]

There are some other points to be drawn from the careers of financial officials during this period: Firstly, both military and civilians assumed the offices of the *ustādār* and *wazīr*, although in principle the former belonged to the military office and the latter to the civil office. A common feature, however, of both types of financial officials is that they often belonged to families specifically engaged in financial affairs. They were different from the so-called *'ulamā'* in that they had financial experience through having served as secretary in the bureaux of the *amīrs* and others, rather than possessing the legal knowledge of the *'ulamā'*.[2] The reason that the Copts (or Copts converted to Islam) occupied a high proportion of civil officials may be their engagement in financial affairs since the early Islamic period.[3]

---

p.95, 152. Armenian: *Sulūk,* IV, p.693, 845.

[1]Service in the military household: *Nujūm,* XIV, p.281, etc. Coptic origin: *Sulūk,* IV, p.568, 938; *Nujūm,* XV, p.378, XVI, p.69, 85, 135.

[2]*Ustādār* and later *kātib al-sirr* Ṣalāḥ al-Dīn Muḥammad was born in the house of secretary, and was famous for his excellent secretaryship (*Sulūk,* IV, p.574, 1011-1012). In contrast with him, al-Ḥāj Muḥammad al-Ahnāsī and his son 'Alī, both *wazīrs*, were criticized for deficiency in literacy and secretarial talent, for they had only experienced the art of administrative execution (*raslīya* and *barddārīya*) (*Nujūm,* XVI, p.135). Other examples: *ustādār* Zayn al-Dīn 'Abd al-Qādir (*Sulūk,* IV, p.845); *ustādār* Nāṣir al-Dīn Muḥammad (*ibid.,* IV, p.645).

[3]The Copt family Tāj al-Dīn b. Kātib al-Manākh and his son both assumed the office of the *wazīr* during the time between 824/1421 and 837/1433 (*Sulūk,*

In time of difficulties it was a necessary condition of being a financial official that one had sufficient wealth and economic power to endure the payment of huge bribes and confiscation of property, had a talent for collecting taxes and other fees whether they were legal or illegal, and had the leadership ability to conduct one's duties and to command subordinates. Financial officials formed a household (faction) like that of legal officials cited in the previous chapter, as some financial officials employed their subordinates to jointly perform confiscation, and in turn a subordinate strove to make money for his master under the confiscation.[1] The social status of financial officials was beginning to rise due to their growing importance in the Mamlūk Government as evidenced by their right to ride horses or donkeys wearing a turban, gown, long boots and spurs, similar to legal officials. Some of them attained the title of *amīr* and wore military dress. They accumulated wealth and endowed religious foundations.[2]

IV, p.568, 645). al-Suyūṭī mentioned the increase of the Copt *wazīrs* in place of the *'ulamā'* in the Mamlūk period(*Ḥusn*, II, p.216). cf. Donald P. Little, "Coptic Conversion to Islam under the Baḥrī Mamlūks, 692–755/1293–1354," *BSOAS*, 39/3, 1986.

[1]Collecting tax in the provinces: *Sulūk*, IV, p.798, 868-869. Zayn al-Dīn Yaḥyā was appointed to the office of *ustādār* eleven times between 846/1442 and 872/1467, and gained so great power in the Mamlūk Government as to deprive the Royal *Mamlūks* of their *iqṭā'* land which he tranferred to *Dīwān al-Mufrad*. He enriched himself by wicked means such as buying goods from poor workers and then selling them double the price, and he endowed many *jāmi'*s and *sabīls* (public fountains). He was dismissed and 500,000 dinars were confiscated in 857/1453. His subordinates were also tortured by the new *ustādār* until they paid the money for which they had been assessed (*Nujūm*, XVI, p.27, 30, 32).

[2]Administrative staff were permitted to wear gowns and to ride donkeys and horses, similar to the legal officials (*Ṣubḥ*, IV, p.43). Ibn al-'Iwad from *fallāḥ* origin ascended to the office of *ustādār* after serving the office of *amīrs*, and wore a turban, but he continued to speak like a peasant (*Badā'i'*, IV, p.376,

Such elevation created a vacuum that was filled by lower ranks of people such as the butcher, who lacked any secretarial ability or legal knowledge, which a contemporary *'ulamā'* regarded as a sign of decline of the state.[1]

VI *Administrative Networks*

The Mamlūk Sultanate tried to remedy its financial defects through various measures. Institutionalized bribes to obtain official appointment and confiscation were perceived as an integral part of the financial policy of the Mamlūk State, not mere acts of arbitrary or vicious injustice. The appointed officials strove to gain profit by receiving fees and bribes from his clients, or by imposing heavy taxes on the people. Bribery was thus rampant from the top to the bottom rank of officialdom.

How was such conduct perceived by the people? Notorious *'ulamā'* such as al-Maqrīzī and Ibn Taghrī Birdī both criticized bribery because it reached the stage where neither religious nor military officials would take action without being bribed, while men who were ignorant and unjust assumed high posts.[2] Otherwise

387). Ṣalāḥ al-Dīn Muḥammad who took the office of *ustādār*, *muḥtasib* and *kātib al-sirr* had a title of *amīr* (*Sulūk*, IV, p.1011).

[1]Shihāb al-Dīn al-Bībā'ī from a guard in a village got a job at the shop of butcher and succeeded in his business so as to provide meat with the *Mamlūks* as assistant of the *wazīr*. Sultan Khushqadam appointed him *nāẓir al-dawla* in 860/1456, though he was ignorant and lacked a talent of secretary. In 868/1463 he was appointed the office of *wazīr*, which was reported as the worst event of Egyptian history by the historian, because it was assumed by such a person of lower class, though the post of *wazīr* was always occupied by leaders of citizens since the Umayyad dynasty until now (*Nujūm*, XVI, p.278, 340-341; *Ḥawādith*, p.771, 780).

[2]*Ḥawādith*, p.783. We also find many poems of satire criticizing the injustice

their criticism of bribery was surprisingly scant; instead the chronicles tended to report the offering of bribes at the appointment as commonplace and refrained from censure. While accusations were leveled against specific bribe-takers, it was directed against their ill conduct,[1] not against the act of taking bribes itself. Bribery was not criticized as long as it did not create administrative disorder and injustice. An Arabic dictionary in the 8th/14th century moreover relates how payment to defend one's proper rights (*ḥaqq*) against the injustice (*ẓulm*) of others is not called bribery.[2] The people may indeed have approved of their officials conducting their work by receiving various kinds of fees and bribes as far as it did not cause social injustice.

The prevalence of bribery and fees in executing administrative affairs had its root in the administrative system of the Mamlūk period. Firstly, the officials either did not receive any regular salary from the State, or it was insufficient. When asked by the Sultan about the salary of the office of *nāẓir al-aḥbās* (superintendent of *waqf* foundation), al-'Aynī, one of the famous *'ulamā'* of the 9th/15th century, replied: A man of probity gains nothing other than from signing the documents, but a man of evil can gain profit by oppressing the livelihood of the citizen.[3] Officials had no means of sustaining their livelihood or of recouping the cost of being an official other than by receiving fees and bribes from clients asking for their services. Al-Maqrīzī who strongly criticized bribery, mentioned bribes (*barṭala*) for official appointment and *ḥimāya* (protection fee) as among the main

---

which bribery engendered (*Badā'i'*, III, p.448, IV, p.92).

[1]*Nujūm*, XIV, p.345; *Mufākaha*, I, p.313. The chronicles also praised one who neither offered nor received bribes (*Sulūk*, IV, p.1006; *Badā'i'*, IV, p.460).

[2]*Lisān*, XIX, p.37.

[3]al-'Aynī, *'Iqd al-jumān fī ta'rīkh ahl al-zamān*, MS. Dār al-Kutub al-Miṣrīya, Ta'rīkh no. 1584, vol. 19, fol. 443.

financial resources of Egypt.[1] The Mamlūk State might regard bribes as a constant resource and condoned official collection of fees such as *ḥimāya* from the people in exchange for their administrative service or protection. The State therefore could not prohibit bribery completely, even if it temporarily declared bribery to be prohibited when confronting great disasters such as an epidemic.[2]

The second problem is that the administration was not operated by an official bureaucracy, but by influential persons and their networks. Usually there existed such influential persons as ʿAbd al-Bāsiṭ *nāẓir al-jaysh* (Controller of the Army) (d. 854/1450) and Ibn Muzhir *kātib al-sirr* (d. 893/1488), who could wield great power whatever their official posts in the 9th/15th century.[3] Such figures exercised real power of the appointment and amassed enormous wealth during their lifetime. The Sultan conferred upon such influential persons administrative authorities to execute state affairs and they transferred their authorities to their subordinates or to their followers. Thus administrative networks emerged, linked together by conferring authorities, which implemented the state administration.[4]

---

[1] *al-Khiṭaṭ*, I, p.111.

[2] *Nujūm*, XV, p.96 (in 841/1438); *Badāʾiʿ*, V, p.117 (in 922/1516).

[3] ʿAbd al-Bāsiṭ: *Sulūk*, IV, p.1146, 1155-1156, 1159, 1168-1169; *Ḍawʾ*, IV, pp.24-27. Ibn Muzhir: *Badāʾiʿ*, III, p.255; *Inbāʾ*, p.288, 297; *Ḍawʾ*, XI, pp.88-89.

[4] Lapidus pointed out the following feature of the institutions of Middle Eastern Islamic societies in his paper: Institutions were conceived to be embodied in individuals and the authority of individuals did not derive from their roles, but rather attached to their whole persons. Subordinates owed loyalty to the man and not just to the role or the office. (id., "Muslim Cities as Plural Societies," p.144).

Conclusion

More careful study is required before concluding whether the administrative networks of the 15th century were irregular and specific to the era of decline or were common to other periods and other regions. It is well known that in the Ottoman Empire bribery prevailed in a more institutionalized form from the end of the 10th/16th century, although the Ottoman Sultan Selim I criticized the *qāḍī*s of the Mamlūk Government who gave and received bribes when conquering Aleppo in 922/1516.[1] In addition we already know of a similar network for the conferment of administrative authority. It was tax farming through the granting of taxation rights in exchange for payment of assessed sums to the State, a system called *ḍamān* in the 'Abbāsid period and *iltizam* in the Ottoman period. Bribery in the Mamlūk period and tax farming were similar in the point that both bartered administrative rights for cash money. The *iqṭā'* system should be defined as the granting of taxation rights to the military in exchange for their military and administrative service. While their domain over the land was weak, due to the incessant changes of their domains, compared to that of feudalism in Medieval Western Europe, we can think of it as a system to distribute taxation rights as a substitute for salaries for the administrative service, similar to *iltizam* system.

Furthermore, both the offices and rights of the administration might be perceived as private property. We can find terms such as *mustaḥiqq* (holder of legal right) or *ḥaqq* (legal right) to express beneficiaries of state revenue or of offices of *waqf* institutions in the Mamlūk period, and such offices could be divided into two

---

[1] *Badā'i'*, V, p.74. Cf. Ahmet Mumcu, *Osmanlı Devletinde Rüşvet*, Istanbul, 1985.

or three to be given, sold, or inherited as *milk* (private property).[1] Islamic law clearly defined the notion of private ownership (*milk*) and usufruct (*manfa'a*) and treated it as absolute unless it were harmful to the public interest. It is well known that trade and commerce, which developed in the Islamic world, especially in the Middle East, since the 9th-10th centuries, were based on a clearly defined and well-protected concept of ownership. The forming of administrative networks by means of distributing administrative authority as a form of private ownership may have been generated in such a well-developed market society, where every kind of property and property right, including goods, capital, usufruct, and even administrative rights, could be exchanged.

The history of Islamic society reveals to us two polarized tendencies; centralization and decentralization, which occurred in the 'Abbasid State, the Mamlūk State and the Ottoman Empire. Centralization has so far been regarded as the sound and prosperous era of the State in contrast to the decline and disorder that accompanied decentralization. Yet if we take account of the existence of tax farming and other contractual systems of administrative affairs in the above-mentioned periods, administrative networks, meaning a system which bestowed rights from above, or a system which bargained for them from below, had usually operated, whether conspicuous or not. Bribery itself was never the cause of decline, rather the State organization could operate by conferment of the authority in exchange for bribery even if state control over the administration became weak.

In this paper we should make it clear that administrative

[1]*Mustaḥiqq. Mufākaha*, I, p.202; *Buṣrawī*, p.229. Division of the office: *Badā'i'*, V, p.370; *Mufākaha*, I, p.30. Buying the office: *Sulūk*, IV, p.619; *Mufākaha*, I, p.18, 22.

networks spread from the capital cities to the rural regions and from high officials to their mean subordinates, and combined them to form a State. Though it is difficult to define the concept of urbanism, we may class such a flexible system of administration as a conspicuous phenomenon of "Islamic urbanism" because it was realized on the basis of a market society which developed in the Islamic Middle East, if further studies of other areas such as Iran and Maghrib will support this tentative finding.

List of Main Sources and their Abbreviations

Badā'i': Ibn Iyās. *Badā'i' al-zuhūr fī waqā'i' al-duhūr*. Muḥammad Muṣṭafā (ed.), 5 vols., al-Qāhira & Wiesbaden, 1960–1975.

Bidāya: Ibn Kathīr. *al-Bidāya wa al-nihāya*, 14 vols., Bayrūt, 1966.

Buṣrawī: 'Alā' al-Dīn al-Buṣrawī. *Ta'rīkh al-Buṣrawī*. Akram Ḥasan al-'Ulabī (ed.), Dimashq & Bayrūt, 1988.

Ḍaw': al-Sakhāwī. *al-Ḍaw' al-lāmi' lil-ahl al-qarn al-tāsi'*. 12 vols., al-Qāhira, 1353–1355A.H. (1934–1937).

Furāt: Ibn al-Furāt. *Ta'rīkh al-duwal wa al-mulūk*. vols. 7–9, Bayrūt, 1936–1942.

Ḥawādith: Ibn Taghrī Birdī, *Ḥawādith al-duhūr fī madā al-ayyām wa al-shuhūr*. William Popper (ed.), 4 vols., Berkeley & Los Angeles, 1930–1942.

Ḥusn: al-Suyūṭī. *Ḥusn al-muḥāḍara fī akhbār Miṣr wa al-Qāhira*. Muḥammad Abū al-Faḍl Ibrāhīm (ed.), 2 vols., n.p., 1967–1968.

Ighātha: al-Maqrīzī. *Ighātha al-umma bi-kashf al-ghumma*. Muḥammad Muṣṭafā Ziyāda & Jamāl al-Dīn Muḥammad al-Shayyāl (ed.), al-Qāhira, 1940.

I'lām: Ibn Ṭūlūn. *I'lām al-warā bi-man wulliya nā'iban min al-Atrāk bi-Dimashq al-Shām al-Kubrā*. 'Abd al-'Aẓīm Ḥāmid Khaṭṭāb (ed.), al-Qāhira, 1973.

Inbā': Ibn al-Ṣayrafī. *Inbā' al-haṣr bi-abnā' al-'aṣr*. Ḥasan Ḥabashī (ed.), al-Qāhira, 1970.

Kawākib: Najm al-Dīn al-Ghazzī. *al-Kawākib al-sā'ira bi-a'yān al-mi'a al-'āshira*. Jibrā'īl Sulaymān Jabbūr (ed.), 3 vols., Bayrūt, Jūniyā & Ḥarīṣā, 1945–1949. Repr. Bayrūt, 1979.

Khiṭaṭ: al-Maqrīzī. *Kitāb al-mawā'iẓ wa al-i'tibār bi-dhikr al-khiṭaṭ wa al-āthār*. 2 vols., Būlāq, 1270A.H.

Lisān: Ibn Manẓūr. *Lisān al-'Arab*. 20 vols., al-Qāhira, 1300–1307 A.H.

Mufākaha: Ibn Ṭūlūn. *Mufākaha al-khillān fī ḥawādith al-zamān*. Muḥammad Muṣṭafā (ed.), 2 vols., al-Qāhira, 1962–1964.

Nujūm: Ibn Taghrī Birdī. *al-Nujūm al-zāhira fī mulūk Miṣr wa al-Qāhira*. 16 vols., al-Qāhira, 1963–1972.

Quḍāt: Ibn Ṭūlūn. *Quḍāt Dimashq al-thaghr al-bassām fī dhikr man wulliya qaḍā' al-Shām*. Ṣalāh al-Dīn al-Munajjid (ed.), Dimashq, 1956.

Ṣubḥ: al-Qalqashandī. *Ṣubḥ al-a'shā fī ṣinā'a al-inshā'*. 14 vols., al-Qāhira, 1913–1922.

Sulūk: al-Maqrīzī. *Kitāb al-sulūk li-ma'rifa duwal al-mulūk*. vols. 1–2, Muḥammad Muṣṭafā Ziyāda (ed.), al-Qāhira, 1939–1958. vols. 3–4, Sa'īd 'Abd al-Fattāḥ 'Āshūr (ed.), al-Qāhira, 1970–1973.

Table 1: Purposes of Bribery

Periods		I	II	III
Civil Officials	*Qāḍī*	22 (36.1)	8 (11.1)	29 (35.8)
	Kātib al-Sirr	14 (23.0)	4 (5.6)	3 (3.7)
	Financial Officials	1 (1.6)	3 (4.2)	2 (2.5)
Civil Military Officials*	*Wazīr*	1+0 (1.6)	0 (---)	1 (1.2)
	Ustādār	1+0 (1.6)	0+2 (2.8)	0 (---)
	Muḥtasib	2+0 (3.3)	2+2 (5.6)	0+1 (1.2)
Military Officials	Province Governors	3 (4.9)	11 (15.3)	6 (7.4)
	Local Functionaries	6 (9.8)	15 (20.8)	2 (2.5)
	Total of Officials	50 (82.0)	20 (27.8)	60 (74.1)
	Total of Military Officials	11 (18.0)	52 (72.2)	21 (25.9)
	Total of Appointment of Offices	61(100)	72 (100)	81 (100)
	Other Purposes	0	3	13
	Total	61	75	94

The number in parenthesis indicates percentage of each distribution.
* The former indicates the number of civil officials and the latter that of military.

Table 2: Amounts taken as Bribes						
Amount	I		II		III	
	Civil	Military	Civil	Military	Civil	Military
highest	90,000	100,000	10,000	70,000	32,000	100,000
over 50,000	3	2	0	2	0	1
over 10,000	11	3	0	10	5	7
over 5,000	4	0	5	3	5	4
over 1,000	7	3	2	8	13	1
less than 1,000	1	0	0	0	6	0
Total Cases	26	8	7	23	29	13
Total Amount	461,800	227,200	39,000	326,500	164,900	241,000
Average	17,762	28,400	5,571	14,195	5,686	18,538
Total of each period	689,000		365,500		405,900	
Average of each period	20,265		12,183		9664	

All units of amount are dinar.

Table 3: Officials subjected to Confiscation				
Periods		I	II	III
Civil Officials	*Qāḍī*	0 (---)	1 (2.1)	12 (11.5)
	Kātib al-Sirr	0 (---)	4 (8.5)	6 (5.8)
	Financial Officials	1(11.1)	6 (12.8)	7(6.7)
Civil Military Officials*	*Wazīr*	1+0 (11.1)	3+0 (6.4)	4+0 (3.8)
	Ustādār	3+2 (55.6)	10+4 (29.8)	7+3(9.6)
	Muḥtasib	0 (---)	1+0 (2.1)	2+0(1.9)
Military Officials	High Officials	0 (---)	0 (---)	4 (3.8)
	Province Governors	0 (---)	1 (2.1)	0 (7.4)
	Local Functionaries	1 (11.1)	5 (10.6)	7(6.7)
	Total of Officials	5 (55.6)	33 (70.2)	78 (75.0)
	Total of Military Officials	4(44.4)	14 (29.8)	26 (25.0)
	Total of Officials	9(100)	47(100)	104 (100)
	Others	0	1	31
	Total	9	48	135

The number in parenthesis indicates percentage of each distribution
* The former indicates the number of civil officials and the latter that of military.

Table 4: Confiscated Amounts

Amount	I		II		III	
	Civil	Military	Civil	Military	Civil	Military
highest	30,000	30,000	205,000	250,000	200,000	200,000
over 100,000	0	0	2	2	5	2
over 50,000	0	0	3	4	5	3
over10,000	4	2	12	2	11	6
over 5,000	0	0	3	2	9	2
less than 5,000	0	0	7	1	7	2
Total cases	4	2	27	11	37	15
Total Amount	100,000	50,000	786,000	615,400	2,104,000	1,086.200
Average	25,000	25,000	29,111	55,945	56,865	72,413
Total of each period	150,000		1,401,400		3,190,200	
Average of each period	25,000		36,879		61,350	

All units of amount are dinar.

CHAPTER THREE

INFORMAL NETWORKS:
The Construction of Politics in Urban Egypt

Diane SINGERMAN

Introduction

As a student of political participation among the *sha'b* (or popular sector) in the contemporary period, I have argued elsewhere that Western social scientists have ignored a range of informal political institutions which are indigenous to the urban milieu and sustained and supported by both men and women from the lower strata of society (Singerman 1995). The *sha'b* only recently written back into history through the efforts of social and labor historians, students of peasant politics, and feminist scholars, still are portrayed largely as the objects of political rule rather than as the architects of political change and struggle, yet they remain essential to the overall political dynamics of national life.[1] Unfortunately, the specificity of my case study in several densely-populated areas in central Cairo did not allow for a historical analysis which

[1]While the noun, the *sha'b*, refers to a collective people, populace or folk and has an implicit collective connotation to it, as an adjective, *sha'bī* demarcates a wide range of indigenous practices, tastes, and patterns of behavior in everyday life. The indigenous nature of things *sha'bī* is key to an understanding of its meaning among Egyptians. Wealthier, more Westernized Egyptians use the term to distinguish themselves and their way of life from the more popular mainstream because for one reason or another they have departed from a lifestyle that they themselves would identify as more Egyptian. A similar but distinct adjective, *baladī*, is associated somewhat more with one's place of origin and lifestyles or practices which are associated with it (see El-Messiri 1978 and Nadim 1975).

would explore the continuities between political participation and collective life within a larger time frame.[1]

My participation in this round table on Islamic Urbanism and Social Networks has provided a welcome opportunity to begin tentatively to delve into the historical continuities of political life among the *sha'b*, or what several scholars in earlier periods have called the *'āmma* (see Lapidus 1967 and Hourani 1970). What is particularly interesting about the analysis of the politics of the Islamic city is that historians have argued that the *'āmma* could never organize beyond the small, localized, particularistic concerns of the quarter, due to the constraints which foreign rulers, in collusion with the *'ulamā'* (who had their own interests and the interests of Orthodox Islam to protect) placed on larger "political" associations (Hourani 1970, 20; Lapidus 1970, 200). Though I find this argument surprisingly global in nature, Hourani argues that "the whole spirit of Islamic social thought went against the formation of limited groups within which there might grow up an exclusive natural solidarity hostile to the all-inclusive

---

[1]My understanding of the popular sector is based on detailed field work of a small community in central Cairo. By that, I refer to four contiguous districts whose histories and growth date back to the medieval period when the victorious Fatimid rulers of Egypt built a new walled, exclusively royal city in A.D. 969 and named it al-Qāhira. These districts include al-Darb al-Aḥmar, al-Gamaliyya, Bāb al-Sha'riyya, and al-Muskī. The study was conducted between 1985 and 1986, although residence in Egypt for several other years and subsequent trips back later also inform this research. From nine independent introductions the group of people I interacted with, interviewed, and came to know, eventually grew to 350 men, women, and, to a lesser extent, children (197 males and 153 females). I have characterized these 350 people as a community because of their associations and networks with each other. In order to understand the political economy of this *sha'bī* community in more detail, I constructed a sub-sample of the economically active population from the larger group of 350 individuals. Included in the economically active sample were 171 men and 121 women.

solidarity of an *umma* based on common obedience to God's commands (1970, 14)."

In fact, the aims and strategies of the *'āmma* are defined as apolitical and impotent, though it is noted that popular rebellions could cause trouble for the rulers and notables at times, but rarely, if ever, could their complaints spark a revolution. It is this characterization of the aims and strategies of the *'āmma*, as apolitical and impotent which I find so problematic with the literature on the Islamic city and networks in the pre-modern period. I find it problematic because it is based upon the same elitist and state-centric notion of politics which also cripples contemporary political analysis on urban politics in the Middle East. In the contemporary period, the *sha'b* have similarly been written off as political actors, since they have largely been unable to challenge the national elite, even after a series of nationalist independence movements and military *coup d'états* brought indigenous leaders to power in the post-War II era. It seems that many political scientists and historians, like the Ottoman, Mamluk or clerical elite, are more concerned about the mechanisms which maintain order and the status quo than entertaining more normative concerns about the implications of political exclusion and investigating the struggles of the common people. While, it is tempting to draw parallels between the informal nature of politics in the medieval period and the modern era, I am sure that the historical specificity of different eras would be lost. Rather, through a brief discussion of the politics of the *sha'b* in contemporary Cairo which will illuminate the importance of informal networks, I will offer a critique of the very "statist" notion of politics and political participation that some historians of Islamic urbanism have relied upon, and suggest that their conclusions about political life, may need re-examination in light of more contemporary debates about the nature of politics and political change.

In particular, my arguments are comparative in nature, focusing on structural factors and state-society linkages which have been critically important in a variety of polities both inside and outside the Islamic world. In my previous research, while Islamic influences on law, morality, and culture are certainly relevant and influential, I am not generally comfortable with interpreting politics in "the Islamic City" as unique because of its Islamic heritage. Or, as Janet Abu-Lughod has argued, "Why would one expect Islamic cities to be similar and in what ways?" (Abu-Lughod 1987, 160). Rather, I would argue that religious structures and belief systems are themselves intricately related to dynamics of power, and thus should be analyzed more organically.

Informality: Politics and Economics in Popular Quarters of Cairo

According to traditional understandings of politics, those who do not participate in private or state-sanctioned formal organizations and who do not join protest movements or clandestine organizations which directly challenge the established political order, remain 'unaccounted for' and 'uncounted.' Constituencies which are intentionally excluded from formal political participation by a ruling power are not only repressed by their governments but depoliticized, ignored and dismissed by reigning typologies of political activities. Prevailing definitions of political participation suffer from an obvious bias towards influencing the elite, governmental institutions and formal, legal associations. Verba and Nie defined political participation as "the activities aimed at influencing the selection of government personnel and/or the actions they take" (1972, 2). Huntington broadened the definition to include any attempt at influencing government decision-making in general (Huntington and Nelson 1976). Nelson suggested, more recently, that violent and non-violent extra-legal protest activities should be recognized as political participation in authoritarian or non-democratic nations. "Participation is simply the efforts of ordinary people in any type of political system to influence the actions of their rulers, and sometimes to change their rulers" (1987, 104). While this revised definition now includes a wider range of political action it only recognizes citizens as politically active if they directly engage the political elite or rulers.

Furthermore, research on political participation in the United States defined women's activities and their organizations as private or social activities, thus rendering them invisible until the path breaking work of feminist political activists and political theorists such as Carole Pateman challenged the very categories and gender-blind assumptions of political analysis (Pateman 1980). Redefining the public and private realms then becomes crucial to a re-interpretation of Egyptian politics. By examining the dynamic interaction of both men and women in extra-systemic, informal political processes I hope to present an alternative view of politics which locates power in a wider range of structures and institutions, in which both men and women participate. In short, I hope to complicate the story of power, interest and participation in Egypt.

Alternatively, Adam's notion of participation as a "structural, dialectical condition of society" recognizes and understands power struggles and communal conflict within and between communities, neighborhoods, provinces, ethnic groups, and religious groups (1979, 13). An interactive notion of the political process captures the participation of less visible members of the community and refutes, or at least modifies, claims that they are apathetic, alienated or repressed.

The success of narrowly-based regimes to control political participation should not blind scholars to the strength of people's ability to adapt, resist and even prevail. If opposition to a regime is too risky and dangerous, and therefore not publicly articulated, it does not mean that political activity has disappeared, or that people are apathetic or apolitical. Rather, it presents a challenge to look harder, and certainly to look outside of conventional political venues and historical accounts. Men and women in any society may find alternative, creative ways to achieve their own ends, at times even subverting state-sponsored organizations which were intended to serve regime, not opposition, interests (see Bianchi 1984).

This realm of politics, which some have labeled "pre-political" activity, has been the subject of much current multi-disciplinary interest by scholars trying to understand how popular resistance evolves and how activists, such as Eastern European dissidents, for example, have been able to direct the "weapons of the weak" or the "power of the powerless" against dominant political forces (see Garton-Ash 1990; Hankiss 1988; and Havel et al., 1985). Scott uses the term infra-politics to describe this hidden, though pervasive political activity, which also characterizes the Cairene urban milieu.

> For a social science attuned to the relatively open politics of liberal democracies and to loud, headline-grabbing protests, demonstrations, and rebellions, the circumspect struggle waged daily by subordinate groups is, like infrared rays, beyond the visible end of the spectrum. That it should be invisible, as we have seen, is in large part by design—a tactical choice born of a prudent awareness of the balance of power (Scott 1990: 183).

My understanding of "informal" politics, while influenced from the conceptual debates on politics mentioned above, is more directly appropriated from the notion of an informal economy, which Keith Hart popularized in an article on the urban unemployed and underemployed in Ghana in the early 1970s, provoking a paradigm of research on economic development and economic policy (1973). One typical definition views the informal sector as "economic activities which largely escape recognition, enumeration and regulation by the government" (Abdel-Fadil 1980, 15). In other words, those activities which escape the authority of government, by default, constitute the informal sector.[1] Large informal economies are characteristic of highly regulated economies both under socialist and capitalist regimes. In the former, individuals and firms organize their activities to avoid the notice, regulation, and control of a centrally-planned economy, profiting on its contradictions. In the latter, capitalist firms try to enhance their profits by avoiding government regulations and reducing labor costs. Under many government regulations, firms which employ few workers escape a range of regulations which allows them to maintain what some have argued are precapitalist labor relations and industrial organization.

A profusion of cross-national research over the past two decades on the informal sector served to make what had been invisible to policy makers and scholars, visible. Mazumdar argued that the extent of employment in the informal sector in urban settings was very significant, reaching 55% in Bombay, just over 50% in Jakarta, 69% in Belo (Brazil) and 53% in Lima (Mazumdar 1975). Portes concluded that "for Latin America as a whole, roughly 60% of the economically active population, or about 80% of all workers, can be estimated to be employed outside the formal sector" (Portes 1989, 21-22). In a comparative study, Franks compiled thirty-seven different estimates of the size of the sector in twenty-nine countries, finding an average of 41 percent of the urban economically active population employed in the informal sector (1989). Despite the various problems of measurement and definition of informal sector employment in

[1]Castells and Portes argue the informal economy is "not an individual condition but a process of income-generation characterized by one central feature: *it is unregulated by the institutions of society, in a legal and social environment in which similar activities are regulated*" (Castells and Portes 1989, 12).

urban and rural, developing and developed economies, the figures convinced scholars of the vitality and diversity of this sector, though arguments remained about a range of questions, particularly normative concerns over the exploitative or developmental aspect of the informal sector, and the role of policy makers and governments in encouraging, formalizing, or shutting down the informal sector.

In Egypt, the informal economy, informal networks, savings associations, informal communal goods and black markets have been devised by men and women as a way to provide for their families, protect their security and further the collective interests of the community and examples of informality are everywhere. As de Soto wrote in his study of informality in Lima, Peru, "you only have to open the window or step onto the street" to witness this phenomenon (1989, 14). One encounters the informal sector when tripping over a woman on the sidewalk and thousands like her who sell cheap consumer goods, newspapers or fast food in Cairo without a license, or when wandering through an alleyway where young boys are crammed into tiny workshops which ignore labor, tax, and industrial regulations, or when visiting sprawling newly-settled residential neighborhoods which have largely been built illegally on government or agricultural land and without regard to building codes or zoning laws. In almost every family in Cairo, children take private, illegal lessons from their school teachers in order to pass competitive national exams which largely determine their occupational and financial future. In most kitchens in Cairo one finds food purchased from black marketers who illegally and extra-legally procure government subsidized and distributed food and commodities for clients (often neighbors and relatives). Many women in these households organize informal savings associations, *gam'iyyāt*, among their relatives, friends and colleagues to finance another wedding, another trip to the Gulf or a family business venture. All of these activities are informal in nature and provide much needed services and resources for *sha'bī* communities.

The conclusions from my study of a particular *sha'bī* community demonstrate that the informal economy is far more extensive than macro and micro analyses have suggested previously. Approximately 62% of the economically active population of the *sha'bī* community I studied was engaged in informal sector activities in at least one of their primary, secondary, or tertiary economic activities (see Singerman 1995 for further detail). A third of the community relied upon informal employment from a primary source of earnings and almost 90% of all secondary sources of income were informal. In other words, a clear majority of this population depended upon the informal sector for their livelihood.[1] The breadth of the informal economy in *sha'bī* communities is further supported by other macro and micro studies in Egypt, employing a variety of methodologies (see also von Sivers 1987; Meyer 1987; Stauth 1991; CAPMAS 1985; Al-Mahdi and Mashhur 1989; Abdel-Fadil 1989; Tadros, Feteeha, and

[1]In this community and others, the informal sector not only employs people, but production itself is organized informally. Small-scale enterprises, which encompass artisanal production, predominate in this community. Family enterprises are another important component of informal systems of production in Egypt. Forty-eight percent of all informal sources of income in the *sha'bī* community under study were derived from family enterprises as a primary economic activity in this community and nineteen percent of all secondary economic activity. The economic logic of family enterprises is not based purely on market principles, but on motives to strengthen and enrich the family, as well as individuals within the family. They provide opportunities for employment and profit for members of the community that might not work in the formal economy (although some family enterprises are part of the formal economy). They also provide a more socially acceptable option for employment for women, who, without an uncle or brother in their place of work, might be forbidden to hold a job (for further detail see Singerman 1995, 199-204 and Singerman 1995b).

Hibbard 1990; Hopkins 1991; Mahmoud Badr et al. 1982; and Assaad and Neyzi 1986).[1]

Informal political activities are conceptually very similar to informal economic activities. Under authoritarian rule in many developing nations, the state has consistently regulated, licensed, and supervised politics, just as much as it has tried to regulate and supervise the economy. Nevertheless, certain excluded, disadvantaged, or "marginal" economic groups depend upon the informal economy and some even prosper within it. In a similar fashion, certain constituencies which are excluded or marginalized from the formal political system depend upon informal political activities to articulate and further their interests, despite the desire of the political elite to control (read: repress) political participation. In most authoritarian nations, particularly in developing nations, one could argue that the state has always tolerated some degree of economic autonomy among its citizens because of the revenue it has brought to national economies. But these same states tolerate much less political autonomy and thus the ground for legal, visible politics is extremely narrow and men and women use informal institutions, outside of the supervision and control of the state, to pursue their collective interests. Like the nature of the informal economy, informal politics remain embedded and dependent upon a larger political arena. Informal political institutions, such as networks or even families in some polities, operate to further the interests of their members, whether or not those institutions are

---

[1]In a recent study of the informal sector which examines the corpus of macro and micro research in Egypt, Rizk presents the range of these estimates: "In 1986, estimates by Birks and Sinclair were 878,000; Abdel-Fadil 876,000; Charmes, 2,281,000. For 1985, the number rises to about 3 million, according to CAPMAS." Nader Fergany estimates that informal sector employment, using the same "size per establishment" criterion, has grown from 2,434,000 in 1980 to 2,887,000 in 1985. Rizk estimates informal sector employment, based on 1976 figures, at 2,416,000 (1991, 171).

regulated or even noticed by the "high" politics of the state. They link up individuals to larger associations that are collective in nature. Despite political marginalization and exclusion, collective life survives through informal political institutions that people design, establish, and sustain to pursue their interests. Unfortunately, scholars have not addressed the political dimension of the informal sector as forcefully as they have its economic characteristics. I argue that the informal sector not only has its own politics and its own political institutions but that popular interests can be pursued more forcefully when the autonomous financial resources of the informal economy support informal political networks.

Thus, when I speak of informal politics, I am referring to an organizational grid that pervades *sha'bī* communities, deeply embedded within a larger structural context, yet hidden to the dominant ruling powers. In the politics of everyday life among the popular sector in Egypt men and women are constantly involved in forging collective institutions which serve common public and private needs. Through the vehicle of informal political institutions women and men both create public space and invade what is conventionally considered the public arena as they connect individuals, households, and communities to state bureaucracies, public institutions, and formal political institutions. They organize informal networks which weave in and out of the bureaucracy, the offices of politicians, religious institutions, private charitable and voluntary associations, workplaces, households, markets, schools, health clinics, the extended family, and the neighborhood in order to fulfill individual and collective needs.

These networks are pervasive, flexible, and efficient. The range of classes, occupations, age cohorts, and kin groups represented in specific networks is wide, since incorporating people with different characteristics, high and low status and a variety of resources and contacts into the network increases their effectiveness. While these institutions may not look the same to us as formal political institutions they are organized and maintained by their members and bound by what I have called "the familial ethos," or rules and norms which are supported by the popular sector (described further below). They are intentionally designed to serve collective needs and they penetrate the public sphere. Because informal networks link the household and extended family to bureaucratic offices, politicians, the marketplace and public services and institutions, the household, conventionally viewed as part of the private sphere, is incorporated into the public realm. Thus, there is a much grayer area between private society and public politics in Egypt, particularly within *sha'bī* communities which depend upon networks more than other segments of the population. Spatially defined boundaries of public and private, which seem to hold such sway in studies of Islamic urbanism, are transgressed constantly through informal networks, calling into question portrayals of strict gender segregation in Islamic societies.[1]

Informal networks not only have an institutional dimension but they are seen as legitimate in the eyes of their constituents. In many developing nations, "communal sanction is as definitive for informal associations as legal recognition is for formal ones"

---

[1]For example, Hourani argues, "[t]he right of the family to live enclosed in its house led . . . to a clear separation between public and private life; private life turned inwards, towards the courtyard and not towards the street; in the thoroughfares, the bazaars, and the mosques, a certain public life went on, policed and regulated by the ruler, active and at times rebellious, but a life where the basic units, the families, touched externally without mingling to form a *civitas*." I would argue that informal networks in the contemporary period, and probably long before it, allowed far more mingling and interpenetration of physical space than is apparent from spatial forms and ideological constructs drawn, in part, from Islamic cosmology (Hourani 1970, 24).

(March and Taqqu 1986, 5) particularly when legal recognition comes burdened with close supervision from, and dependence on, the state.[1] Again, the role of informal institutions must be seen within the context of authoritarian politics in Egypt where the boundaries between individuals, groups, and state authority are still highly contested and many citizens may not see formal and governmental institutions as legitimate (the illegitimacy of the present Egyptian government has been a central argument of more radical Islamist groups who have challenged the government in a variety of open and clandestine strategies).

Networks are the political lifeline of the community, allowing individuals and groups to cooperate with other members of the community to achieve individual and collective goals. Informal networks provide a mechanism for individuals and households to influence the allocation and distribution of public and private goods (such as security, education, health care, food and credit mechanisms) in their community and in their nation. Informal networks organize, coordinate, and direct individual actions. In short, they aggregate the interests of the *sha'b.* They are a concrete manifestation of extra-systemic political participation not controlled by formal political institutions or the political elite. Neither state institutions nor the political elite dominate informal networks, although the *sha'b* consciously strive to incorporate local state bureaucrats and political elites into its networks to

---

[1]Note how political parties in corporatist or authoritarian regimes may indeed be created by the state to control political participation. For example, in order to offset the remaining power of Nasserists within the bureaucracy and elsewhere, President Anwar Sadat decided to create three "platforms," a rightist, centrist, and leftist one, to participate in parliamentary elections in the fall of 1976. Shortly thereafter these state-created institutions became legal political parties. The centrist platform became the National Democratic Party, the Tagammu', the Leftist party and the Ahrar, the rightist party (Waterbury 1983, 355-359).

facilitate access to public goods controlled by the state. Informal networks are penetrative, efficient, flexible, and encompass a diverse membership. They fill a political need in the community by representing and furthering the interests of the *sha'b*, which have little access to, and influence over, the formal political system. Formal and informal networks permeate daily life and are a critical, though ambiguous and concealed, arena of micro and macro political processes in Egypt. In fact, informal networks now compete with the government's provisionary role which has been a key source of its legitimacy since the 1952 Free Officer's Revolt. According to many historians, the expectation that urban-based governments have an obligation to provide for the basic welfare of urban residents has often been a factor in popular rebellions and protests in Middle Eastern and European cities (see Khouri-Dagher 1996; C. Tilly 1975; L. Tilly 1971; Kaplan 1984; Lapidus 1967; Shoshan 1980; and Raymond 1984).

Networks are designed not only to obtain more frozen chicken or soap from food cooperatives, but to solve intra-family and inter-communal conflicts and promote morality in the community. Through informal networks, the *sha'b* not only seek access to public goods and services, but promote the ideals of the familial ethos, which, in turn, supports the smooth working of informal networks. Without the level of trust necessary to ensure the reciprocity of informal networks, naked self-interest would mitigate against any collective activity on the part of the *sha'b*. Rather, women and men rely on the familial ethos to ensure that individuals subscribe to communal morals and preferences, many of them shaped by the prescripts of Islam. The familial ethos, fashioned by the *sha'b*, supports channels of arbitration, conflict resolution, economic assistance and cooperation in the community. Many of its values and mores seek to ensure the continued reproduction of the family (or marriage and children) which holds such an important place in Egyptian society (both Muslim and

Christian) due to a variety of religious, cultural, economic, and social factors. At the most fundamental level, the family serves its members by providing material and political security, by formulating the obligations and responsibilities of family members to one another, and by supporting family members in the local neighborhood, the larger community, and in their dealings with the state and its bureaucracy. Within these communities, the family provides a structure and a context through which resources are allocated and distributed, disputes are arbitrated, and behavior is closely monitored. Apart from the critical importance of the familial ethos in Cairo, the family itself serves as a political institution for the *sha'b.*

Clifford Geertz describes an ethos as "the moral (and aesthetic) aspects of a given culture, the evaluate elements . . . A people's ethos is the tone, character, and quality of their life, its moral and aesthetic style and mood; it is the underlying attitude toward themselves and their world that life reflects" (Geertz 1973, 126). Although Geertz sets an ethos in a distinctly cultural context, while I would not diminish its cultural meaning, an ethos is also a product of economic and political dynamics and my arguments about the significance of the familial ethos have to be placed within a context of financial insecurity, considerable government intervention in the economy, and a tradition of political exclusion in Egypt.

An ethos of cooperation, arbitration and association with trusted individuals, which promotes a certain code of morality and propriety is situated within the realities of everyday life among the *sha'b*. The Egyptian government through its legal system, executive power and its intervention in the economy also promotes its own vision of justice, development, "the good," and propriety. Its public relations vehicles attempt to influence values and norms in Egypt as well, so that a certain tension between communal norms and "official" norms and priorities pervades daily life within *sha'bī* communities. Communities which are oppressed both politically and economically struggle to control resources and promote their authority and their vision of "the good" even more forcefully (Chazan 1988, 123).

A community's understanding of "the good," of justice, and of fairness, based on a widely shared consensus of values and norms, can obviously serve as the foundation of a wider-reaching political and philosophical outlook. There is a convergence between the familial ethos at the local level and the way in which the *sha'b* judge national events and politics and envision a better Egypt. A communal philosophy can set the parameters for theory construction and praxis. Sheldon Wolin explains how creating alternative norms and visions has an implicit political dimension to it which ultimately sets the ground for challenges to the prevailing order.

> The politics of founding or theory destruction, refers to the critical activity of defeating rival theoretical claims. Theoretical founding has both a *political* dimension and *politics*. The former is the constitute activity of laying down basic and general principles, which, when legitimated, become the presuppositions of practices, the ethos of practitioners. The point of engaging in the politics of theory is to demonstrate the superiority of one set of constitutive principles over another so that in the future these will be recognized as the basis of theoretical inquiry. Thus the founder's *action* prepares the *way* for *inquiry*, that is, for activity which can proceed uninterruptedly because its presuppositions are not in dispute (1981, 402-403).

As Gramsci has suggested in his theory on the role of ideology and culture in political transformation, though the *sha'b*'s organizational and economic resources may be meager, a deeply felt alternative ethos may be utilized to challenge the ideological hegemony of the state through what he called a more gradual and non-violent cultural war of maneuver, rather than a much riskier frontal war of position (see Forgacs 1988, 222-245). The familial ethos in *sha'bī* communities, then, is quite powerful. It orders individual lives, sets parameters of behavior in the community and shapes the political vision of many Egyptian citizens. Like all structures, the family is not wholly benevolent or harmless and the familial ethos is deeply contested within the community. It is an ideal which is shaped by an ever-changing variety of new material, social and political forces.

People understand the ties that join an individual to his or her household, family, school, marketplace, neighborhood, mosque, food cooperative and even to national institutions such as the army or the Parliament. Their political perspective extends to both very personal and more distant institutions. A constant articulation and refinement of right and wrong and propriety pervades daily discourse. This propensity to judge, to voice one's opinions on a particular issue and relate one's experience, is not circumscribed by a Western division between what is public or private. In Egypt, the household is neither isolated nor secluded, but incorporated into the public life of the community through informal networks.

Informal networks have not only a pragmatic dimension, but within the authoritarian context of Egyptian politics, they serve as a collective institution to pursue common objectives, based on a normative commitment of cooperation and mutual reciprocity. Material interests however, are only one component of informal networks and the familial ethos, an ideological current and outlook, legitimizes the principles which sustain informal networks.

Alternatively, many scholars reduce informal networks to a purely materialistic base, stripping them of any ideological legitimacy. Graziano argues that clientalistic exchange is based on "extrinsic benefits, that is, individualized or non-collective advantages." Ideology, on the other hand, is " . . . the polar opposite of exchange in the specific sense that exchange subjects the person to an instrumental logic which facilitates the social and political control over him, while ideology gives an individual autonomous ends on which material and immediate rewards have no hold" (Graziano 1975, 44-45). While social exchange will not undermine the status quo, "ideology, in contrast, has an expressive value and may allow the transformation of the system" (Graziano 1975, 44-45). The tenacity with which urban residents (and peasants in the countryside) protect their autonomy and communal solidarity may be influenced by specific material issues, but to argue that these concerns lack ideological content or the potential to transform the status quo reflects a condescending view of people's ability to understand their relative position and daily struggle in political and ideological terms. It suggests a false dichotomy between the context in which people live, and their beliefs and political preferences.

Too often, a neat distinction is drawn between political and apolitical behavior, the former consciously directed at collective behavior to influence public decisions and the latter merely individual, self-interested behavior directed toward private ends. However, to delink political behavior from self-interest is misguided considering the complex motivations that influence behavior, particularly among people who live daily with scarcity and cannot afford to misjudge their options. As Scott explains in his class discussion of peasant politics in *The Weapons of the Weak*,

> To require of lower-class resistance that it somehow be 'principled' or 'selfless' is not only utopian and a slander on the moral status of fundamental material needs; it is, more fundamentally, a misconstruction of the basis of class struggle, which is, first and foremost, a struggle over the appropriation of work, production, property, and taxes. 'Bread-and-butter' issues are the essence of lower-class politics and resistance. Consumption, from this perspective, is both the goal and the result of resistance and counter resistance. It is precisely the fusion of self-interest and resistance that is the vital force animating the resistance of peasants and proletarians. When

> a peasant hides part of his crop to avoid paying taxes, he is both filling his stomach and depriving the state of grain (1985, 295-296).

The needs, desires, and political preferences of the *sha'b* are inextricably linked to their material condition and they develop institutions, outside the formal framework of institutions to fight their "bread and butter" issues, and articulate an ideology which legitimizes them.

Informal Politics and Islamic Urbanism

The linkages between networks, politics, and patron/client relations is particularly relevant in studies of Islamic urbanism. As noted earlier, historical studies of the Islamic City are laced with arguments that the urban population, outside of some marginal groups, was never able to transcend small, local, particularistic ties to forge political communities and political organizations that had some autonomy. Hourani points to the role of the *'ulamā'* and Islamic law in supposedly obstructing the growth of intermediate associations between the individual and the larger Muslim community or *umma* (Hourani 1970, 14).[1] Furthermore, collusion between the *'ulamā'* and foreign military rule largely thwarted popular participation and occasional rebellions. Lapidus argues that the Mamluks "used their ultimate powers of arms and money in dealing with the *'ulamā'* and the common people to create clienteles which helped serve the needs of city-wide administration, and to control and channel violent popular outbursts so that the equilibrium of the society would be preserved

[1]While this debate certainly lies outside my area of expertise, I would imagine that many students of civil society in the contemporary Arab world, as well as Islamic political activists, would find this argument somewhat problematic and essentialist in nature.

(Lapidus 1970, 205)." Later, adding to the debate about the Islamic city and communes, he suggests why autonomous structures did not emerge during the Mamluk era:

> In Muslim society, which did not cultivate purposive voluntary associations, and whose social life was not so highly segmented as to foster a keen sense of isolation and independent objectives, communes could not develop. Administrative and bureaucratic forms of organization were equally irrelevant except for the central government. The personal loyalties essential to the Mamluk military system militated against it. Hierarchical management of the society was also impossible when administrators could not be found whose loyalties were basically with the regime. There was no base for administration, for there were no agents free of other roles, functions, and social commitments. Insofar as the cooperation of local notables was needed, it would have to be won on a different and unbureaucratic basis. *In the Muslim world politics was not defined in terms of institutions or structures. Politics as the task of coordinating different purposes, people, and interests for the sake of some common goal was defined in terms of networks of overlapping and crisscrossing relationships which were typical of urban life in general* [emphasis added]. Thus, political ties took the form of patronage-clientage relations, relations between two people such that one protected and sustained the other, who in turn provided his patron with certain resources or services. Patronage relations were in principle mutual, but they entailed an element of dependency for the client. While the patron had others who could supply the resources and services he needed, the client risked safety and his life if he abandoned the patron (1967, 186).

In Lapidus' framework, networks cannot be institutions, nor are they structures due to their patron/client character and their inegalitarian nature. Yet, the evidence drawn from contemporary Cairo and other areas, suggests that informal networks are institutionalized, though they do not bear the official imprimatur of the state, even if the state also utilizes networks to further its own interests. Furthermore, informal networks are not mere embodiments of exploitative patron/client relations, but can be more accurately characterized by Lomnitz's notion of "reciprocity networks" (Lomnitz 1977, 209). In her case study of shantytowns on the outskirts of Mexico City, she found that reciprocity networks guaranteed economic security for recent migrants from the countryside which neither market forces nor the state could do. In Cairo, networks provide not only economic but political security.[1] An understanding of networks as both a political resource and a political institution for the *sha'b,* moves beyond the negative connotations surrounding clientelism.

Western social scientists typically condemn the inequality of these relationships while minimizing their mutual reciprocity since inequality conveys an idea of dependency. However, in *sha'bī* communities, dependency is not a wholly negative relationship, since people do not view themselves as individual entities perpetually competing with one another. While competition and self-interest prevail at times, individuals are connected to kin, neighbors and colleagues in more interdependent relationships than is common in the industrialized West. Even the most hierarchical relationships, which reflect a stratified society, also involve reciprocity. People who utilize networks to fulfill individual and collective needs, and to influence the distribution of public and private goods and services, engage other people in their efforts. Although far from altruistic, the system allows people who have access to different types of resources to contribute to, and prosper within the community,

---

[1]Within the Middle East, research on Palestinian refugee communities and shantytown communities in Lebanon have also pointed to the critical role that networks play in providing economic and political security. Anthropologists have frequently suggested that tribal and kinship solidarities provide a cultural explanation for the maintenance of these ties. Although I do not mean to suggest that kin and communal solidarities are not strengthened by Egyptian or Arab culture, it is just as important to re-affirm that *sha'bī* communities rely on these familial and communal ties as a response to government repression and exclusion (see Sayigh 1981, 1985; and Joseph 1985).

despite vast differences in status, wealth, education, piety, or property. The logic of the system promotes the proliferation of one's networks in an ever-widening web, including, not excluding, more and more people. Personal networks supplement wealth, property or status as a determinant of economic or political power.[1] Those who may be wealthy, but have not cultivated a complimentary system of networks, may be more disadvantaged than an uncritical assessment of their assets would infer.

The question of autonomous groups, or the lack thereof, for Lapidus then becomes part of a larger argument about class formation and the question of revolution during the Mamluk period. Strangely, the discussion of class formation lacks any reference to changes in technology or the factors of production.

> [R]ebellions and crimes never sought to change the government but only to ameliorate specific wrongs. As such they belonged to an equilibrium of political actions among the Mamluks, their officials, the notables, and the various classes of the common people. The people were not utterly alienated, but only imperfectly assimilated into the society. They had severe grievances, but accepted limited objectives which could be accommodated by the Mamluks and the notables. A true proletariat, productive of new ideologies and communal forms, and so resentful of disinheritance as to wage war on the established order, never developed in Muslim cities. The *zu'ar*, or the *harafiish*, and the commoners generally all had interests in common with the Mamluk regime as well as in opposition to it. The politics of the excluded became part of the politics of inclusion. The lower classes were caught between violence and impotence (Lapidus 1967, 184).

Or, as Hourani summarizes Lapidus' position,

---

[1]In Morocco people accepted and even encouraged indebtedness, monetary or otherwise, to increase the interdependency of the community and decrease the risk of communal discord. People involved in a network with unsettled claims would hesitate to harm one another for fear of forfeiting their claims (Waterbury 1970).

> [T]he only effective popular associations were those based on the quarters, there were no effective professional or 'political' organizations on a city-wide basis, except for certain 'marginal' and 'anti-social' associations whom the higher orders of the city could only control and use up to a point. . . . At times indeed the 'popular' forces, the instruments of political action, could escape from the control both of the government and of the urban leaders and throw up their own leaders . . . They might continue to exist for centuries, but, as Lapidus has shown, their basis was not the city as a whole but a small unit, the quarter or group of quarters, and their aims were essentially non-political. They could trouble ruler and urban leaders alike, but could not take their place (1970, 20).

While the question of revolution is always of interest, unfortunately too much political analysis conflates political life with "successful" attempts to overthrow the government. The "success" of informal institutions to gain power or their ultimate ability to displace the elite was not the focus of my research in Cairo, nor should it be the central question when analyzing the politics in previous historical eras. There is more to political life than resistance to the state or the possibilities for revolution and more emphasis should be placed on identifying and analyzing the institutional mechanisms which excluded groups create to further their claims and interests. Gusfield has critiqued research on social movements for its linear preoccupation with the question of "success." A "linear image of social movements . . . directs attention to a discrete association of people whose activity is perceived as using means to gain an end . . . The focus of attention on empirical events is on how they advance or deter the achievement of goals consciously stated in organizational programs." Gusfield proposes that

> a more fluid perspective toward the meaning of a movement emphasizes the quickening of change and the social sharing of new meanings in a variety of areas and places. It is less confined to the boundaries of

> organizations and more alive to the larger contexts of change at the same time as it is open to awareness of how the movement has consequences and impacts among nonpartisans and non members as well as participants and devotees. Rather than success of failure of a movement, it is more likely to lead to questions about consequences: What happened? (1981, 319, 323)

Paradoxically, as Lapidus notes, informal networks strive for both autonomy from and integration with the bureaucracy and political elites, because the end-goals of networks are diverse. At times people try to escape the state and, in other circumstances, to exploit it. What they do gain is a modicum of political space, which comes at the cost of extensive organization and intricate webs of association.[1] Building an organizational grid in a society where associational life is tightly controlled and where the *sha'b* have little likelihood of upsetting powerful constituencies with far greater resources at their disposal, still allows these communities room to pursue their interests and expand their political space. Again, the dimensions of this space may be narrow and constantly shifting, but the institutional framework of networks remains in place, responding to changing material and political circumstances. Furthermore, because the Egyptian government has pegged its legitimacy to a social contract with the *sha'b*, it is left with fewer options in the contemporary context of structural adjustment and privatization pressures from national and international forces. The government maintained its commitment to the *sha'b* by providing basic goods and services, in return for political acquiescence. That is, citizens participate

[1]In the context of contemporary social movements, it is just the demand for public space and political inclusion, on the part of formerly excluded constituencies, that has fueled a range of new social movements in Latin America, and Eastern and Western Europe (See for example Hellman 1990; Maier 1987; and Mainwaring 1987).

by consuming, and the government maintains its legitimacy through distribution. To consume, is to be political and stay out of danger. To participate directly in formal politics is to be political but to court danger and the retribution of the state. If the Egyptian government abandons its part of the bargain, and her citizens can no longer consume, there is no reason for them to be politically acquiescent as well.

At the same time, there are recognized limitations to political autonomy and expression in Egypt. Individual or collective will and organization can rarely overpower the resources, power and authority of the centralized, pervasive, bureaucratized Egyptian state. Political demonstrations have been forcibly repressed whenever the population has taken to the streets to oppose increased food costs or other government legislation on labor issues or associational life. On the other hand, the government has often been ineffective in controlling or repressing ubiquitous networks that counteract state policies, such as informal commodity distribution networks for food, unregulated and untaxed savings associations, a black market in foreign currency, the unlicensed and unregulated construction of housing, and clandestine religious and political associations which seek political power and, at times, the overthrow of the government.

Explanations of an atrophied political life in the Islamic City rested on the role of the foreign rulers and religious and merchant notables in circumscribing an autonomous indigenous political life. In the contemporary period, in a variety of Middle Eastern nations, the military still rules, but it is an indigenous military. After the promises of nationalist leaders of independence movements, the fetters which remain on the political participation of the *'āmma* are far more explosive and the costs of repression for regimes, far higher. Despite the vicissitudes of "high politics," the informal networks of "low politics" organize and enhance the political fortunes of the popular sector.

Works Cited

Abdel-Fadil, Mahmoud. 1980. "Informal Sector Employment in Egypt." *Series on Employment Opportunities and Equity in Egypt*, no. 1. Geneva: International Labour Office.

_____. 1989. "Labor in the Unorganized Sector." *Al-Ahrām al-Iqtiṣādī*, No. 1086 (November 6): 18-21.

Abu-Lughod, Janet L. 1987. "The Islamic City—Historic Myth, Islamic Essence, and Contemporary Relevance." *International Journal of Middle East Studies* 19: 155-176.

Adams, Richard Newbold. 1979. "The Structure of Participation: A Commentary." In *Politics and the Poor: Political Participation in Latin America*, eds. Mitchell A. Seligson and John A. Booth, vol. 2. New York: Holmes & Meier Publishers.

Assaad, Ragui and Neyzi, Leyla. 1986. "Locating the Informal Sector in History: A Case Study of the Refuse Collectors of Cairo." Paper presented at the Workshop on the Informal Sector of the Economy in the Middle East, The Social Science Research Council, Munich, 28-31 July.

Badr, Mahmoud et al. 1982. "Small Scale Enterprises in Egypt: Fayoum and Kalyubiya Governorates, Phase 1 Survey Results." *Michigan State University Rural Development Working Paper* no. 23.

Bianchi, Robert. 1984. *Interest Groups and Political Development in Turkey*. Princeton: Princeton University Press.

Castells, Manuel and Portes, Alejandro. 1989. "World Underneath: The Origins, Dynamics, and Effects of the Informal Economy." In *The Informal Economy: Studies in Advanced and Less Developed Countries*, eds. Alejandro Portes, Manuel Castells, and Lauren A. Benton, 11-37. Baltimore: The Johns Hopkins University Press.

Central Agency for Planning, Mobilisation, and Statistics. 1985. "A Study on the Labor Market in Egypt: the Unorganized Sector." Cairo: CAPMAS, June.

Chazan, Naomi. 1988. "Patterns of State-Society Incorporation and Disengagement in Africa." In *The Precarious Balance: State and Society in Africa*, eds. Naomi Chazan and Donald Rothchild, 121-148. Boulder: Westview Press.

de Soto, Hernando. 1989. *The Other Path: The Invisible Revolution in the Third World.* Translated by June Abbott. New York: Harper & Row.

Duben (Dubetsky), Alan. 1977. "Class and Community in Urban Turkey." In *Commoners, Climbers and Notables,* ed. C.A.O. Van Nieuwenhuijze, 360-

371. Leiden: E. J. Brill.

Eickelman, Dale F. 1981. *The Middle East: An Anthropological Approach.* Englewood Cliffs, NJ: Prentice-Hall.

Forgacs, David, ed. 1988. *An Antonio Gramsci Reader: Selected Writings, 1916-1935.* New York: Schocken Books.

Franks, Jeffrey R. 1989. "Unravelling the Riddle of the Informal Sector: A Survey." Harvard University-World Institute of Development Economic Research, unpublished.

Garton-Ash, Timothy. 1990. *The Magic Lantern: The Revolution of '89 Witnessed in Warsaw, Budapest, Berlin, and Prague.* New York: Random House.

Geertz, Clifford. 1973. *The Interpretation of Cultures.* New York: Basic Books.

Graziano, Luigi. 1975. *A Conceptual Framework for the Study of Clientelism.* Western Societies Program Occasional Paper, no. 2. Ithaca, NY: Cornell University.

Gusfield, Joseph. 1981. "Social Movements and Social Change: Perspectives of Linearity and Fluidity." *Research in Social Movements, Conflict and Change* 4: 317-339.

Hankiss, Elemér. 1988. "The 'Second Society': Is There an Alternative Social Model Emerging in Contemporary Hungary?" *Social Research* 55: 13-42.

Hart, Keith. 1973. "Informal Income Opportunities and Urban Employment in Ghana." *The Journal of Modern African Studies* 11: 61-89.

Havel, Vaclav et al. 1985. "The Power of the Powerless." In *The Power of the Powerless*, ed. John Keane, 23-96. Armonk, NY: M.E. Sharpe.

Hellman, Judith Adler. 1990. "The Study of New Social Movements in Latin America and the Question of Autonomy." *LASA Forum* 21 (Summer): 7-12.

Hopkins, Nicholas S. 1991. "The Informal Sector in Egypt," *Cairo Papers in Social Science* 14 (Winter).

Hourani, A. H. 1970. "Introduction: The Islamic City in the Light of Recent Research." In *The Islamic City: A Colloquium.* Papers on Islamic History: I, eds. A. H. Hourani and S. M. Stern, 9-24. Philadelphia: University of Pennsylvania Press.

Huntington, Samuel and Joan Nelson. 1976. *No Easy Choice: Political Participation in Developing Countries.* Cambridge: Harvard University Press.

Joseph, Suad. 1985. "Family as Security and Bondage: A Political Strategy of the Lebanese Urban Working Class." In *Arab Society: Social Science Perspectives*, eds. Nicholas S. Hopkins and Saad Eddin Ibrahim, 241-256.

Cairo: The American University in Cairo Press.
Kaplan, Steven Laurence. 1984. *Provisioning Paris: Merchants and Millers in the Grain and Flour Trade in the XVIII Century*. Ithaca: Cornell University Press.
Khouri-Dagher, Nadia. 1996. "The State, Urban Households, and Management of Daily Life: Food and Social Order in Cairo." In *Development, Gender, and Change in Cairo: A View from the Household*, eds. Diane Singerman and Homa Hoodfar. Bloomington: Indiana University Press.
Lapidus, Ira M. 1969. "Muslim Cities and Islamic Societies." In *Middle Eastern Cities: A Symposium on Ancient, Islamic, and Contemporary Middle Eastern Urbanism*, ed. Ira M. Lapidus, 47-79. Berkeley: University of California Press.
_____. 1967. *Muslim Cities in the Later Middle Ages*. Cambridge: Harvard University Press.
_____. 1970. "Urban Society in Mamluk Syria." In *The Islamic City: A Colloquium*. Papers on Islamic History: I, eds. A. H. Hourani and S. M. Stern, 195-205. Philadelphia: University of Pennsylvania Press.
Lomnitz, Larissa Adler. 1977. *Networks and Marginality: Life in a Mexican Shantytown*. Translated by Cinna Lomnitz. New York: Academic Press.
Al-Mahdi, Alia and Amira Mashhur. 1989. "The Informal Sector in Egypt." Cairo: National Center for Sociological and Criminological Research.
Maier, Charles S. 1987. "Introduction." In *Changing Boundaries of the Political: Essays on the Evolving Balance Between the State and Society, Public and Private in Europe*, ed. Charles S. Maier, 1-26. New York: Cambridge University Press.
Mainwaring, Scott. 1987. "Urban Popular Movements, Identity, and Democratization in Brazil." *Comparative Political Studies* 20 (July): 131-159.
March, Kathryn S. and Rachelle L. Taqqu. 1986. *Women's Informal Associations in Developing Countries: Catalysts for Change?* Boulder: Westview Press.
Mazumdar, Dipak. 1975. *The Urban Informal Sector*. Staff Working Paper 211. Washington, D.C.: International Bank for Reconstruction and Development.
El-Messiri, Sawsan. 1978. *Ibn al-Balad: A Concept of Egyptian Identity*. Leiden: E. J. Brill.
Meyer, Günter. 1987. "Socioeconomic Structure and Development of Small-Scale Manufacturing in Old Quarters of Cairo." Paper presented at the Middle East Studies Association Annual Meeting, Baltimore, November.

Nadim, Nawal al-Messiri. 1975. "The Relationship Between the Sexes in a Harah of Cairo." Ph. D. dissertation, Indiana University.

Nelson, Joan. 1987. "Political Participation." In *Understanding Political Development*, eds. Myron Weiner, Samuel P. Huntington, and Gabriel Almond, 103-159. Boston: Little, Brown & Co.

Pateman, Carole. 1980. "The Civic Culture: A Philosophic Critique." In *The Civic Culture Revisited*, eds. Gabriel A. Almond and Sidney Verba, 57-102. Boston: Little, Brown & Co.

Portes, Alejandro, Manuel Castells, and Lauren A. Benton, eds. 1989. *The Informal Economy: Studies in Advanced and Less Developed Countries*. Baltimore: The Johns Hopkins University Press.

Raymond, André. 1984. *The Great Arab Cities in the 16th-17th Centuries*. New York: New York University Press.

Rizk, Soad Kamel. 1991. "The Structure and Operation of the Informal Sector in Egypt." In *Employment and Structural Adjustment: Egypt in the 1990s*, eds. Heba Handoussa and Gillian Potter, 167-188. Cairo: The American University in Cairo Press.

Sayigh, Rosemary. 1985. "Encounters with Palestinian Women Under Occupation." In *Women and the Family in the Middle East: New Voices of Change*, ed. Elizabeth Warnock Fernea, 191-208. Austin: University of Texas Press.

_____. 1981. "Roles and Functions of Arab Women: A Reappraisal." *Arab Studies Quarterly* 3 (Autumn): 258-274.

Scott, James C. 1990. *Domination and the Arts of Resistance: Hidden Transcripts*. New Haven: Yale University Press.

_____. 1985. *Weapons of the Weak: Everyday Forms of Peasant Resistance*. New Haven: Yale University Press.

Shoshan, Boaz. 1980. "Grain Riots and the Moral Economy: Cairo 1350-1517." *Journal of Interdisciplinary History* 10:3 (Winter).

Singerman, Diane. 1995. *Avenues of Participation: Family, Politics, and Networks in Urban Quarters of Cairo*. Princeton: Princeton University Press.

_____. 1995b. "Where Has All the Power Gone? Women and Politics in Popular Quarters of Cairo." In *Reconstructing Gender in the Middle East: Tradition, Identity, and Power*, eds. Fatma Müge Goçek and Shiva Balaghi, 174-200. New York: Columbia University Press.

Stauth, George. 1991. "Gamaliyya: Informal Economy and Social Life in a Popular Quarter of Cairo." *Cairo Papers in Social Science* 14 (Winter): 78-103.

Stern, S. M. 1970. "The Constitution of the Islamic City." In *The Islamic City: A Colloquium*. Papers on Islamic History: I, eds. A. H. Hourani and S. M. Stern, 25-50. Philadelphia: University of Pennsylvania Press.

Tadros, Helmi R., Mohamed Feteeha, and Allen Hibbard. 1990. "Squatter Markets in Cairo." *Cairo Papers in Social Science* 13 (Spring).

Tilly, Charles. 1975. "Food Supply and Public Order in Modern Europe." In *The Formation of National States in Western Europe*, ed. Charles Tilly. Princeton: Princeton University Press.

Tilly, Louise. 1971. "The Food Riot as a Form of Political Conflict in France." *Journal of Interdisciplinary History* 2.

Verba, Sidney and Norman Nie. 1972. *Participation in America: Political Democracy and Social Equality*. New York: Harper and Row.

Von Sivers, Peter. 1987. "Life within the Informal Sectors: Tunisia and Egypt in the 1970s." In *Mass Culture, Popular Culture, and Social Life in the Middle East*, eds. George Stauth and Sami Zubaida, 243-257. Boulder, CO: Westview Press; Frankfurt: Campus Verlag.

Waterbury, John. 1970. *Commander of the Faithful: The Moroccan Political Elite—A Study in Segmented Politics*. New York: Columbia University Press.

_____. 1983. *The Egypt of Nasser and Sadat: The Political Economy of Two Regimes*. Princeton: Princeton University Press.

Wolin, Sheldon S. 1981. "Max Weber: Legitimation, Method and the Politics of Theory." *Political Theory* 3 (August): 402-403.

CHAPTER FOUR

POLITICAL POWER AND SOCIAL-RELIGIOUS NETWORKS IN SIXTEENTH-CENTURY FES

Mohamed MEZZINE

Is it possible to speak of a concept of Islamic urbanism proper to Morocco (itself part of Maghrib), in traditional or colonial historiography? What place is there for such a concept in the current essays and studies on the history of the Moroccan city?

And if there is indeed such a thing as a concept of Islamic urbanism, would it be possible to apply it to the city of Fes at the beginning of modern times?

—What was the role of political power in the Islamic city?

—What was the role of the socio-religious network?

—Is it possible to evolve a specifics of the Moroccan (and the Maghribi) city for that period?

These are questions which will be addressed, either directly or indirectly, in this overview through the examination of the case of the city of Fes. Founded in the 9th century by Idriss I,[1] political capital of Morocco for over seven centuries and spiritual capital up to now, Fes is the Islamic city *par excellence* in its urbanism, its social, religious and even economic organization.

[1]According to the traditional sources on the history of Fes, Idriss II—son of Idriss I—would be the real founder of the city. See Lévi-Provençal, "La fondation de Fès," *Annales de l'Institut d'Études Orientales* [Algiers] 4 (1938): 23-52. Reprinted in *Islam d'Occident* (Paris, 1948).

I *Preliminary*

The main purpose of this paper is to show the evolution of an Islamic city over a century (specifically the 16th).[1] Its evolution, as seen from within, that is through the dialectical relations of its socio-religious components face to the representatives of (temporary) political power.

The choice of Fes, one of the most ancient and prestigious cities, is deliberate as it makes it possible to apprehend the various shades of these relations in the long term, given the sum total of data that have thus far been gathered on this city. A large number of archival sources and studies have had for object this city,[2] spiritual capital of Morocco (when it does happen to be also its political capital).

Fes held a very special position on the political scene of the Sa'did dynasty which was in power in 16th century Morocco. At the same time, it was a primordial stake for the socio-religious networks of the period—the saints of all the *tariqa*s (*sufi* ways) had their *zawiya* in the city (Fes, the shrine of shrines). The *ulama*, for their part, had the great mosque of the Qarawiyin University with the principal *mederssa*s (schools of higher education) standing next to it and supporting it.

Last but not least, Fes is at the center of a rich plateau (Sais), at the junction of the Maghrib/Mashriq roads via Tlemcen, and of the North to the South roads towards the Tafilalet, and hence towards the caravanning routes.

---

[1]Actually the century under consideration (the Sa'did period in Fes) extends from 1549 to 1642.

[2]See the *Bibliographie de Fes* published by the Moroccan Ministry of Culture. See also the bibliography appended to Mohamed Mezzine's *Fas wa Badiyatuha: Musahamatun fi Tarikh al-Maghrib al-Saadi* [*Fes and its Rural Surroundings—A Contribution to the History of Sa'did Morocco*] (Rabat, 2 vols., 1986) which contains 294 references.

Fes is thus the epitome of the city where the interests of the different components of 16th-century Moroccan society intermingle, at times supplement, but often oppose and cut across each other.

The tribes of the area (Sais) who work *waqf*[1] or *jmaa*[2] lands which provide food for Fes *suqs* organize trade in their own way between the city and its rural surroundings.

Fes accordingly epitomizes the Moroccan city, and in this quest after a system that would eventually help account for the evolution of Islamic urbanism, it would eventually make it possible to examine the relations between political power and urban, rural and socio-religious networks.

But for our approach to be clear it would be useful, and even necessary, to relocate this *problématique* in its historical context on the one hand, and on the other to provide a few elements of information concerning the history of the Moroccan city in general.

1. The Moroccan Historiographic Context

The history of Morocco has always been seen and written as a history of tribes, of dynasties and of cities.

First, Arab historians such as Ibn Abi Zara al-Fassi,[3] and then Ibn Khaldun,[4] organized it along dialectical relations between Bedouin tribes and city-based dynasties. In the *Qirtas* of Ibn Abi

---

[1]Pious bequeathal property.

[2]Collective lands.

[3]Author of the celebrated history of Fes—*Rawd al-Qirtas*—which has now been edited by the Kingdom's Historiographer, A. Benmançour, (Rabat, 1972). French trans. by Beaumier—*Histoire des souverains du Maghreb et annales de la ville de Fès*—(Paris, 1860).

[4]Celebrated author of *al-Muqaddima* [The Proregomena] (Les Proregomènes, trans. Slane), *Histoire des Berbères* [A History of the Berbers], Trans. Slane, 4 vols. (Paris: Geuthner).

Zara, as well as in the *Prolegomena* or even in *A History of the Berbers* by Ibn Khaldun, the great lords of the Sanhadja, the Masmuda, and even the Ghomara are reported to have managed the ten (if not more) centuries of Morocco's history, before even the arrival of Islam in the country, towards the end of the 6th and the beginning of the 7th centuries. Ibn Khaldun has even evolved out of the changes in power a system controlled by what he terms the *'assabiya* (cohesive power)[1] of the tribes.

Later on, court historians of Shereefan dynasties[2] (from the 16th century onwards) were to focus their analyses on the dynasties in power. They described these from within, barely touching upon the socio-religious networks which seemed to be there only to support or oppose the power in place.

In the 19th century and beginning of the 20th, when Moroccan historians of the colonial period came about[3] the historiographic landscape was one of the most complex. History was shared between the *fiqh*, biographical narratives, *tarajim*, and the writings of the *ulama*—scholars who endowed history with an oppositional rhetoric. The urban phenomenon then supplanted the mode of dwelling in rural areas.

The explorers of colonization in the 19th and beginning of the 20th century moved towards a history where exoticism and preliminary inquiry assumed a major importance. The city was then neglected for rural areas in a dichotomy where the tribe was

---

[1]See the study by Yves Laroste, *Ibn Khaldoun* (Paris: Maspéro, 1966). See also the study by Ali Oumlil entitled "al-'Assabiya wa ad-Dawla" ['Assabiya and the State].

[2]Such as al-Fichtali, author of *Manahil as-Safa* (ed. A. Kriem, Rabat, 1972) and al-Ifrani, author of *Nuzhat al-Hadi* (ed. Houdas, Paris, 1888).

[3]Such as Ibn Zaydan, author of *al-Ithaf*, 5 vols. (Rabat, 1929). Mokhtar Soussi, author of *Maâsoul*, 20 vols. (Casablanca, 1960). Mohamed Dawud, author of *Tarikh Titwan*, 8 vols., the last one having been published in 1979 (Rabat: Imprimerie Royale).

opposed to the city—the *Bled Siba* (lands devoid of *Makhzan* authority) being opposed to *Bled Makhzan* (the city in particular).

It was only at the beginning of the 20th century[1] that cities like Fes[2] and Marrakesh[3] were to be subjected to systematic study. And already with the Marçais brothers there were going to appear tentative attempts of comparison between the management of the Islamic city and that of the Greco-Roman, then Christian, then European city.

Interest was directed towards monuments, then customs and habits, then urban society.

Deverdun with *Marrakech des origines à 1912*, the Tarraud brothers with *Fès ou la bourgeoisie de l'Islam*, H. Terasse with *La Qarawiyine* and then *al-Andalus*, and finally Le Tourneau with his work on *Fès avant le protectorat* propose other analytical views. They apprehend the city through the perspective of its monuments, and often through that of its *ulama*, saints and, at a far distance, through its merchants and craftsmen. The socio-religious network then started to make a place for itself in colonial historiography.

On the morrow of independence (1956) the city took over in terms of the amount of written history. Being at the center of nationalist movements (as Fes and Casablanca were),

---

[1]H. de Castries with his series, *Sources inédites de l'histoire du Maroc* which started publication in 1907. L Massignon, *Le Maroc dans les premières années du 16ème siècle* (1906). R. Montagne, *Les Berbères et le Makhzen dans le sud du Maroc* (Paris, 1932). Jacques Berque, *Structures sociales du Haut Atlas* (Paris, 1954). P. Martin, *Quatre siècles d'histoire marocaine* (Paris: Felix Alcan, 1923).

[2]R. le Tourneau, *Fès avant le protectorat* (Casablanca, 1949) and G. Deverdun, *Marrakech des origines à 1912* (Rabat, 2 vols., 1959–1966).

[3]See Mohamed Mezzine's doctoral thesis "Le temps des *marabouts* et des *chorfat*" [The Times of *Marabouts* and *Sharifs*] (2 vols., forthcoming), esp. vol. 1, pp.7-44.

investigations multiplied in ancient and new archives. A new generation of historians, with a view of re-writing a national history of Morocco, at a remove from colonial interpretations, would re-read ancient archives, look for and find new ones.

New texts were edited, annotated and published, and numerous were those which cast a new light on the city, on its social and religious movements, as well as on its relations with political power:

al-Ithaf (5 vols.) by Ibn Zaydan was reissued.

Nashr al-Mathani by al-Qadiri was edited and published.[1]

The *Jadwa* by Ibn al-Qadi (2 vols.) was likewise edited and annotated.[2]

Texts dating from the 16th, 17th and beginning of the 20th centuries, rich in data, were scrutinized by a new generation of academic researchers.

Towards the 1980s new studies on the city come to light. The new sources are utilized and worked out through sharper and more up-to-date *problématiques*. The relations between the rural surroundings and the city are tackled. Attempts at quantitative (serial) history appear with the publication of articles in specialized periodicals.

And the writing of the history of Fes witnessed itself changes similar to those proper to the general history of Morocco except that Fes—standing as it does in the subconscious of Moroccan intellectuals for a heavily studied, if not overstudied city—does not seem to have attracted the attention of researchers after 1956.

Admittedly A. Benmançour edited and saw through publication celebrated texts on Fes:

---

[1] Al-Qadiri, *Nashr al-Mathani,* ed. and annotated by M. Hajji and A. Tawfiq (Rabat, 1977).

[2] Ibn al-Qadi, *Jadwat al-Iqtibas* (2 vols.), ed. and annotated by A. Benmançour (Rabat, 1976).

—The *Jadwa* by Ibn al-Qadi
—*Buyutat Fas al-Kobra* by Ibn al-Ahmar
—The anonymous *Rawdat an-Nisryn*
—*Rawdat al-As* by Maqqari.

But this type of work on Fes was to remain rather limited. The few articles published in specialized periodicals in the 60s and 70s did not qualify Fes as a city at the center of preoccupations of the new generation of historians.

Towards the end of the 70s, when I myself started work on the relations between Fes and its rear rural areas (in the 16th century), I had at my disposal but a limited amount of data. One had to wait for the coming forth of private archives on the occasion of the Hassan II prize which rewarded the most original private documents.[1]

A harvest of unparalleled documents accordingly saw the light of day, and subsequently the relations between Fes and its rural surroundings took another aspect.[2]

Deeds of sale and purchase, *waqf* deeds, *adul* testimonials of all types, manuscripts long considered lost, religious litigation writings. A whole set of documents was to allow for a new approach to the history of Fes, in its newest aspects: namely the relations between political power and the city and rural socio-religious networks.

2. Background Data on the Moroccan City

The Moroccan city has thus come to be studied no longer in comparative terms with model Greco-Roman city, or the Latin city, as colonization historians used to approach it, but as a city whose characteristics wrought themselves through centuries,

---

[1]This prize was started in 1976 and has carried up until now, but the harvest is no longer as rich as it used to be.
[2]See Mohamed Mezzine, *Fas wa Badiyatuha*.

admittedly in relation with its cultural and human environment.

A model evolution of the Moroccan city has accordingly come to be outlined on the basis of the major historical (and chiefly political) stages it went through.

—First with the advent of Islam in Morocco, the city or cities were but—often ephemeral—small military-religious boroughs. These did not start assuming the aspect of a city until the arrival of the Idrissids who redeveloped a part of Volubilis (the Roman city) but who have above all founded and built the city of Fes in the 9th century, making it their capital.

—Later on, at the beginning of the 11th century, the Almoravids were to found Marrakesh on the southern Atlantic plateaux, at the foot of the Deren mountain chain—the High Atlas.

—Other small towns, along the coastline and inland were in the meantime to crop up at the junction of trade routes (Oujida), at the watch posts of major wadis, and at oasis as the latter operated as rallying points for caravans (Sijilmassa).

—During the 12th and 13th centuries as relations with al-Andalus developed and multiplied—Ceuta, Tangier, Arzila, Besora . . . flourished. Fes was expanded through the Fes-Jdid extension.

—During the 14th and 15th centuries, after a period of building and consolidating of the great cities such as Fes and Marrakesh . . . the urban phenomenon was significantly going to decline. For more than a century the destructions initiated by socio-political conflicts were to mark the Moroccan city—Sijilmassa was wiped out of the map. Marrakesh and Fes suffered the excesses of the crisis backlash.

It was only in the 16th century with the Sa'did dynasty that a semblance of rebirth was to proliferate at the horizon. The great capitals were rebuilt—Fes, Marrakesh, Tetuan, Sale, Safi... pending the building in the 17th and 18th centuries of Meknes—by the Alawit dynasty—the recovery Larrash, and consolidation of Anfa (which was to become Casablanca in the 20th century).

In the 20th century when Morocco was made into a protectorate (March 1912), the French were going to privilege what they called useful Morocco, namely that part of the country enclosed between the Atlas mountains and the sea. By the side of the great traditional cities new and smaller ones were then to see the light of day. Each having an economic function of its own—trade city, mining city, and farming city.

Actually the towns which are representative of Moroccan cities and of their evolution are the oldest two—Fes and Marrakesh, the major two political (down to the 20th century), religious and spiritual capitals of Morocco (up until now for Fes at least).

II *Fes—A Model City*

In the 16th century, during the Sa'did period, two powers marked through their presence political life in the country—dynastic power, and the religious power of saints—in the city as well as in the rural surroundings.

Admittedly, when one spoke of political power at the time, one first meant central dynastic power but also religious or military local powers—the fact being that in the 16th century many powers competed with or supplemented central power. The survival of the latter often depended on the balance it managed to work out with the former.

In fact, there was also a socio-religious network which represented indeed a spiritual but also an economic power. It was embodied through the coalition between the *zawiya* heads, through the *ulama* (traditional scholars) and the great city-based families, especially at Fes. The Jazuliyins—linked through their practices and ceremonials to the order of the great Jazuli (d.

1465) were the most represented in Fes.[1] On the other hand, the Qadiriyins—followers of the order of the great Moulay Abdelkader Jilani from Iraq—were also numerous.[2]

These large two religious networks branched off in the surrounding cities and rural areas. These two orders, together with dynastic power, were to be the prime movers of the century in politics, economic matters, and spirituality.

The city of Idriss (its patron saint) was at the time one of the most influential spiritual centers not only in Morocco but also in the Islamic West—and this for over four centuries, that is from the 13th century, under the Marinids, to the 17th under the Alawits. The city, was to be a live stage for the relations between political power and the power of saints.

The position held by the city of Fes in the 16th century in the strategy of Sa'did power was of prime importance. The crown prince (*khalifa*) was its designated administrator. He was in charge of keeping a balance between the representation of the political power based in Marrakesh (the capital) and representation of spiritual and religious powers in general—that of the saints and *ulama*.

The 16th century came out to be a crucial period for the relations between central power and that of sainthood—some historians speak actually of the exacerbation of relations between political power and religious power (or socio-religious network). Morocco had actually experienced earlier in the 15th century the rise of this phenomenon. And its origins must surely be looked for in the Wattassid period (15th century)—even if one reaches beyond this century in a search for origins or consequences.

---

[1]See "Mumti al-Asmaa fi Dikri al-Jazli," undated lithograph by Mohamed Mehdi al-Fassi.

[2]See Hashem Alaoui's *Iltiqat ad-Durrar* [The Gathering of Pearls] (Casablanca, 1984).

But it was not until the 16th century (corresponding to the 10th and beginning of the 11th in the Hegira calendar) that a balance—or imbalance—between the two powers starts to take shape. It is the century which marks the transition from a form of political power supported by tribal *'assabiya* to a power with shereefan origins.

Jacques Berque, *Intérieur du Maghreb,*[1] observes judiciously—at least for the 16th century—that the period of stability Morocco—and especially the city of Fes—went through was the indisputable outcome of the balance struck between shereefan Sa'did (political) power and the power of *zawiyas* and confraternities—the latter being the conjunction of interests between a social network on the one hand, and religious one on the other.

In order to contextualize this, we will need to introduce these two powers, before outlining the major stages in their relations during the 16th century. This should then help to articulate part of the dynamics which activated the Islamic city at the time—through our examination of the city of Fes.

1. Two Powers with Religious Origins

The city of Fes experienced in the 16th century two forms of power. It was Sa'did from 1554 to 1642, and at the same time the pole of attraction of Moroccan sainthood.

—The first one is a monarchical power which derives its legitimacy from its ancestry which links it to the Prophet—that was shereefan Sa'did power.

—Admittedly informal and subjacent, the second one is a religious power whose borderlines take shape in the 16th century and which derives its legitimacy on the one hand from its call for *jihad* (holy war), and on the other from its aptitude at reforming

---

[1]Jacques Berque, *L'intérieur du Maghreb* (Paris, 1978).

Moroccan society—the power of *zawiyas*, chiefly the Jazuliya one.

Fes society at the time had no trouble adapting to these two powers. And even though, as I have already indicated, their aims and objectives intermingle, run into—and sometimes across—each other, written sources make it possible for us to outline the structural, ideological and human framework of their relations.

1. Dynastic Political Power in Fes

Sa'did power is a dynastic power the origins of which (i.e. the *baiaa*), for historians, may be traced back to 1510.[1] Chroniclers, indeed remind us that *baiaa* (investiture) is a politico-religious acknowledgement of the rightful heirs to power in Islam. Yet, *baiaa* also stands as the confirmation of a warlord calling for a defensive *jihad*, now become a necessity for survival. It was a matter of breaking through the noose which was tightening around the country—all of the Atlantic and Mediterranean ports were practically occupied. And this occupation stretched through time—Ceuta being captured in 1415, Agadir in 1505, and Safi in 1513.[2]

a. *The Shereefs of Fes*

The Sa'dids would spend nearly half a century in an attempt to prove their will and determination to loosen this noose and liberate ports (*tughur*)[3] before arriving at Fes in 1549 and settling definitively in it in 1554.

Five great Sa'did princes would succeed one another at Fes

---

[1]The *baiaa* of Mohamed Ibn Abderrahmane, alias al-Qaim bi-Amri Allah, took place at Tidsi, in the Draa valley.

[2]See J. Brignon et al., *Histoire du Maroc* (Paris: Hatier, 1967), 205-222.

[3]They liberated Agadir and Safi in 1541, and then Larrash.

in the wake of the founder al-Qaim bi-Amri Allah—

Mohamed Cheikh	(1549-1557)
al-Ghalib	(1557-1574)
al-Mutawakkil	(1574-1576)
Abdelmalik	(1576-1578)
al-Mançour	(1578-1603)

Apart from al-Mutawakkil about whose alliances with Christians texts keep a self-conscious silence,[1] the other four princes stand out as the heroes of an entire period. Writings on Fes draw out their portraits, repeating tirelessly the inventory of their achievements, with a particular insistence on their generally positive relations with the saints and *marabouts* of different *zawiyas*.[2]

Mohamed Cheikh is cited as being the first to have ever tried with success to bring to toe the line the masters of *zawiyas* and the great *ulama* of Fes and its surroundings. His action would mark the city's written memory.

The episode of the Siege of Fes (1549) and the refusal of the great scholar *(alim)* al-Wansharissi to recognize the Sa'dids and call for their *baiaa* was to complete this image of a hard difficult and uncompromising prince in the subconscious of the common Fassi.

During the ensuing episodes, the struggle for a balanced power Mohamed Cheikh engaged in with the great saints of the period (al-Habti . . .), as well as his endeavors to tax all the *zawiyas* into subservience were to be accounted for as a consequence of that initial stance.

One needs only to glance through Ibn Askar's *Dawhat an-*

---

[1]For the recapture of power, especially during the Battle of Wadi al-Makhazin, or Battle of the Three Kings, which took place on 4 August 1578.

[2]See in particular—"Tarikh ad-Dawla as-Sa'diya," ("A History of the Sa'did State") by an anonymous historian; Fichtali's "Manahil as-Safa"; Al-Ifrani's "Nuzhat al-Hadi".

Nasir in order to assess the impact of Sa'did policy *vis-à-vis* the *marabouts* (saints) and the position which these held in the preoccupations of shereefan princes.

During the period of al-Ghalib (1557-1574), Fes gained in prosperity, equilibrium and security. Although the prince did not live in the city, the latter was at the center of Sa'did policy. It was the northern capital of the country, facing on the one hand the Iberians who were still occupying Ceuta and Tangier . . . and on the other hand the Ottomans who were camping along the eastern border of the country. This privileged situation was to condition the urban politics of central power *vis-à-vis* Fes as well as every single socio-religious reaction in the city during al-Ghalib's reign.

The *khalifa* of the Sultan at Fes was actually to make capital out of this situation—over nearly twenty years central power benefited from the support of *marabouts* and *zawiyas*. This support was actually gained on the basis of an agreement on all the major issues of the period.

When Abdelmalik arrived in power in 1576 through supplanting his cousin Abdelmalik, and notwithstanding the difficulties he met with in trying to establish his authority, Fes *ulama* accorded him their *baiaa* and supported him when he decided to embark upon that momentous battle against the Portuguese Don Sebastian in 1578. The illustrious saint Abu al-Mahassin al-Fassi, with his tremendous hold over Fes, called all the components of Fassi society for *jihad* and for the support of al-Ghalib.[1]

Fes had already had to take position in 1574 *vis-à-vis* the pretender upon his laying claims to his father's throne—when al-Mutawakkil sought the *baiaa* of its *ulama*, Fes granted it first but then withdrew it when he forsook it upon the arrival of his

---

[1]See *Nashr al-Mathani*, vol. 1.

uncle Abdelmalik. The Fassis were thereafter to bear him a grudge for his attitude.

Over the succeeding two years, the city with its various components went through hard times. Insecurity and the break in food supplies were to bring discredit upon Sa'did power: uncertain, as it was seen through the eyes of the city's inhabitants. This is why Abdelmalik and Abu al-Mahassin's call was heeded—the Fassis were thereby giving the Sa'dids a second chance.

It was only in the wake of victory over the Portuguese, in the Battle of Wadi al-Makhazin (1578), that the Sa'dids were able to resume the position that had been theirs in Fes. Al-Mançour—the victorious king—came first to Fes for his investiture (*baiaa*). And this once the city's *ulama* were unanimous in their support, with the great *mufti* al-Humaidi at their head.

And over a period of twenty-five years (1578-1603), Fes was to become anew the kingdom's second city. The Sultan's *khalifa*, crown prince Mohamed Cheikh, was to reign as a master over a subjugated city, even though it was still prey to social uprisings and religious demonstrations. *Ahl Fes* with all their components were following very closely what political power would organize, decide or achieve.

The city thus took part to all the major decisions Sultan al-Mançour often came to take therein—the conquest of the Sudan (1591), the alliance with the Ottomans and later on with the Spaniards.[1] The council whose advice he often sought, in Fes, before taking his decisions consisted of *ulama*, saints, merchants and *sharifs*.[2] This is actually the network which contemporaneous sources labeled *ahl Fes*, a label where filiation to the city transcended affiliation to a dynasty, a religious order or a craft.

Under the reign of Moulay Ahmed al-Mançour Sa'did policy

---

[1]See Fichtali's *Manahil as-Safa*.
[2]*Ibid*.

in Fes maintained the same supports and the same principles—the preservation of a balance between the various forces in presence—with the *ulama* and *marabout*s on the one hand, and the *amma* consisting of merchants, craftsmen and landlords, on the other. So long as that balance was maintained, stability prevailed in the city.

In 1603, upon the death of al-Mançour, the city was to suffer the full backlash of the crisis of succession the Sa'did dynasty went through. Fes even became an object of covetousness—the *baiaa* of its *ulama*, the support of its saints, the money of its merchants were alternately sought by the different pretenders.[1]

For a start Zaydan (1603-1605) therein obtained his first *baiaa*, and his supplies, set up his clans and alliances, but could not last. As Fes and Marrakesh were between the hands of his brother Abu Faris and then of his brother Mohamed Cheikh, Zaydan could not preserve a solid balanced and stable mode of administration.

The politico-religious frictions that ensued out of alliances and misalliances never made it possible, either for Zaydan or for the other brothers who succeeded him in Fes, to bring the city back to the state of stability it experienced under their predecessors. The main religious figures at Fes were actually looking away—towards the *zawiya* of Dila. The latter was a dynasty-type religious organization which had succeeded in setting up a real "seigneury" with an administration, an army, a proper management of economic matters, etc. all of its own.

Towards the middle of the 17th century, when the *marabout*s of this *zawiya*—settled along the borders of the Fazzaz (Middle-Atlas) mountains—reached the city gates and besieged it, the latter hardly put up any resistance. *Ahl Fes*, in their quest for

---

[1]See Naciri's *l'Istiqsa*, vol. 6, pp.7-15.

peace and stability did not miss the opportunity of disposing of a moribund dynasty for a *zawiya* in full prosperity.

b. *Sa'did Achievements in Fes*

Yet the different Sa'did princes who succeeded each other at Fes (or Marrakesh, the political capital) never spared their efforts to give the town the character of a great Islamic city.

They redeveloped old religious temples and built new ones. The large central mosque of the Qarawiyin was then expanded and redecorated. Its present-day huge library stands out as the work of Sa'did princes. The ornamentations of the great *sahn* [patio] with coloured *zellidj* (mosaics), the marble basins which pour forth limpid and purifying water—as well as the two kiosks which shade them—are all the work of Sa'did princes, al-Ghalib and al-Mançour.[1]

A large number of places of prayer have nowadays been dated back to the period of *sharifs*. Quarter mosques were built, chiefly towards the southern eastern section of the city in the then new housing areas—al-Ayoun, Qlaqlyin, Bab Jdid, al-Makhfia.

The Sa'dids did all they could to consolidate the city's religious and cultural infrastructure, thereby confirming their undeniable resolve to win over the saints and *ulama*.

Around the Qarawiyin mosque, trading quarters developed and carried transactions where the licit often competed with the illicit. Large shopping streets ran across the *medina* from west to east and were cut across by a network of alleys and culs-de-sac which were teeming with life and offering a favorable environment for the propagation of religious ideologies. Shops stood by the side of *funduqs*, *mederssas* and quarter mosques, all of the latter being sites where religious, trading and political projects formed

[1]A. Tazi, *Jami al-Qarawiyin*, vol. 2, pp.340-341.

and dissolved. The large number of the scribes, *adul*s and *tullab*s who gravitated around the Qarawiyin shared in the recording of this swarming into their *kunnashat* (school notebooks).

By the beginning of the 16th century Leo Africanus (al-Wazzan)[1] already described these quarters as the most active, the most populated and the most commercial. Some forty years later Marmol,[2] a Spanish prisoner in Morocco during the Sa'did period described these same quarters and reported on their development.

The al-Andalus refugees, in the wake of the Reconquista, settled in Fes and were to reinvigorate trade in the city.

Contemporary accounts, such as al-Qadiri's "Kunnasha,"[3] report definitely on the arrival and settling of these refugee populations in the main quarters of Adwat al-Qarawiyin. A large number of families—known to the present-day in Fes—had settled during that period—

The Tahiri Jouti family
The Debbagh family
The Cheddadi family
The Mançouri family
The al-Bayad family
The Bergi family
The Bazzaz family
The Bennouna family

Sa'did princes, as a matter of fact, contributed efficiently to the development and reorganization of the city.

On the one hand they rebuilt the ramparts, set up *bordj*es (the North Bordj and South Bordj)—namely control

---

[1]Leo Africanus, *Africae Descripto* (1526), French trans.—*Description de l'Afrique*—by Epaulard (Paris, 2 vols., 1956), vol. 1, 192-204.

[2]Marmol de Carvajal, *Description de l'Afrique,* French trans. by P. d'Albancourt, vol. 1.

[3]Al-Qadiri, "Al-Kunnasha," Rabat: Bibliothèque générale, N° 676.

towers—around Fes Jdid so as to provide security for the city against the Ottomans as well as against the often discontented tribes who lived around Fes—such as the Sheraga, Ouled Jamaa, and the Kholts.[1]

On the other hand, they decontaminated by means of hydraulic works—gigantic by the standards of the period—all the surroundings of Wadi Fes which streams across the city from the South-West to the North-East. They set up a dam—Abi-Tuba—at the gates of Bab Jdid in order to stop the recurrent overflowing of Wadi Fes, thereby setting up water reservoirs which could be of use in case of drought.

The Sa'did period was admittedly a period of stability and, according to some reports, of prosperity for Fes. Yet, allusions to famine, epidemics and spells of drought remain frequent, notwithstanding the Sa'did princes' efforts to build, in Adwat al-Andalus, granaries and silos for the storing up of grain in anticipation of hard times—an age-old tradition which was developed by Sa'did princes.

These difficulties are probably the real reason that could account for the development and multiplication of the phenomenon of *marabouts*—in Fes and its rural surroundings.

Uncertainty during those difficult periods of drought often went hand in hand with insecurity and disorder thereby creating a need for moral and religious support. The *zawiyas* with their *sheikhs* and followers were always there to provide food for the needy and to teach them prayers and panegyrics.[2]

The multiplication in the number of *zawiyas* for the sheltering of the hordes of the needy and the poor who then became followers of a saint or a *tariqa*, in Fes as well as elsewhere in Morocco—to

[1]See *Manahil as-Safa*, *loc. cit.*, pp.162-170.
[2]See B. Rosenberger and H. Triki, "Famines et épidémies au Maroc aux XVIe et XVIIe siècles," *Hespéris-Tamuda* 14-15 (1973–1974).

the extent of embarrassing dynastic political power—was to generate a new situation. The relations between political power and society had more and more to be transacted through these religious intermediaries. In each city, in each region there used to settle one or many saints, according to contemporaneous accounts, in answer to an unprecedented social solicitation, thereby setting up a solid and powerful politico-religious sainthood.

2. *The Socio-Religious Network*

As a network, sainthood is a phenomenon which developed especially in 15th and 16th century Morocco in general, and in Fes and its rural surroundings in particular. A large number of orders, or *tariqa*s, thus formed in Fes. But the most powerful ones, that is those which managed to infiltrate Fassi society at the time were the Jazuli order and the Qadiri order.

a. *Jazuliya*

Fes, given its status as a spiritual capital, was to attract the great names of Moroccan sainthood of the period. Al-Jazuli Mohamed Ibn Abderrahman Ibn Suleiman, one of the great renovators of Shadilism (13th century), created an unprecedented *marabout* movement in Morocco. Between 1465, date of his death, and 1578, date of the Battle of Wadi al-Makhazin victory, the followers having themselves become masters were to swarm throughout the country. Both in the rural areas and in the city of Fes, *marabouts*, and saint-headed confraternities, were to multiply.

With the support of all the social components of society, calling for *jihad* against the Christians occupying coastal towns, substituting themselves for temporal power both in the city and in the rural surroundings through the relief provided to the needy and the poor during the great famines, the saints were becoming for central power an inescapable interlocutor.

At the origin of both the *baiaa* of the Sa'did dynasty's

founder,[1] and of the gathering which rallied around the *sharifs*, the *muridin*—disciples and followers of the Jazuli movement—had structured themselves into an omnipresent veritable network. They were in Fes, as well as in the Ghomara country (North of the city) or the Sais plateau (South and South West), the spiritual guides of an often troubled population. Schoolmasters on occasions, directors of conscience, ideologues in times of trouble, the *awliya* (saints) were to mark the century with their religious imprint.

Fes used to harbor a large number of saints—some of them rose to fame as they were close to power, or on the contrary because they opposed it.

According to Ibn Askar's *Dawha,*[2] more than 125 *wali* or *marabouts*, having links with the Ghomara country, lived in Fes at the time. Ibn al-Qadi's *Jadwa* reports that practically all the Fes *ulama*, over a period of three generations, had more or less solid links with Jazulism, when it was not with its rival movement—the Qadiriya. They expounded its principles, advanced its reform of religious practice and taught its songs and dances.

b. *Qadiriya*

Qadiriya, the second *tariqa* then practiced and followed by a large number of *marabouts* or *ulama* in both Fes and Morocco, is slightly different from Jazulism.

Referring themselves to the great master Moulay Abdelkader Jilani, whose shrine is in Baghdad, the followers of this movement were less numerous in Fes. Already known in 14th century Morocco, Qadiriya did not actually develop until the 15th and

---

[1]The Saint Sidi Mohamed Ibn Mubaraq was, according to some sources, the instigator of this *baiaa* (investiture).

[2]Ibn Askar, *Dawhat an-Nasir*, ed. M. Hajji (Rabat, 1976).

16th centuries with the arrival of the Ottomans in North Africa.

Qadiriya is a *tariqa* which is more practiced in Tunis and Algeria. And as a result of the often difficult, nay bellicose, relations between Fes, Algiers or Tlemcen, all the followers of this movement were held in suspicion. The network which Qadiriya evolved had none of the solidity of that developed by the Jazuliya.

One of the great scholars of the period, Ahmed Zerrouk, had actually attempted to evolve a doctrine, and hence a movement, which would subsume the two *tariqas*, the Zerroukiya. However, the Jazuli network dominated on the whole the sites of the sacred, of knowledge, and of trade. Accordingly, both Qadiriya and Zerroukiya did but supplement an already powerful socio-religious system.

The success these movements achieved originated in their simplicity and their accessibility even to the *amma* (the common people). This made it easier for their ideas and practices to permeate all compartments of Fassi society.

From *alim* to *sufi*, from craftsman to countryman, from tradesman to politician, from the guilds of craftsmen which had saints of their own to the quarters which venerated their own *marabouts*, sainthood came to be everywhere and thus filtered literally through society—on both the horizontal and the vertical levels[1].

The sites of the sacred in Fes—mosques, *zawiyas* and even *mederssas*—provided ideal locations for the propagation of the *tariqa*'s ideas and for direct contact with the followers. These were visited by heterogeneous congregations consisting of *talib* (students), *muridin* (disciples), of merchants from the shopping arcades, of countrymen on visit to Moulay Idriss, of soldiers

[1]See A. Tazi, *Jami al-Qarawiyin, loc. cit.*, especially the latter part of vol. 2 dealing with the biographies of *ulama*.

waiting for a new campaign.

The sermons and the *awrad*—a form of panegyric in the recitation of which the congregation shared during ceremonies or at prayer times—often facilitated the debating of current political economic and religious events. Links came thus to weave themselves between the various components of a civilian society in quest after equilibrium. Facing political power, a network of influence was now getting organized and gaining in importance.

With their participation to the administration of the city through water distribution, the regularization of commercial transactions via the *ulama* (*mufti*), their contribution to facilitating social interaction by means of sermons and public preaching, saints became for shereefan power an intermediary, an unmatched regulator of social tensions, a warrantee for stability. Actually, the major bargains of the period involving the administration of the city of Fes were often transacted in close collaboration between the princes and the socio-religious network.

2. The Administration of the City of Fes Between Political Power and Socio-Religious Networks

Traditionally Islamic city administration has been the concern of political power (in place) as much as a matter of collaboration between that power and the city's social network, on the basis of a set of customs and traditions which have acquired with time the power of laws and which have been fashioned by the *sunna*. However, what has been peculiar to 16th century Fes is that its administration became more the concern of corporation representatives, of quarter *sheikhs* and of *zawiya naqibs* than that of central power. Besides, this occurred not only because this power was settled in another capital (Marrakesh) but because Moslem urban societies were managed by veritable networks, and that these were more religious and above all closer to the saints than ever before, in the 16th and 17th centuries.

1. Managing the Sites of the Sacred and of Knowledge

The very urban structure of the city is, furthermore, a structure which highlights the rise of the religious within society. The city is actually an interweaving of quarters (*hawmat*) and constructions where religious buildings seem, symbolically, to win over buildings with a political or administrative character.

a. *Implantation of Mosques and Mederssas in the Social Fabric*

The green tiled roofs stand out clearly when the Fes *medina* is watched from above. The sites of the sacred, then those of knowledge, wearing the green for emblem, seem keen on holding the city, on framing it, on having it live through a dense cultural spirituality standing halfway between a regular and stable orthodoxy and an often radical *sufi* observance.[1]

Over one thousand religious buildings (782 during the Marinid period, just for mosques) carve out a place for themselves in an urban fabric which is also occupied by buildings accommodating the everydayness of the city.[2]

Administrative buildings were rare in the *medina*. The Boujlud Kasbah had indeed been dominating the city with its high walls ever since the Almoravid period, relayed in this by the Marinid Fes Jdid, with its palaces, towers and ramparts. But all these constructions remained relatively at a distance from the *medina* center where mosques, *mederssas* and *zawiyas* maintained a certain primacy.

These religious buildings, most of which date back to earlier

---

[1]"Fès Médiévale," special issue of the French review *Autrement* [série "Mémoires," 1 N° 13 (Février 1992), ed. Mohamed Mezzine. See in particular the articles by Lucien Golvin, Catherine Cambazard-Amahan, Abdelaziz Touri and Abd el-Ghani Maghnia on the sites of the sacred and of knowledge in Marinid Fes.

[2]See Ibn al-Qadi, *Jadwat al-Iqtibas, loc. cit.*, vol. 1, pp.48-49 and 51.

periods, seem to structure themselves around the nucleus formed by the Qarawiyin, emblematic of religious and scholarly orthodoxy (the *ulama*), and the Moulay Idriss mausoleum, symbol of the city's patron saint, and also of the period's triumphant sainthood.

The other *zawiyas*, *mederssas* and quarter oratories are dotted around that nucleus in a pattern of concentric circles. Controlling the main itineraries, located at the far end of alleys and culs-de-sac, welcoming at the city's main gates the newcomers from the areas around Fes, or from al-Andalus, Tlemecen, or even the Mashriq, these sites of the sacred generated a scholarly or at least devout society which trained craftsmen and merchants and thereby turned them into potential allies.[1]

b. *Everyday Administration*

The administration of these sites, itself inspired by the *shariaa*, gave the socio-religious network an unparalleled force of cohesion.

The *nadhir al-ahbas*, a personage as important as the *muhtassib* who has complete control over the management of the *waqf* of each of the *medina*'s different institutions, is at the heart and center of this network.

Designated by the Sultan, this personage is an *alim* priding himself on understanding mysticism and considering himself, at least during the 16th century, a follower of the saint of saints—al-Jazuli.

Actually the *nidharat al-ahbas*, being in charge of administering *waqf* property, is itself an early municipality. Its self-administered fortune in land and real estate was beyond comparing with individual fortunes.

Under the Marinids, when a fire had destroyed the Qarawiyin's records, the Sultan (Abu al-Hassan) decreed that all

[1]See Ibn al-Qadi's *Jadwat al-Iqtibas, loc. cit.*, vol. 1, pp.48-49 and 51.

houses, shops and workshops were property of the Qarawiyin *awqaf*, and of Fes *mederssa*s and mosques, until proof to the contrary was provided—by means of an *adul* testimonial.[1]

Each mosque had its own land and real estate property which provided it with a budgetary autonomy that facilitated its management.

The Qarawiyin, for example, had *habus* property in terms of shops, houses as well as arable land (*jnanat*) outside the city. It even owned olive orchards in the Sais, the pre-Rif and on the hills to the East and South-East of the city, as well as in the Beni Yazgha[2]. Some Qarawiyin *hawalat* concerned also real estate property in the Tafilalet, some 200 miles away from Fes.[3]

Moulay Idriss' mausoleum—which shelters the tomb of the city's founder is of a more recent construction than the Qarawiyin (1437), as it was built on the location of the former Shurafa mosque—owns for its part a whole fortune in terms of land and real estate property accumulated by *waqf* through donors and benefactors.[4]

The different *mederssa*s, both at the periphery and the center, all benefited either from their own *waqf* or from that of the mother house which is the Qarawiyin.

Last but not least come the *zawiya*s and their quarter mosques, the first being meeting, prayer and seminar venues often acquired by the *sheikh* through purchase or donation. Their administration is simpler as it is private. *Zawiya* followers are themselves in charge of the profitable management of its possessions, by enlarging these and storing them up through offerings made by new members.

---

[1] A. Tazi, *op. cit.*, pp.340-347.
[2] See *Hawalat Fas al-Qara*, microfilm, N° 135.
[3] *Hawalat Fas al-Qara*, microfilm, N° 137.
[4] *Hawalat Fas al-Qara*, microfilm, N° 145.

Yet, the fact is that the city of Fes has always been difficult to manage by the different dynasties which have succeeded one another in it. And more particularly ever since the Wattassid period, that is since the propagation of the Jazuliya *tariqa*, after 1465.

From that time onwards, Wattassid and then Sa'did princes had to reckon with the *ulama* on the one hand, but also and especially with the followers of the Jazuli movement and more particularly with their saints. The major names, famous at the time, include—al-Habti, Ibn Khajjou, al-Ghazouani, Abu al-Mahassin, at-Taba, al-Ghomari, etc. In point of fact the administration of the city of Fes, during the Sa'did period, was to prove very difficult.

All occasions were suitable for *ahl al-hall wa al-aaqd* (those with the power to do, and undo) to oppose power, take issue with its legality, dispute the legitimacy of its laws.

During nearly a century of power in Fes (1554–1642) the city was to experience a large number of problems. It had to take stand on political matters, on issues relating to administration and water distribution, and on everyday matters.

2. *Political Administration*

Politically, the city of Fes, regimented as it was by that veritable network of saints and merchants, was going to be solicited for two types of problems under Sa'did power—the problem of the *baiaa*, and that of *jihad*.

a. *The Problem of Baiaa and of Succession*

The *baiaa* is that act of allegiance whereby a city, a community or a social category proclaim their subservience to the prince who requests it. In general *baiaa* is enacted by the *ulama* who are supposed to represent the entire population. And given that the city of Fes held a very special position within the context of other Moroccan cities—thanks to its university mosque, its *ulama* and *fuqahas*, its shrines and its different sites of prayer—its *baiaa* was mandatory for any prince aspiring to acquire a definitive legitimacy. This applied for the Almoravids, the Almohads, the Marinids and then the Wattassids, as well as for the Sa'dids.

With the very first conquests and successes, the Sa'dids thought of the Fes *baiaa*. After the conquest and *baiaa* of Marrakesh, they arrived in Fes in 1549. The city first refused this *baiaa* and held up a siege of more than six months, surrendering only through force. Thus all through a century of Sa'did power, Fes was to act as an arbiter in the proclamation of princes. The city's *ulama* and *sheikhs* had become an important element in/for the progress of power. A large number of *ulama* and *zawiya* have made themselves famous through their refusal to give support to a given prince or through grating it to another.

Al-Wansharissi had refused *baiaa* to Mohamed Cheikh and was eliminated for that. Two other *ulama* were to suffer the same fate—Harzuz and Zaqqaq.

Later on, al-Qasar lent his support to al-Mançour (1578) and then to his son Zaydan (1603), but then turned against the latter and called for the proclamation of his brother Abu-Faris, and subsequently of Mohamed Cheikh.

Actually, all along their exercise of power Sa'did princes needed the support of both the *ulama* and the saints. The fact was that succession rules were not always respected, when there were any at all. Zaydan relates—in a now celebrated letter addressed to Cheikh Abu Abdallah al-Hahi—that it was his grandfather who had set up the "from the eldest to the eldest" succession rule.[1]

Contemporaneous reports relate diverse accounts on the

[1]*Nuzhat al-Hadi*, which quotes the entire text of the letter, pp.172-180.

relations between power and the socio-religious network concerning the enforcement of this succession rule.

Ibn Askar mentions, in his *Dawha*,[1] the case of the celebrated saint al-Yasluti who had always refused to give his backing to Sa'did princes. He declined throughout his life meeting any one of them. Ibn Askar also recalls the case of Shatibi who used to say—"I am poor and I don't need to see them . . ." All these refused their support to the Sa'dids. And yet, the same Ibn Askar relates that Abdallah al-Habti never disdained meeting Mohamed Cheikh.[2]

During the period which followed—that of al-Ghalib and then al-Mançour—a period of relative prosperity, the *ulama* and the saints gave their support to the Sa'dids. Such was the case of Ali Ibn al-Hadj al-Aghçaoui who would always answer al-Ghalib's call in Fes.[3] And such was also the case of Abu an-Nuaim and Bensuda who gave their support to al-Mançour and publicized it in both Fes and the rural surroundings.

After 1603, during the difficult period the city went through, al-Humaidi, and then al-Qasar, would change sides in accordance with circumstances. They were to contribute with other *ulama* and saints to the departure of the Sa'dids and the arrival of the Dilaites. The followers of the *zawiya* of Dila who had arrived and settled in Fes in 1642 were paving the way for the arrival of a new dynasty—the Alawits.

b. *The Problem of Jihad*

Next to the debate on *baiaa*, another debate vital as much for power as for sainthood in Fes was to graft itself on the first. *Jihad* (holy war) had been the Sa'dids' argument into power. At

---

[1] *Dawhat an-Nasir, loc. cit.*, p.14.
[2] *Idem.*, p.14.
[3] *Idem.*, p.40.

Fes, the dynasty had emphasized its success in *jihad* against the Christians, at Agadir and Safi (1541), by means of seeking the Fassi population's *baiaa*.

Fassi *ulama* and saints, for their part, never relented from calling for *jihad* for the liberation of occupied sites. Some of them even contributed to the supervision and training of troops.

Cheikh Abu al-Mahassin[1] distinguished himself in Fes through his appeal for *jihad* and his taking part to battles.

Sidi Ali Ben Ottman Shawi, Sidi Mohamed Ibn Raissun al-Alami also took part in the Battle of Wadi al-Makhazin.

Later on, when Sa'did power started to degenerate, Ibn Bakkar al-Ghomdi, Abdelwahed Ibn Achir, Abdelhadi Ibn Tahir appealed for *jihad* and sought political leaders for that purpose.

In this context, two reproaches have been leveled at the Sa'dids by the *a'yan* of Fes (notables, merchants, religious figures and *ulama*) concerning *jihad*.

The first one related to the Sa'dids' deemphasizing of *jihad*, towards the end of al-Ghalib's reign and during al-Mançour's, and above all to their signing accords with the Christians.

The second one, especially after 1603, focused on their having compromised with Christians—Mohamed Cheikh gave them up the port of Larrash in 1610.

This Sa'did retreat in the fulfilling of the promises made to the Fes *a'yan*—in their failure to lead a proper and constant *jihad*—was to contribute to the rupture between the two parties.

The Sa'dids sought by all means to subjugate a city which had already opened its gates to the Dilaites who were promising a redemptive *jihad*.

Al-Ayashi, a saint and fighter for the faith, was to show them how *jihad* should be properly led.

The city now followed its new spiritual leaders, even though

---

[1]See al-Ifrani, *Safwat man Intachar*, p.46.

neither al-Ayashi, nor the Dilaites could fulfil all of the Fassi population's expectations, or resolve the city's economic and everyday problems.

The alliance with these new spiritual leaders was ephemeral. Other *sharifs* were already soliciting the city's support.

3. The Economic Administration of the City

Traditionally, Fes city markets followed the law of supply and demand. During normal periods of political and economic stability, trade carried on between the rural areas and the city in the following manner.

On the one hand Fes rural surroundings—Sais, Zouagha, Beni Yazgha, Shraga—provided the city with farm produce. Wheat, barley, olives, wood, flax, etc. were sold in the city's different *suqs*. Political power, represented through the *muhtassib*, did not control the quality of goods, the honesty of merchants and the security of the markets. Merchants' corporations saw to the proper use of authority. On the other hand, the city flooded these rural surroundings with the wares of its craftsmen. Its different workshops (538 according to Leo Africanus) manufactured utensils, farming tools and everyday consumer products.

Contemporaneous texts report on this regular come and go between the rural surroundings and the city, at times of stability. The role of sainthood is then relatively minor, but that of merchants and craftsmen in seeing to the balance of exchanges is then momentous. Frauds are censured by corporations and the *ulama* lend the support of their condemnation to any deviation. Contemporaneous religious jurisprudence texts—especially those relating to *Muâmalat*—depict a business minded society, keen on profit, where the authority for regulating commercial transactions is shared between the *mufti*, the *shariaa* (Islamic law) representative, and the *qadi*, representing the *sultan* (political come in power).

This is particularly clear at times of hardship and crisis. And Fes, during the Sa'did age, suffered several years of drought, famine and epidemics, in addition to periods of political trouble and instability.

Except the few crises which are cited in contemporaneous documents only through allusion and which are limited in both time and space, several momentous crises shook 16th century Fassi society:

—The great famine of the turn of the century (1519–1520-1), coupled as it was with the spread of epidemics, was most terrible.

—The 1569 crisis, provoked by drought, was to deal a major blow to Fes and its rural surroundings.

—The great 1581 epidemic then those of 1601, 1602 and up to 1607, were to mark the memory of Fes population. The disruptions of trade circuits, political disorders triggered off by insecurity as well as famine were all reducing the city and closing its gates, its shops, its towers.

—The ensuing years of drought which occurred in 1611, 1617 and 1623 were to bring to completion the destruction of age-old trade networks.

In point of fact, the entire 16th Sa'did century was marked out with long or short subsistence crises. Fes knew them all as its entire urban and commercial structure had been affected through them. And no sooner had the first crises set in than the authorities, representative of central power, had proved unable efficiently to manage the city.

Demonstrations here, rebellions there, mutinies and desertions yonder, dear prices, dishonest speculation—these were the fate of a city in times of hardship.

Merchants—especially towards the end of the century—were weary of the exactions of power itself. Farmers were affected by the requisitions of warring troops. The common people—the *amma*—were unable to face the exorbitant prices of basic necessity goods.

The entire urban society was affected. People then turned towards the network of holy men which was developing in Fes. The *zawiya*s of these saints became real charity centers geared towards providing food and at times shelter. Through a profitable use of benefactors' donations, saints redistributed a wealth accumulated at times of prosperity.

The saints' network thus became increasingly powerful whilst dynastic power was losing in prestige. The city's everyday management, towards the middle of the 17th century, passed over into the hands of *zawiya*s, *ulama* and merchants. This would account for the success of the *zawiya* of Dila at creating a real politico-religious power, with a hierarchy of its own and a dynasty of saints, and at imposing itself in Fes as the only viable power in those hard times.

Conclusion

From within the perspective of a tentative generalization of the concept of Islamic urbanism, it would be difficult to provide definitive and precise answers to the questions raised at the beginning of this paper on the role of political and religious powers in the administration of the Islamic city, and on the specificity of the Moroccan city. For that, one would need to multiply examples, develop analyses and extend examinations. Yet, it would not be inopportune to observe first:

1—that the viability of the Moroccan city in modern times depended on the balance, struck at the expense of one or the other, between political power and religious power;

2—that no temporal power in the Islamic city could be viable unless it enlisted the strength and support of religious power;

3—that the socio-economic administration of a Moroccan city, during that period, was chiefly the concern of sainthood, and that the latter had ended up attaining that political power it had been aspiring to ever since the turn of the century;

4—last but not least, that the social dimension in Islamic urbanism was, during periods of stability and prosperity, the concern of central political power, and during crisis periods the concern of religious power.

However, even though this paper has not specifically sought to offer a systematic comparison between the "classical" Islamic city and the local Islamic city—the Moroccan one in this occurrence—and on the basis of our examination of the case of Fes, the view may now be advanced that the very concept of Islamic urbanism is one which is too general, if not too large. This becomes all the clearer when one elaborates the examination of local cases, especially that the general cannot—from the standpoint of method—be the sum total of the particular in all its diversity. The Moroccan city is admittedly an Arab-Islamic city, endowed with the general characteristics of Islamic urbanism, but it also retains conjectural and even structural specificities which are entirely its own.

This is the reason why the study of the Islamic city should no longer be carried the way it used to at the time of the Protectorate by historians in Morocco who "imperatively" imparted the Islamic city with a Latin or Greco-Roman referent. It should not either be undertaken the way it currently inclines in general studies on the Arab-Islamic world where the so-called attributes of Islamic urbanism are often arranged into schemes by means of sweeping generalizations. One should rather premise the study of Islamic urbanism on local studies which would give primacy to the records and manuscripts on specific cities and areas for the writing of urban monographs. This, in any case, is the trend in current historical writing in Morocco. And this by itself is a way of contributing, however unassumingly, to a rewriting of the history of the Islamic city.

CHAPTER FIVE

THE PASTORAL CITY AND THE MAUSOLEUM CITY:
Nomadic Rule and City Construction in the Eastern Islamic World[1]

HANEDA Masashi

Introduction

In a pioneering work that first drew attention to the individuality of Iranian cities in the Islamic world, Jean Aubin examined the causes for the growth of settlements on the Iranian Plateau from the three aspects of geography, economics and politics.[2] His wide-ranging arguments may be summarized as follows. Geographical factors took precedence in the development of cities on the dry Iranian Plateau, in that they were built on the edges of the plateau where there was a supply of water. These cities were surrounded by an extensive rural zone, from which they cannot be considered separately. Even when natural conditions were disadvantageous, though, economic factors might prevail, as where cities grew up on trade routes. Such cities however would decline when trade routes changed, as is well illustrated in Southern Iran. Cities also

---

[1]This is a revised version of my article "Bokuchi-toshi to Bobyō-toshi," originally published in Japanese in *Tōyōshi-kenkyū*, 49-1 (1990). I thank Charles Melville for his helpful suggestions and useful comments. I regret, however, that I could not always make the best use of them. The paper was at the final stage of the redaction when he kindly read the draft.

[2]Jean Aubin, "Eléments pour l'étude des agglomérations urbaines dans l'Iran médiéval," in *The Islamic City*, ed. by S. M. Stern and A. Hourani, Oxford, 1970, pp.69-71.

developed through political factors, such as by occupying an important strategic position, or by being connected with a particular interest group. Those cities which grew up in the period political power was exerted by nomads fall into the same categories. Their routes were different to the regular trade routes and passed through many areas of adverse geographical conditions, yet particularly in the Mongol period a large number of structures were built along them. These however had only a temporary existence, owing to princely whim, and they disappeared once the rulers grew to favour the traditional cities. Only Sulṭāniyya survived to the seventeenth century. This city followed a pattern well known in Central Asia from early times, that of a union of a town with a surrounding pastoral area (*association de ville-pâturage*), and its survival owes to three factors: that it was a commercial centre for nomadic people, that it was strategically important, and that it was situated on the east-west trade route.

Aubin's concept of the *association de ville-pâturage* in particular has attracted scholarly interest. This I would like to call the "pastoral city." Turko-Mongolian nomadic tribal incursions into the Iranian Plateau after the eleventh century influenced Iranian society in a number of areas. The "pastoral city" was one such, and numbers of them grew up during the Mongol period, when nomadic power was particularly strong. First and foremost of the characteristics of such cities is that they combine the pastures where the nomads had their quarters and an urban area, but we can also consider the three conditions that contributed to the survival of Sulṭāniyya to be in themselves general characteristics of the "pastoral city."

As research progresses regarding city plans and construction in the eastern Islamic world after the Mongol period and we have come to know more about specific cities,[1] it has become

---

[1]See M. Haneda & T. Miura eds., *Islamic Urban Studies: Historical Review*

clear that new cities were built that cannot be explained by the concept of the "pastoral city" alone. Therefore it would appear that the time is ripe to amend systematically the way we have understood the history of city construction under nomadic rule. Accordingly, this paper will first examine in as much detail as possible based on historical sources the conditions under which a city was built, its location, and its later history, using the example of Ghazaniyya, a forerunner of full-scale urban construction by the Mongols. It will then examine Sulṭāniyya (first half of the fourteenth century) and Naṣriyya (latter half of the fifteenth century) and discuss features in common among the three cities, with the intention of making it clear that (a) these cities should not be considered only as "pastoral cities" but as "mausoleum cities" as well; (b) the *waqf* played an important part in the survival of a city; and (c) city construction by nomads was not a passing phenomenon but its influence continued through to the building of the new Iṣfahān by Shah 'Abbās at the beginning of the seventeenth century.

I *Ghazaniyya*

1. The Conditions under which Ghazaniyya was Built

Ghazaniyya is the general name given to the mausoleum Ghazan Khan (1295–1304), the seventh Īlkhānid ruler, built for himself and to the charitable and religious institutions associated with it. Centring on this complex of buildings there came into being an urban centre, called variously Shām, Sham, Shamb, and Shamb-i Ghazan.[1] For sake of convenience I will transcribe

---

and Perspectives, London, 1994, pp.242-250.

[1]Opinions vary concerning the original name. D. Wilber discusses whether the word Shām came from Shām, which means Syria, or from shanb, that is, a

it here as Shām. Let us begin by examining the process by which Ghazaniyya came to be built.

It had been a custom from ancient times among the Turks to erect, when a tribal leader or an influential person died, a splendid grave recalling his achievements in life, as well as on occasion a commemorative stele. The plains of Northern Asia are still today dotted with such graves and memorials. The so-called Orkhon inscriptions of the Türküt are good examples. This custom did not change when the tribes were converted to Islam, and the majority of Muslim Turk rulers have left mausolea. The Turks who entered West Asia were no exception; in Iran many mausolea were built during the Seljuq dynasty. The so-called mausoleum of Tughrul Beg (1038–1063) in Ray and the great domed mausoleum of Sultan Sanjar (1117–1157) in Merv are typical examples.[1]

The Mongols, by comparison, though similarly a nomadic people, had always kept the location of the graves of their leaders a secret. The whereabouts of the grave of Chingiz Khan, thought to be somewhere in the Mongol highlands, is famously unknown. The same tradition was continued by the Īlkhānid Mongol state founded by Hülegü in Persia, and the graves of the Īlkhānid rulers continued to be built away from settlements and the knowledge of people. The whole area around them was made a sanctuary (*ghurūq*) to which entry was strictly prohibited[2]. During

---

cupola (*The Architecture of Islamic Iran. The Ilkhanid Period*, Princeton, 1955, p.124). According to M. G. Mashkūr, the word is Azeri and means a flat and green place ("Taḥqīqī dar bāra-yi Shanb-i Ghāzān," *Bāstānshināsī va hunar-i Īrān*, no. 3, été 1348/1969, pp.23-24). The same phrase is repeated in another work by the same author: *Tārīkh-i Tabrīz tā pāyān-i qarn-i nuhum-i hijrī*, Tehran, 1352, pp.472-473.

[1]A. U. Pope, *A Survey of Persian Art*, 1964–1965, Tehran & Tokyo, III, p.1018, VIII, p.282.

[2]Honda Minobu, "Iruhan-no tōeichi, kaeichi (The Winter- and Summer-

the time, however, of Ghazan Khan, this tradition was greatly dented. According to the *Jāmi' al-tavārīkh*, this renowned Khan, converting to Islam, overthrew old customs and brought about innovations in many aspects of society. It describes the traditional attitude to graves in the following way:

> Because the traditions (*rasm*) of our ancestors were such, and because it was not desirable for a Muslim to erect his own tomb, there was no confusion in [our] beliefs. There was however no advantage in this (not building a tomb). Since we had become Muslims, our customs (*shi'ār*) had to be according to the way of Islam, for the ceremonial forms of Islam (*rusūm*) were far superior to our practices (*'ādāt*).[1]

After this passage there is a description of how Ghazan made a pilgrimage to a number of sacred mausolea, including that of Imām al-Riḍā in Mashhad, and how, impressed by their splendour, he determined to build a mausoleum for himself. His thoughts at the time are recorded in the following words:

> How many of the dead can there be that have such mausolea? In their death they are happier than others still living. Though our piety cannot be compared with such holy men, we can learn from them and build some pious foundations ("portals of piety;" *abvāb al-birr*) about my own eternal abode. May that through such work (*barakāt*) we can attain the grace of

---

Quarters of the Il-khans)," *Tōyōshi-kenkyū*(The Journal of Oriental Researches), 34-4 (1976) p.104. On the discovery of Arghun's tomb and its exact location, see R. Zipoli, "The Tomb of Arghūn," in *The Proceedings of Primo Convegno internazionale sull'arte dell'Iran islamico*, Venezia-Tehran, 1978. Devin DeWeese discuss in detail the meaning of the word "goruq" and shows how the word is used in various Mongol states. *Islamization and Native Religion in the Golden Horde*, The Pennsylvania State University Press, 1994, pp.179-203. On the Ilkhanid case, see particularly pp.190-193, where he emphasizes a link between the word qoruq and the enthronement sites of the new khans.

[1]Rashīd al-Dīn, *Jāmi' al-tavārīkh*, III, ed. A. Alizade, Baku, 1957 (abbreviation: JT), pp.415-416.

> Almighty God, performing charitable works and giving alms as perpetual pious deeds (JT, p.416).

From this we can discern at least two reasons behind the building of a mausoleum by Ghazan. First, he would fulfil his duty as a Muslim and attain God's grace by constructing charitable institutions, often called in his time "portals of piety," near his mausoleum, and donate his wealth to them. Second, he wanted to sleep in a splendid and well-managed mausoleum, such as he had visited on his pilgrimage, that would be visited by many people. Needless to say, his hope was that by so doing his spirit would be tranquil and his name and works resound down the ages. Causing people to gather together at charitable institutions was for Ghazan killing two birds with the one stone.

Selected as the site for the mausoleum was a place called Shām in the middle of the Bāgh-i 'Ādiliyya on the south-west outskirts of Tabrīz (JT, p.324). Here Ghazan's father, the ilkhan Arghūn, had already ordered the building of several structures. The *Jāmi' al-tavārīkh* notes:

> Arghūn Khan liked undertaking large-scale building and made a sizable suburb in the village of Shām of Tabrīz. There he built a large caravanserai (*khān-hā*). Here [the Khan] ordered any who would to build houses and construct waterways (*kahrīz*). He called it Arghūniyya (JT, pp.346-347).

Having selected Shām, with its connections with his father, Ghazan immediately ordered the construction of a mausoleum. He was extremely enthusiastic about the work and would visit the site whenever he had the time. It is said he personally supervised the workmen and answered technical questions (JT, pp.324, 410sq.). His fervour can be gauged by his strict orders to make the dome larger than that of Sultan Sanjar's mausoleum so that it would be the greatest in the world (JT, p.416). The construction began on

October 5, 1297 (Dhū al-Ḥijja 14, 696) and was still to be finished when Ghazan died in May, 1304.[1] When completed, the mausoleum was as splendid as the Khan had planned, duodecagonal in form, and with a dome that measured to the vault of the cupola 130 *gaz* in height. The interior was illuminated by eighty lamps, each of which was made of gold and silver weighing fifteen *man*, and 300 *man* of lapis lazuli were used to decorate the ceiling and walls.[2]

A number of charitable institutions were built in Shām together with the mausoleum. The main ones were, according to the contemporary *Jāmi' al-tavārīkh* of Rashīd al-Dīn and *Tārīkh-i Vaṣṣāf* of Vaṣṣāf:[3]

1. The mausoleum (*'imārat*)
2. The Friday Mosque (*masjid-i jāmi'*)
3. Two *madrasas* (belonging to the Shāfi'īs and the Ḥanafīs)
4. A Sufi convent (*khānqāh*)
5. A residence for descendants of the Prophet (*dār al-siyāda*)[4]
6. A hospital (*dār al-shifā*)
7. A library (*bayt al-kutub*)
8. An observatory (*raṣad*)

---

[1]Cf. C. Adle, "Le prétendu effondrement de la coupole du mausolée de Qāzān Xān à Tabrīz en 705/1305 et son exploitation politique," *Studia Iranica*, 15-2 (1986), pp.267-270.

[2]On the architectural features of Ghazan's mausoleum, see A. U. Pope, op. cit., pp.1054-1056, D. Wilber, op. cit., pp.16-22, 124-126.

[3]JT, pp.417-424, Vaṣṣāf, *Tārīkh-i Vaṣṣāf*, Tehran, 1338 (offset printing of the Bombay edition of 1269), pp.382-383.

[4]On the function of this institution, see Akio Iwatake, "Nizāmuke-no wakufu-to 14 seiki-no Yazudo (Vaqf of Niẓām Family and the City of Yazd in 14 Century)," *Shirin*, 72-3 (1989) p.27. Iwatake asserts that the *dār al-siyāda* in Yazd had two functions: a residence for descendants of the Prophet (*sayyids*) and a base of charity for the *sayyids*. Ghazan treated the *sayyids* respectfully and built several *dār al-siyādas*; besides that in Tabriz, they were built in Isfahan, Shiraz, Baghdad, etc. See JT, p.399.

9. A "house of the law" (*bayt al-qānūn* or *bayt al-ḥikmiyya*)[1]
10. The administrator's mansion (*bayt al-mutavallī*)
11. A reservoir (*ḥawḍ khāna*)
12. A public bath (*garmāba-yi sabīl*)

Once the buildings were finished, a residential quarter grew up around them, which, joined with the existing Arghūniyya, formed a new town. It could not have been large, since Mustawfī refers to it in the *Nuzhat al-Qulūb* as a "small city" (*shahrcha*).[2] It was doubtless the place where those who worked in Ghazaniyya lived. In fact, the walls that Ghazan planned for the town were said to be longer than those of Old Tabrīz, which suggests he included both the residential district of Shām and a wide green belt around it in the area to be protected (JT, p.414). Ultimately, Ghazan's early death resulted in the suspension of building work and the walls were never completed. Nevertheless it should be noted that Ghazan had intended to create a city that included areas of greenery, or *bāgh*. As I shall point out below, this was a feature of the type of city built by the nomads.

The *Jāmi' al-tavārīkh* records in considerable detail the endowments made over to Ghazaniyya (JT, pp.417–424). It is not my purpose to mention them all, but two or three examples will suffice for illustration. Each morning and evening food was to be distributed at the Sufi convent to the residents and to the poor, and clothing and footwear was also to be made available to those in distress. Money was provided for the care of one hundred orphan boys, who were to be circumcised and taught the Koran. Lectures were given at the *madrasas* and at the observatory, and of course patients were treated at the hospital. What is also of

---

[1]Khwāndamīr reported there was a code of taxes fixed for the welfare (*rifāhiyat*) of soldiers and peasants in this building. See Gh. Khwāndamīr, *Ḥabīb al-siyar*, ed. Dabīr Siyāqī, Tehran, 1333, vol. 3, p.188.

[2]Ḥamd Allah Mustawfī Qazvīnī, *Nuzhat al-Qulūb*, ed. G. Le Strange, London, 1915, p.76.

interest are the provisions for the maintenance and management of the mausoleum. Foundations supplied it with carpets, wax for lighting, and money for the purchase of oil, the wages of workers and sweets to be distributed every Friday evening. Soup was provided in the kiosk in the garden for those visiting the mausoleum, and on Ghazan's memorial day a special meal was to be offered those who had been invited, and alms given afterwards. In this way attention was given equally to maintaining the mausoleum and providing for those who visited it, and to giving to charity. If we consider that a principal aim of Ghazan's endowments was to merit the grace of God, then his charity was principally for his own benefit.

Rich financial resources were necessary to manage, maintain and run a huge complex like Ghazaniyya and it is said that Ghazan endowed all of the wealth that he had accumulated lawfully (JT, p.412). Since the endowment documents are no longer extant we unfortunately do not know exactly what the nature of that wealth was. However, considering the contents of other contemporary endowment deeds, it is more than likely that Ghazan set aside a part of the income derived from royal lands within Īlkhān territory[1]. This surmise is supported by a reference in the *Jāmi' al-tavārīkh* that Ghazan had a canal made in the Karbala district, bought the water and land rights, and donated them to Ghazaniyya (JT, p.412).

2. The Location of Ghazaniyya

A great deal remains unresolved concerning the running of the institutions at Ghazaniyya, the financial backing for the

[1]On the endowment of Rab'-i Rashīdī, built at almost the same period as Ghazaniyya, see S. S. Blair, "Ilkhanid Architecture and Society: an Analysis of the Endowment Deed of the Rab'-i Rashīdī," *Iran,* vol. XXII (1984), pp.67-90.

endowments, detailed plans of the buildings, and features of interest from the viewpoint of architectural history. Here I would like to take up the question of location. Why did Ghazan choose Shām, on the outskirts of Tabrīz, for his mausoleum? Because he desired above all else a splendid tomb that would cause his name to be remembered down the ages, he would have taken great pains over the selection of a suitable site for it. Let us consider this point more closely.

Once they had conquered settled areas, members of the Mongol ruling class developed connections with cities which were political, economic and cultural, and whether they liked it or not, they had to associate with urban centres. All the same, they rarely ventured into the inner parts of the cities, with their closed quarters and narrow winding lanes, and certainly had no wish to live there. Urban living had no appeal to the nomad mentality. They never had capitals in our modern understanding of the concept, with for example, a royal palace and administrative institutions, like Istanbul. When they had to visit a city they would pitch their tents in the *bāgh* dotting the outskirts. For instance, Ghazan had a tower, a bath and large buildings erected on the grassland (*marghzār*) on the outskirts of Ūjān, a city that for a time could be said to have been his capital, and pitched a "tent made of golden tissue" (*khargāh-i zarrīn*) on the *bāgh* for his own quarters.[1]

Leaving aside for a moment whether or not buildings were erected, this phenomenon of the nomad ruler staying outside urban areas on the *bāgh* is, as has been pointed out by Jean Aubin and many scholars after him, not confined to the Īlkhānids but can be seen throughout the eastern Islamic world after the

---

[1]JT, pp.346-347. Honda Minobu, "Surutānīya kentokō (On the building of Sulṭāniyya)," *Tōhō-gakkai sōritsu 40-shūnen kinen tōhōgaku-ronshū,* 1987, p.735.

thirteenth century, when Turko-Mongolian nomads held sway.[1] Though Tīmūr loved Samarqand greatly, he would always return from his campaigns to the *bāgh* on its outskirts, not to the city itself. His audience with the Castilian ambassador Ruy Gonzalez de Clavijo and the banquet he held for him both took place at one of the parks (*bāgh*) in Samarqand's surburbs.[2] Timur's son Shāh Rukh and most of the succeeding Timurid rulers had many parks dotted around their capital, Herat.[3] In 1506, just prior to the fall of the dynasty to the Uzbeks, the Timurid prince Bābur was greeted by the last ruler of the dynasty, Badī' al-Zamān, at Bāg-i Jahān ārā, a park made by his father Sulṭān Ḥusayn.[4] The cities of the Āq-Qoyūnlū and Safavid dynasties also showed a similar pattern, with the rulers basing themselves in *bāgh* in the suburbs. I shall deal with this in more detail below.

Shām too, seems to have been a camp for nomads. The building initiated by Arghūn already indicates this, and it can also be verified through historical documentation. The geographical conditions of the district are demonstrated in

---

[1]Aubin, op. cit., p.71, Haneda, "Maydān et Bāġ," ed. A. Haneda, *Documents et archives provenant de l'Asie Centrale*, Kyoto, 1990, p.97.

[2]R. G. Clavijo, *The Embassy of Ruy Gonzalez de Clavijo to the Court of Timour*, tr. by Clements R. Markham, originally published by the Hakluyt Society and reprinted in New York in 1970, pp.129sq. Bābur described the location and nature of the *bāgh*s in Samarqand. We know the approximate location of each *bāgh* through the work of Golombek & Wilber, *The Timurid Architecture of Iran and Turan*, vol. II, map 7.

[3]See T. Allen's two monographs on Herat. *A Catalogue of the Toponyms and Monuments of Timurid Herat*, Cambridge, Mass., 1981, *Timurid Herat*, Wiesbaden, 1983.

[4]On the Bāgh-i Jahān ārā, see W. Ball, "The Remains of a Monumental Timurid Garden outside Herat," *East and West*, 31 (1981), M. Szuppe, "Les résidences princières de Hérat. Problèmes de continuité fonctionnelle entre les époques timouride et safavide (1ère moitié du XVIe siècle)," éd. J. Calmard, *Etudes safavides*, Paris-Téhéran, 1993, pp.272-276.

Mustawfī's near-contemporary record, the *Nuzhat al-Qulūb* (1340):

> In Tabrīz itself water is found in the wells at a depth of around thirty *gaz*. At Shām it occurs at ten *gaz*, but at Rab'-i Rashīdī it is only reached at seventy *gaz* (*Nuzhat al-Qulūb*, p.76).

Thus Shām appears to have had one of the more easily accessible supplies of water in the Tabrīz area. Evliya Çelebi, who visited there in the seventeenth century, wrote that the water in the wells was as cold as ice, even in summer.[1] Where there is water, plants can grow. The *Jāmi' al-tavārīkh* employs the expression "Shām of the luxuriant grass (*marghzār-i Shām*)," one that is used for Ūjān also.[2] Thus Shām had both the necessities required by a nomadic people, rich supplies of both water and grass. The Mongol Khans may well have pitched their tents at Bāgh-i 'Ādiliyya.

Ghazan stayed at Shām when he went to Tabrīz after vanquishing his political rival and predecessor, Baidu (JT, p.300). History records too that many powerful nomad leaders after him stayed there also. Malik Ashraf, Timur,[3] and, in the sixteenth century, the Safavid Shahs Ismā'īl (1501–1524) and Ṭahmāsp (1524–1576) used Shām, which they also called Shamb-i Ghāzān, both for themselves and as a mustering base for their armies.[4] It is clear in view of Shām's strategic importance to Tabrīz that it

---

[1]Evliya Çelebi, *Seyahatnamesi*, Istanbul, 1314, vol. 2, pp.265-266.

[2]Rashīd al-Dīn, *Tārīkh-i mubārak-i ghāzānī*, ed. K. Jahn, London, 1940, p.94.

[3]Ḥāfiẓ Abrū, *Dhayl-i jāmi' al-tavārīkh-i rashīdī*, ed. Kh. Bayānī, Tehran, 1350, p.234, Abū Bakr al-Quṭbī al-Āhrī, *Tārīkh-i Shaykh Uvays*, fac. ed. & tr. J. B. Van Loon, 's-Gravenhage, 1954, pp.77, 177, Sharaf al-Dīn 'Alī Yazdī, *Ẓafar Nāma*, fac. ed., Tashkent, 1972, fol. 179a.

[4]Khwāndamīr, op. cit., vol. 4, p.600, Ḥasan Rūmlū, *Aḥsan al-tavārīkh* (vol. XII), ed. 'Abd al-Ḥusayn Navāī, Tehran, 1357, p.424.

functioned both as a camp for nomads and as a military base, two conditions of the "pastoral city".

Not only nomads came to Shām. The following account in the *Jāmi' al-tavārīkh* gives us a deeper appreciation of the careful planning that went into Ghazan's choice of Shām.

> He [Ghazan Khan] constructed another city larger than Old Tabrīz at a place called Shāmb or Shām where he built a pious foundation surrounded by many gardens and parks. This was called Ghazaniyya. Merchants from Rūm and Europe (*afranj*) had their goods inspected there. To avoid bad feeling, the *tamghachī* there were the same as those of Tabrīz (JT, p.214).

While there is much that remains unclear about the role of *tamghachī* in the eastern Islamic world, it is certain that they were concerned with collecting the tax on commerce called *tamgha*. Unfortunately our view is restricted by the fact that there are no detailed records surviving of commercial transactions in Shām; however from the above quotation and the former one concerning Arghūniyya, it seems clear that Ghazan intended that Shām, on the western approach to Tabrīz, should be an entrepot for merchants arriving form the west, and so a large-scale trading centre, where abounded merchants, goods and all the types of people who came in response to trade. This town, newly built on an international trade-route, must have drawn many people besides nomads.

We thus have ample evidence from historical documents that Shām amply fulfilled all the conditions for a "pastoral city". It is very apparent why Ghazan chose it as the site of his tomb. Being a place where nomads and sedentary people could mix freely, it was an ideal location, since the tomb would dominate the surroundings and be visited by large numbers of pilgrims.

Though Shām was a "pastoral city", it had one characteristic quite different from the earlier Arghūniyya and Ūjān, and other cities of the same type. This was the presence in its centre of the ruler's mausoleum surrounded by pious institutions supported by a large number of endowments. When we consider that Ghazan's own motivation for building the city was above all to support his tomb we cannot ignore the fact that it was also a "mausoleum city". This will become even clearer when we examine the later history of Ghazaniyya.

3. Ghazaniyya after Ghazan

How did Shām develop after Ghazan died, and, following his wish, became the occupant of the mausoleum built for him? Was the prosperity of the "pastoral city" to be only momentary? To anticipate my conclusion, Ghazaniyya, and Shām around it, continued to survive. Ibn Baṭṭūṭa was in the party of the ninth Īlkhān ruler, Abū Sa'īd when he visited it *en route* from Baghdad to Tabrīz, and stayed at a hospice there.[1] Niẓām al-Dīn Shāmī, Tīmūr's renowned chronicler, was only one of a number of prominent people who had the *nisba* of Shāmī or Shāmb-i Ghazanī.[2] Somewhat later, when the last ruler of the Timurids in Herat, Badī' al-Zamān, was driven out of Herat by the Uzbek leader Muḥammad Shaibānī, he received for a time the protection of the Safavid ruler Shāh Ismā'īl, who settled him at Shāmb-i Ghazan.[3] We have already seen how nomadic rulers too visited the town from time to time. Thus contrary to Jean Aubin's thesis, the "pastoral city" of Ghazaniyya survived, in addition to Sulṭāniyya, for more than two hundred years.

Even after the collapse of the Īlkhānid dynasty, administrative rights of endowments were continued by succeeding rulers.[4] No

[1]H. A. R. Gibb, *The Travel of Ibn Baṭṭūṭa*, vol. II, Cambridge, 1959, p.344.

[2]Ḥāfiẓ Ḥusayn Karbalāī Tabrīzī, *Rawḍat al-jinān va jannāt al-janān*, ed. J. Sulṭān al-Qurrāī, Tehran, 1349 (abbreviation: RJ), vol. I, p.434, vol. II, p.655, M. J. Mashkūr, *Tārīkh-i Tabrīz*, p.864.

[3]*Aḥsan al-tavārīkh* (vol. XII), p.198.

[4]Rashīd al-Dīn is said to have been nominated as administrator of the Ghazan's

pertinent documents exist from the fifteenth century, but we know from the records of Iskandar Munshī that in the sixteenth century the Safavids appointed endowment administrators[1]. During the reign of Ṭahmāsp, the second Safavid ruler, two brothers, Amīr Abū al-Valī and Mīr Abū al-Muḥammad were appointed joint supervisors of Ghazan's endowment (*awqāf-i ghāzānī*). Before he took up that position, Amīr Abū al-Valī had supervised the mausoleum of Imām al-Riḍā in Mashhad, and later, during the latter part of Ṭahmāsp's reign, he was made supervisor of the Safavid mausoleum at Ardabīl (*Āstāna-yi muqaddasa-yi ṣafaviyya*), both of which had special significance for the Safavids, both politically and economically. Imām al-Riḍā's tomb was a sacred place for Shī'ism, then the official religion in Persia, and had been a centre for pilgrimage from at least the time of Ghazan. The wealth donated to it was said to have been enormous. The Safavid mausoleum was the resting place of the Safavid family members up to and including Ismā'īl (d. 1524), and so had political and religious importance. Jean Aubin's research has revealed how great were the donations made to that mausoleum after Shaykh Ṣafī.[2] That Amīr Abū al-Valī was associated with these two special mausolea before and after his appointment to Ghazaniyya speaks clearly of the undeniable economic importance that Ghazaniyya must have had in the early part of the Safavid period. Thus for two hundred years after the fall of the Īlkhānids, Ghazaniyya had retained the form that Ghazan had desired. What changed the situation drastically was the border dispute from the late sixteenth and

---

mausoleum by its founder. This however cannot be proven through contemporary sources. Cf. *Tārīkh-i Tabrīz,* p.481.

[1]Iskandar Munshī, *Tārīkh-i 'ālam ārā-yi 'abbāsī,* ed. I. Afshār, Tehran, 1350 (abbreviation: TAA), p.148.

[2]J. Aubin, "La propriété foncière en Azerbaydjan sous les Mongols," *Le monde iranien et l'Islam,* IV (1976–1977), pp.79-132.

early seventeenth centuries between the Safavids and the Ottomans.

The war began when the Ottoman army invaded Azerbayjan and occupied Tabrīz during the internal unrest that followed the death of Ṭahmāsp in 1576. The Safavid army counter-attacked, until finally a truce was reached when Shāh 'Abbās won back most of the former territory. The effects of this thirty year war were felt in every part of Azerbayjan, but particularly in Tabrīz, which became a battleground several times. In 1011–1012 / 1602–1604, when 'Abbās I routed the Ottomans and entered Tabrīz, the city was in ruins, with no dwelling suitable for him. He therefore stayed at Shāmb-i Ghazan (Shām), where he received the people of Tabrīz who had come out to greet him (TAA, p.639). In 1018–1019 / 1609–1611 the Ottoman army again set out to attack Tabrīz. At that time 'Abbās stored cannon, guns and ammunition in the Ghazaniyya complex and sent trusted musketeers (*tufangchiyān*) to guard the city to the death. 'Abbās, a fine strategist, knew that once Ghazaniyya fell to the Ottomans, it could be used as an advance base for an attack on the city (TAA, p.822). The Ottoman army finally retreated, without taking the city. 'Abbās however predicted that it would return and built a new stronghold to fortify the city. The site he chose for this was the Rashīd quarter to the east. He ordered building material to be brought there from buildings that had been destroyed in the fighting or had fallen into ruin. According to Iskandar Munshī, a lot came from Shāmb-i Ghazan in particular, which was then in a desolate state (*vīrānī ba-ān rāh yāftah būd*) (TAA, p.826). However, it seems the mausoleum itself remained intact at that time, and we find mention of it in documents after this time. At very least, the *madrasa*s and the Sufi convent would have been removed, since they would have fallen into disuse once the Safavids had authorized Shī'ism as the state religion.

Besides destruction at human hands, another cause for the

collapse of the old buildings was the earthquakes that occur frequently in this area.[1] Evliya Çelebi, who visited Shāmb-i Ghazan in the 1640s, noted that part of the mausoleum had been damaged by earthquake.[2] Tavernier reported cracks in the dome of the mausoleum caused by the 1651 earthquake,[3] and Jean Chardin, who passed that way in 1666, wrote that the dome had fallen into ruin.[4] Thus by the seventeenth century, Ghazaniyya, which had continued to have been maintained and managed on the old basis until the sixteenth century, had rapidly declined. Eugène Flandin, who travelled around Iran with Pascal Coste between 1840 and 1842, mentioned that the Ghazaniyya mosque had been completely destroyed in an earthquake at the end of the eighteenth century and was now abandoned.[5] It is safe to assume that all of the buildings had fallen into ruin by the nineteenth century.

Until the 1960s, the site of Ghazaniyya could be known by a high mound of rubble that gave hints of its former glory. However information from Professors Honda Minobu and M. Y. Keyani indicates that this mound has now been flattened as a result of the development and expansion of Tabrīz in recent years and modern buildings are now erected on the site. Six hundred years and several decades since it was built, Ghazaniyya has disappeared from the face of the earth, in stark contrast with the tomb of Imām al-Riḍā in Mashhad, visited by Ghazan and

---

[1] On the damage and destruction of buildings in Tabrīz by earthquakes, see C. Melville, "Historical Monuments and Earthquakes in Tabrīz," *Iran*, XIX (1981).

[2] Evliya Çelebi, op. cit., p.266.

[3] J. B. Tavernier, *Les six voyages en Turquie & en Perse*, ed. S. Yerasimos, Paris, 1981, vol. I, p.109. C. Melville corrected the date of earthquake to 1641. Cf. Melville, op. cit., p.166.

[4] J. Chardin, *Voyages du Chevalier Chardin en Perse et autres lieux de l'Orient*, éd. L. Langrès, Paris, 1811, vol. II, p.323.

[5] E. Flandin, *Voyage en Perse*, Paris, 1851–1852, vol. I, p.175.

providing his inspiration, and still the object of thousands of pilgrims.

Though there is no doubt that war and earthquake were the main causes of Ghazaniyya's destruction, it is plausible that it might have survived after the seventeenth century if the Safavids had made more efforts to preserve the religious facilities by close supervision of the endowments. Certainly rulers were ready to do so until the middle of the sixteenth century and the reign of Ṭahmāsp. A change of policy under 'Abbās I was what decided the eventual fate of Ghazaniyya. Such a policy change may have encompassed the abandonment of endowment supervision and the diversion of the endowment assets; 'Abbās is likely not merely to have stopped the supervision of assets but actually to have diverted them to other purposes. Unfortunately I have been unable to come across any direct documentary evidence for this assertion. However, the vast wealth of Ghazaniyya's endowments would have had great appeal to a government struggling to overcome the country's financial problems, in a perilous state as a result of the costs of putting down internal conflicts, financing continuing wars against the Ottomans and Uzbeks, and paying for the numerous large-scale engineering and building works that were being undertaken in all parts of the country.

The research of R. D. McChesney has pointed out that 'Abbās, in order to publicize his devotion to Shī'ism, in 1013 / 1604–1605 endowed for the benefit of the descendants of the Shī'ite Imāms and those living in places closely connected with Shī'ism, all the personal wealth that he had accumulated legitimately over the years.[1] The endowments of Ghazaniyya may well have been confiscated or diverted to that "holy" purpose. Whatever the case, 'Abbās did not see any point in employing Ghazaniyya's

---

[1]R. D. McChesney, "Waqf and Public Policy: the Waqfs of Shāh 'Abbās, 1011–1023/1602–1614," *Asian and African Studies*, 15 (1981), pp.165-190.

endowments as they had been intended, and he certainly would not have been criticized for diverting the more than three-hundred-year-old endowment of a Mongolian ruler to other purposes, even if such action resulted in the ruin of the mausoleum. This leads to the conclusion that the survival of Shām and Ghazaniyya to the beginning of the sixteenth century was largely the result of the survival of the mausoleum and its endowment. As long as the endowment assets were employed in a sound fashion, people would continue to congregate at the mausoleum and so ensure the continuity of the town in some form. The secret of Ghazaniyya's long life was that it was not simply a "pastoral city", but that it had the dual function of "mausoleum city" as well.

II *Sulṭāniyya*

My thesis here is that the construction of new cities with characteristics similar to those of Shām was a particular phenomenon seen in those places and at those times when people of more or less nomadic custom and outlook were in possession of political power. As an example I will now discuss Sulṭāniyya, built by Ghazan's brother and successor, the eighth ilkhan, Öljeytü. This new Īlkhānid "capital" has been discussed in detail by Honda Minobu and others;[1] I refer to that research in the following discussion of Sulṭāniyya and the conditions under which it was built.

Sulṭāniyya's site was originally known by the name Sharūyāz. When it came to be used by the Mongols as their summer quarters it was called Qūnqūr Ūlāng ("rusty meadow");

[1]Honda Minobu, op. cit., S. S. Blair, "The Mongol Capital of Sulṭāniyya, "the Imperial," *Iran,* XXIV, 1986.

the name Sulṭāniyya dates only from the time of Öljeytü.[1] Known for its abundant pastures, Arghūn had already erected some buildings there in the thirteenth century and built a wall.[2] Öljeytü continued his work, but greatly extended it in scope. Thus we see already a similarity to Ghazaniyya, in that it represents the continuation of a father's project by a son. This is emphasized by the fact that the *Jāmi' al-tavārīkh* speaks of Arghūn's construction of Arghūniyya at Shām and of Sharūyāz (later Sulṭāniyya) in consecutive articles (JT, p.223). The *Nuzhat al-Qulūb* describes the site as follows:

> The climate of this place is somewhat cold. Water is obtained both from wells and underground channels, both excellent sources. Wells here are sunk to a depth of between two or three *gaz* to ten *gaz*. Within a day's journey of this place are both cold and warm regions, so that everything people need is produced in abundance. The pastures are rich and excellent. The area is also well-off in hunting grounds (p.55).

Thus Sharūyāz was ideal as a summer pasturage for nomads, with rich supplies of water and grass. Öljeytü's vizier, Tāj al-Dīn 'Alī Shāh, is said to have built a splendid park (*bāgh*) for the ilkhan on the outskirts of the new town. Traces of it remained down to the seventeenth century. The sites of Sulṭāniyya and Shām were very similar in that they were nomad camps, even though the former was used in summer and the latter in winter.

Soon after his accession in 1305, Öljeytü ordered large-scale work to begin at Sulṭāniyya. It is clear from the fact that he had *bazars* and public facilities erected there and made it the hub of the six national routes (*shāh-rāh*) that were also trunk roads for all the international traffic of the time that he intended it to be

---

[1]Honda, op. cit., p.736.
[2]*Nuzhat al-Qulūb*, p.55.

the centre of political and commercial life.[1] There can be no doubt that this place had an important meaning as an intersection concerning Aubin's *réseau pastoral* (network of nomads) and *réseau caravanier* (trade network).[2] Here too Sulṭāniyya shares another common characteristic with Shām. In the middle of the town, too, was Öljeytü's majestic tomb, around which were erected pious foundations. The complex is referred to by various names; in the *Tārīkh-i Öljeytü* and the *Dhayl-i Jāmi' al-tavārīkh* it is called *Abvāb al-birr* ("Portals of Piety").[3] Like the complex at Ghazaniyya, that at Sulṭāniyya was supported by a massive endowment.[4]

Sulṭāniyya and Shām were built for fundamentally the same reason, both being sites of nomad camps, commercial centres, and sites of a mausoleum.[5] One reason that Öljeytü decided to build a town here where people would gather was without doubt related to his plans to activate and make more efficient the economy of his summer quarters by making their site a trading centre. Like his brother Ghazan, this ilkhan too erected a splendid tomb in the middle of the town which attracted large numbers of pilgrims, and he hoped by his charitable works that the greatness of his name would be remembered perpetually and that he would through them be the recipient of God's grace. Honda sees the building of Sulṭāniyya as an "expression of sovereign will and the embodiment of a civil administration policy" on the part of

---

[1]Honda, op. cit., pp.743-744.

[2]J. Aubin, "Réseau pastoral et réseau caravanier. Les grand'routes du Khurassan à l'époque mongole," *Le monde iranien et l'Islam*, 1 (1971), pp.105-130.

[3]Blair, "The Mongol Capital," p.144.

[4]Ḥāfiẓ Abrū, *Dhayl-i jāmi' al-tavārīkh-i rashīdī*, p.68.

[5]There are, of course, some differences between them. For example, Shām had no *qal'a* (fortress) like Sulṭāniyya. Honda, op. cit., pp.739-741, Blair, "The Mongol Capital," pp.142-143.

Öljeytü;[1] from a different point of view, it can be said that the whole town, as a "mausoleum city", was a device to ensure the eternal preservation of his tomb. We can therefore add to Aubin's three conditions determining the existence of cities a fourth factor, that of the mausoleum city. Like Shām and its mausoleum of Ghazaniyya, which continued to exist because of the wealth of its endowments, Sulṭāniyya too survived through to the seventeenth century.

III *Naṣriyya*

In the latter part of the fifteenth century, over a century after the collapse of the Īlkhānids, the region extending from western Iran to eastern Anatolia came under the sway of the Aq-Qoyūnlū Türkmen nomads. The most important leaders of this dynasty, Abū Naṣr Ḥasan Beg, usually known as Uzun Ḥasan (1457–1478), and Sulṭān Ya'qūb (1478–1490) both engaged in notable building work.

North of Tabrīz there was an area of greenery called Bāgh-i Ṣāḥibābād.[2] Its name is said to derive from a minister (*ṣāḥib-i dīvān*) called Shams al-Dīn Muḥammad Juvaynī who lived early in the Īlkhānid period.[3] It appears to have been an ideal place for nomads to camp, and indeed records note that Jahānshāh

---

[1]Honda, op. cit., p.745.

[2]The area was known later as Maydān-i Ṣāḥib al-amr. Cf. *Tārīkh-i Tabrīz*, pp.240-241. We can find the name on the map included in Mashkūr's book (drawn in the nineteenth century) on the right bank of the Maydān-i Chāī river, a little bit north of the city centre. According to J. E. Woods, there remains no trace any more. Cf. J. E. Woods, *The Aqquyunlu: Clan, Confederation, Empire*, Minneapolis & Chicago, 1976, p.150, note 47. See also the map in Melville's article (op. cit., p.165).

[3]RJ, vol. I, p.470.

(1436–1467) of the Qarā-Qoyūnlū dynasty had his court there.[1] Uzun Ḥasan renovated the site and made his quarters there. After his death he was buried there as well. We find in the *Rawḍat al-jinān* an interesting tale:

> As his death approached, Uzun Ḥasan called an ulama serving him called Darvīsh Sirāj al-Dīn Qāsim and said: "It was a great mistake not to build for myself a tomb (*maqbara*), a *zāwiya*, and a mosque. You are the only person I trust. After my death, relinquish your official duties, look after my tomb and build around it a mosque and a *zāwiya*. Commemorate me eternally through charity (*zayr*) and good works (*iḥsān*)." When Ḥasan died and Sulṭān Ya'qūb became ruler, Darvīsh appeared before him and announced Ḥasan's dying wish and his own desire to make it reality. Ya'qūb gave him his complete approval, and in 882 (1477-78) building was commenced on an auspicious day. A large amount of money was used and seven years later in 889 (1484-85) the 'Imārat-i Naṣriyya was finished (RJ, vol. I, pp.90-91).

Thus the tomb of Ḥasan at Naṣriyya was not built by the ruler himself. It did not take the form of a separate mausoleum but was built inside the *madrasa*. The tenor of Uzun Ḥasan's words, that the religious facilities, including the tomb, perpetuate the name of the dead ruler and seek God's grace for him, is identical to the ideas prevalent among the Īlkhānids.

The two characteristics of a "new city" of the Īlkhānid dynasty, quarters for nomads and the existence of the ruler's grave, are also to be found at Ṣāḥibābād. The remaining condition, that of a trading centre, is also fulfilled amply here. The late sixteenth century *Rawḍat al-jinān* contains the following report:

> Bāgh-i Ṣāḥibābād, known today in Tabrīz as the Maydān-i Ṣāḥib al-amr, was previously a large *maydān* where villagers sold various goods. Large

[1] Ibid., Abū Bakr Ṭihrānī-Iṣfahānī, *Kitāb-i Diyār Bakriyya*, ed. N. Lugal & F. Sümer, 2 vols., Ankara, 1962–1964, p.437.

> numbers of merchants displayed their wares under tents they erected. Gradually the street-stalls (*chadrnishīnān*) became shops (*dukkān*), and today there is a splendid bazar here. There does not remain anywhere here what is properly called a *maydān* (RJ, vol. I, p.570).

Ṣāḥibābād thus possessed all the basic characteristics of an Īlkhānid "new city", being both a "pastoral city" and a "mausoleum city". In this sense it was a successor of Shām and Sulṭāniyya. However, this town, built well over a hundred years after Ghazaniyya, had a remarkable new characteristic: the existence of a *maydān*.

The *maydān* of Ṣāḥibābād predated Naṣriyya, for when Uzun Ḥasan, who overthrew Jahānshāh, first entered the Qarā-Qoyūnlū stronghold of Tabrīz, he passed through it.[1] Situated on the outskirts of the city, it was similar to the two *maydān*s of Iṣfahān in that it was a multi-purpose space used variously for a riding ground, a polo ground and a market.[2] An important account of the Naṣriyya district, which included this *maydān*, was penned by a Venetian merchant who visited Tabrīz in the beginning of the sixteenth century. It attests that Naṣriyya could broadly be divided into two areas, the palace and its park, and the *maydān* and the buildings around it. Let us recreate Naṣriyya through his eyes.

> The palace is built in the centre of a large and beautiful garden, close to the city, with only a stream dividing them to the north, and in the same circumference a fine mosque is built with a rich and useful hospital attached. The palace is called Astibisti (Hasht Bihisht, "eight paradises"). . . The palace, as I already said, is situated in the centre of the garden, and is built on a terrace . . . Within the palace, on the ceiling of the great hall, are represented in gold, silver and ultramarine blue, all the battles which took place in Persia a long time since; and some embassies are to be seen

---

[1] *Kitāb-i Diyār Bakriyya*, p.523.

[2] On the character of two *maydān*s of Iṣfahān, see Haneda, "Maydān et Bāġ."

> which came from the Ottomans to Tauris presenting themselves before Assambei, with their demands and the answer he gave them written in the Persian character. There are also represented his hunting expeditions . . . The ceiling of the great hall is all decorated with beautiful gilding and ultramarine . . . On the floor of the hall is spread a magnificent carpet; . . . likewise in the other rooms the floor is all covered . . .
>
> About a bowshot from the palace there is a harem of one storey . . . (The garden is surrounded by a wall) and has three entrances, one to the south, another to the north, and the third to the east. That to the south . . . leads to the garden, the palace being a bowshot distant . . . On the north side, one must enter a certain place like a cloister, paved with bricks, with seats of marble around it. This place is so large that it will hold three hundred horses . . . In this place there is a door entering the garden on the way to the king's palace . . . The other door, towards the east, is on an immense maidan or piazza . . . Over this there is a large edifice with many rooms, and a covered hall looking over the garden. On the side towards the maidan there is an arched gallery . . . Into this building Assambei used to retire with many lords whenever a feast was made on this maidan, and frequently when ambassadors came they used to put them up there, as it was a fine place and had many apartments. This door is further from the others from the royal palace, with a splendid view of the maidan, on which are the mosque and the hospital.[1]

Persian records tell us that the Hasht Bihisht palace, here said to have been built by Uzun Ḥasan (Assambei), was in fact erected by his son, Sulṭān Ya'qūb, in 894 / 1488-9.[2] Further, though the Venetian merchant does not mention it, the *maydān* is known to have also contained religious buildings, such as a *madrasa* and a Sufi convent.[3] Nevertheless, while we should not rely upon the above account implicitly, it gives a good general indication of the contemporary situation.

---

[1] *The Travels of a Merchant in Persia*, London, 1873, pp.173-178.

[2] Ḥasan Rūmlū, *Aḥsan al-tavārīkh* (vol. XI), ed. 'Abd al-Ḥusayn Navāī, Tehran, 1349, pp.622, 627.

[3] *Tārīkh-i Tabrīz*, pp.744-745.

The phenomenon of both religious and commercial functions being concentrated in the *maydān* and its surroundings did not originate in Naṣriyya, for a similar phenomenon existed earlier in Seljuq Iṣfahān.[1] There is no earlier example, though, of a town plan which organically joins together, with the *maydān* as node, the nomads' quarters of the *bāgh* and the town with its religious and commercial functions. Naṣriyya is therefore highly significant in the lineage of the "new city" that developed under nomadic rule.

The Naṣriyya district, centring on the *maydān*, continued until at least the seventeenth century as a venue for all kinds of urban activities, such as executions, polo, archery contests, and large-scale festivals like *'Āshūrā*. The Safavid rulers built a new mosque there, and used the *maydān* to receive envoys and foreign ambassadors visiting Tabrīz.[2] At the time of the Ottoman-Safavid wars, Naṣriyya was used as a kind of front-line fortification.[3] Nothing further is known, as far as present scholarship is concerned, till the nineteenth century, when it appears to have been absorbed into the expanding city, which means that it could not have fallen completely into ruin.[4] Its continuation can be ascribed to its closeness to Old Tabrīz, the existence of a core centreed on the *maydān* and the ongoing prosperity of its commercial activities.

---

[1]H. Gaube, *Iranian Cities*, New York, 1979, pp.76-78.

[2]On executions, TAA, p.160, on polo and archery contests, TAA, pp.298, 678, on 'Āshūrā, TAA, p.298, on the building a mosque, TAA, p.124, on receptions, TAA, pp.100, 300, 681.

[3]TAA, pp.317, 343.

[4]Melville informs us that Naṣriyya was restored completely by Mīrzā Mahdī Qāḍī in 1826 after its collapse due to an earthquake in 1780. Melville, op. cit., p.171.

Conclusion

My investigation has shown that three new cities built in the fourteenth and fifteenth centuries by nomadic rulers were similarly both "pastoral" and "mausoleum" cities. In all cases the existence of the *bāgh*, where nomadic rulers and leaders established their quarters, was crucial. In the vicinity of the *bāgh*, and surrounding it, there came into being a town whose core was a complex of religious facilities centring on a mausoleum. Such cities served simultaneously as places of prayer, a market for the nomads, and a trading hub. Crowds of people gathered in them, due to the existence of charitable institutions supported by royal endowments.

The existence of *bāgh* on the outskirts of cities was a very common phenomenon in Iran and Central Asia. Here, though, the only role of the *bāgh* was to supplement urban life, functioning for example to produce vegetables and fruit for the city, or to provide recreation for the city's inhabitants. It was when nomadic rulers took power that the city and the *bāgh* were connected on more of an equal basis. It is in this sense that research into the *bāgh*, so characteristic of the eastern Islamic world, is of great importance.

The cities I have discussed in this paper owed their existence and prosperity largely to the nomadic rulers and their court, by whose political power people could be forcibly brought together and whose economic power stimulated large-scale consumption. Thus it is easy to imagine that when those rulers died and their dynasties collapsed such cities would immediately have declined. However, as we have seen, they did not in fact fall into ruin and actually continued to exist for long afterwards. The main reason for this was that they were all "mausoleum cities". The endowment (*waqf*) system peculiar to the Islamic world played an important role in their building and maintenance. For example, Hayashi

Kayoko has shown that immediately after the conquest of Istanbul plans were in hand to restore the city and its core of religious facilities (*imâret*).[1] Further research on this basis might well serve to clarify the origins (in place and time) of this type of city construction.

Towns with the characteristics of a "pastoral city" continued to be built until the sixteenth century. Good examples include Sa'ādatābād in Qazwīn, built by Ṭahmāsp, the second Safavid ruler, and Naqsh-i Jahān in Iṣfahān, built by Shāh 'Abbās I, the fifth. Both have the *maydān* as the node connecting the *bāgh* area and the commercial and religious district and so morphologically closely resembles Ṣāḥibābād in Naṣriyya.[2] In this sense, the urban construction undertaken by Ghazan after the nomads came to power at the beginning of the fourteenth century, and continued in Ṣāḥibābād during the Aq-Qoyūnlū dynasty at the end of the fifteenth century, culminated in the building of Iṣfahān by Shāh 'Abbās I at the end of the sixteenth century.

However there is one difference between the three cities discussed here and the new Safavid cities that cannot be overlooked, and that is the absence of the mausoleum of the founder. Ṭahmāsp's tomb was built within the sanctuary of Imām al-Riḍā's mausoleum in Mashhad, while that of 'Abbās lies within

---

[1]Hayashi (Yamamoto) Kayoko , "15 seiki kōhan-no isutanburu: Mehumeto 2 sei-no fukkōsaku-wo chūshinni (Istanbul in the Latter Half of the Fifteenth Century: On the Restoration Policy of Mehmet II)," *Ochanomizu-shigaku*, 25 (1981) pp.7-13.

[2]On the Sa'ādatābād district of Ṭahmāsp, we can find brief accounts in TAA, p.124 and Qāḍī Aḥmad Qumī, *Khulāṣat al-tavārīkh*, ed. I. Ishrāqī, Tehran, 1359, p.312. It had a *maydān* in its centre and seems to have resembled the Naṣriyya district in Tabrīz and the Naqsh-i Jahān district in Iṣfahān as well.

the mausoleum of Imāmzāda Ḥabīb ibn Mūsā in Kāshān.[1] A great change in attitude by the ruler to his mausoleum is thus apparent among the Safavids, a change which is probably closely connected with the Shī'ite policies of that dynasty. A fascinating field of research remains to be studied regarding the connections between the development of the cult of Imāmzāda and Muslim ideas about tombs in the eastern Islamic world.

Cities combining the characteristics of "pastoral city" and "mausoleum city" ceased to be built in the eastern Islamic world at the end of the fifteenth century. Furthermore, in a narrow sense, true "pastoral cities" built by rulers who had strong nomadic elements, were no longer erected once Iṣfahān had been built. This may be seen to be due to the comparative wane of nomad power.

---

[1]TAA, pp.123, 526-528, 1079. The remains of Ṭahmāsp were buried, at first, in Yūrt-i Shīrvānī and then transferred to Mashhad by Ismā'īl II. At the beginning of the reign of 'Abbās I, Uzbek troops occupied and plundered the holy city. Miraculously, however, the Ṭahmāsp's remains reportedly did not fall into the hands of the Uzbeks, and were re-buried in Ardabīl after Mashhad was retaken by 'Abbās I. On the location of the tomb of 'Abbās I, see A. Godard, "The Tomb of Shah 'Abbās," *Bulletin of the American Institute for Persian Art and Archaeology*, IV-4 (1936). Cf. also 'A. Iqbāl, "Az ibtidā-yi Ṣafaviyya tā ākhir-i Qājāriyya pādshāhān-i Īrān har yak dar kujā madfūnand?" *Yādgār*, 3-2 (1946–1947).

CHAPTER SIX

Water Village until the Foundation of the Land-Based Settlement: A Malay Muslim Community and State in Brunei Darussalam

Iik A. MANSURNOOR

Introduction

Although it is argued that a political entity had developed prior to the coming of Islam to present day Brunei, it is clear that Islam became the most important factor in the development of Brunei as a Malay multi-center by the sixteenth century, or even earlier. How can the phenomenon be explained? First of all, the fact that the Brunei Muslims concentrated in the Brunei town proper, while the people in the interior remained for most of them and most of the time non-Muslims needs to be examined further in order to clarify the issue. Indeed, Islam became the centripetal point for urbanism—to live within a burgeoning community with its various urban elements and activities. Moreover, despite the acknowledgement of the early development of "Brunei" by some external sources, especially Chinese,[1] local historical evidences are still wanting to corroborate the early glory of Brunei.

Like many other centers of Muslim polity, Brunei built various institutions and other facilities. The emergence of the sultanate connotes the presence of ruler, palace and principal

[1]Such names as Poni and Bunlai are usually associated with early Brunei, see Brown 1970:132-134.

religious institutions. The formal identity of Brunei as a Muslim state was expressed in the acceptance of Islam by the ruler, Awang Alak Betatar, long before the visit of Pigafetta to Brunei in 1521.[1] The acceptance of Islam by the ruler brought about several changes into the capital. A mosque was built; and it became the symbol and place for identification of the ruler with Islam. Indeed, during the presentation of the Friday sermons, a special prayer was read for the ruler.[2] In Brunei the intensive Islamization of the capital as well as the administration was attributed to the various efforts made during the reign of the third ruler, Sharif 'Ali. His marriage to the ruling family and his eventual appointment as sultan must also be seen as an evidence of the growing influence of Islam and the centrality of Brunei in the trading network.

In arguing that Islam played a major role in the development of Brunei Town (or Bandar Brunei) as both a state capital and urban center, some issues have to be clarified. Following Abu Lughod's argument that Islam can be properly seen only as a factor in urbanism during early Islamic history (1989), this study maintains that Islam in Brunei has been an important factor in the development of Bandar Brunei properly known as Kampong Ayer (Water Village). Indeed, from the descriptions given by several earlier observers, travelers and historians, it is clear that Kampong Ayer was a very large settlement whose important economic activities centered mainly on trade. Within the context of Southeast Asia, the period in the Kampong Ayer florescence was concomitant with intensive Islamization and the strengthening

---

[1]Indeed, during his visit, Pigafetta presented to the sultan of Brunei, among other things, a vest in the Turkish fashion. This clearly shows that Pigafetta was aware about the influence of Islam and the Ottoman ruler in Brunei court. For further discussion on the Islamization of Brunei see Brown 1970; Mohammad 1992.

[2]For further discussion on a similar phenomenon, see Lambton 1984.

of trading networks between Muslim centers and ports in the Indian Ocean. Put differently, increasing Islamization in the region was closely related to the intensification of trade among the centers in the region and beyond. The development of Kampong Ayer as an urban center by the 16th century clearly shows the significance of Islam in pushing urbanism into Borneo.

This paper examines the Islamic factor in Brunei urbanism. The study looks at carefully the historical development of Kampong Ayer since the 16th century until the founding of the land-based town of Bandar Brunei since the beginning of the 20th century.

The writing of this paper was first stimulated by my curiosity about the aquatic life in Brunei Town. It was different from many other Islamic centers. From the very beginning I strongly believed that a better understanding of urbanism in Brunei might contribute to the reshaping of the current debate about "Islamic urbanism".

The network model of studying Islamic town has been widely applied by various scholars.[1] In looking at Brunei Town, the network model partially, even if substantially, provides a useful tool for our understanding about urbanism in Brunei. Yet the fact that Brunei was surrounded by territories and peoples who were not fully integrated to urban centers requires other ways of examining the history of Brunei. The historical experience of duality between the coast and the interior, the decline and later the dismemberment of Brunei clearly show that the formal network controlled by the center had only partial operation in the life of Brunei Town.

In my study of Brunei Town, I maintain that the interactional

---

[1]For further discussion on this issue see A. Goto, "Urbanism in Islam," in *Historical Studies in Japan (VIII) 1988–1992* (Tokyo: Yamakawa Shuppansha, 1995), pp.223-229.

or institutional approach, while more appropriate than formal political and legal analysis, has to be supplemented by research into the cultural as well as the social processes underlying the working of an urban society. To understand the functioning of a socio-political community, such as Brunei Town, it is necessary to explore not only social action but the concepts and values that bear on the ordering of social relationships, the religious and mythic symbols of social order, and the worldview of the peoples. Again, a full understanding of a Malay town requires the study of historic institutions, social action, and cultural vocabularies which together regulate the patterns of human behavior that make them society. While cities and town represent important concentrations of populations and activities and an imposing physical presence, they cannot be viewed as unitary economic, political, or cultural entities or as total societies. Such a town as Bandar Brunei is not a special form of human society, but is the physical setting of a larger social system, the place which concentrates population, and the center for economic, political and cultural transactions. Bandar Brunei is not ordinarily independent political body. It is subject to the ruler who governed a much larger territory. It is composed of, among other things, Muslim religious institutions and associations which are not territorial at all. On the other hand, it inherited an ancient pattern of parochial communities integrated into commercial market organizations, socio-religious associations, and state institutions. Indeed, it has developed its particular colloquial culture, even though they cannot claim of having an exclusive local culture. It remains parts, even if indispensable, of the organization of more complex, wider Brunei and perhaps Islamic, society. Put differently, Brunei Town is not to be understood merely in terms of formal political, legal, religious and social structures, but rather in terms of informal relations among individuals and groups.

Early Kampong Ayer

Our present knowledge of early Kampong Ayer is mostly based on observations and descriptions written by foreign travelers, including Pigafetta and other Europeans.[1] The Brunei sources, particularly *Syair Awang Semaun* (*SAS*) and *Silsilah Raja-Raja Brunei* (*SRB*),[2] also provide interesting basic historical information of the Brunei rulers and the foundation of the dynasty. However, they say little about the town or Kampong Ayer. Yet it is interesting to cite some of their views about the capital. *SRB* gives several accounts on the origin of Kota Batu and Kampong Ayer proper. For example, it states that Kota Batu, which became the capital prior to the emergence of Kampong Ayer, was founded by Sharif 'Ali, the third ruler of Islamic Brunei (Sweeney 1968:A2). Among the principal workers in the foundation of this capital were Chinese. The participation of the latter in the early history of Brunei is undeniable. Several local sources confirm their presence and activities in Brunei.[3]

Kota Batu quickly developed into an elaborate center of the sultanate. Palace, mosque and adjoining educational centers, for instance, were built (Sweeney 1968:A31-3; B5). During the reign of Sultan Muhammad Hassan, Kota Batu housed two palaces within a square compound surrounded with a wall (Ibid., A4, 16).

---

[1]Chinese sources are rich with political and economic information on "Brunei" even before the sixteenth century. For further discussion of these sources see Groeneveldt 1960.

[2]*SRB* continued to be reedited and elaborated until 1936. It thus had some information on the changes that took place in Kampong Ayer after the installment of British resident in the country. We shall return on this point later.

[3]Several versions of *SAS* indeed are full with the mentioning of Chinese involvement in Brunei society from quite early period, see also Brown 1970.

Kampong Ayer proper emerged as a center following the civil war during the second half of the seventeenth century. When Sultan 'Abdul Mubin assumed the rulership sometime in the second half of the seventeenth century, he was challenged by Pengiran Muhyiddin.[1] During the crisis the sultan was forced to move his center from, more probably, Kota Batu to the island of Chermin, on the mouth of the Brunei river. Meanwhile Pengiran Muhyiddin built his base upriver around Kampong Ayer proper (Sweeney 1968:B16-18; cf. Franz 1990:164-165). Following the destruction of the forces at the Chermin island, Pengiran Muhyiddin emerged as the sole ruler in Brunei, although he had to share his victory with the princes of Sulu. He made Kampong Ayer proper his power base, even the location of his palace eventually became the locus of power center until the 20th century.

An important, but difficult to use, source is *SAS*.[2] According to *SAS* Brunei was founded after Awang Alak Betatar and his 13 other brothers moved to and around the region, consolidating power. First Awang Alak Betatar settled with his followers in Bukit Berayong; at the same time one of his brothers, Jerambak, founded a settlement at Butir. When Patih Berbai, another brother, suggested to move to a strategic and healthy place, called "Brunei,"[3] Awang Alak Betatar agreed. His move to "Brunei"

---

[1]For further details about the background to the civil war, see Brown 1970:143-144; Saunders 1994.

[2]It has been mentioned and used by Brown (1970). Since that time Brown has insisted on the pressing need to come up with a serious edition of *SAS* for the benefit of future scholars. But until today no complete edition was published, even though reference to it is widely made, especially among Brunei scholars and writers. In utilizing *SAS* I have relied on a draft copy which I have an access to and a series of articles written by Awang Matassim Hj Jibah in *Berita Muzium* (1980). It should be mentioned that one of our staff at University of Brunei Darussalam is finishing a thesis on SAS.

[3]*SAS*: Bisainya tiada lagi terperi
Bukit mendinding yang kanan kiri

was announced to all his followers who scattered in different settlements.

After securing his position in "Brunei" Awang Alak Betatar sent his brothers to the west and east for territorial expansion. Although this mainly involved conquests, the expansion also suppressed piracy in water around, and coast along, north-western Borneo (Matassim 1980:71). The continuing expansion, pursued by different rulers, resulted among other things in the acceptance of the Brunei supremacy by various local chiefs and in the increasing prosperity realized in Kampong Ayer. It became the capital of burgeoning sultanate. It is claimed in *SRB* that the legitimacy of Brunei rule over the outlying territories in the west was provided by the ruler of "Johor" (Sweeney 1968:A1; cf. Treacher 1889:66).

The development of settlements around Kampong Ayer is also illustrated in *SAS*. For example, legends related to the foundation and the naming of Sumbiling, Pusar Ulak and Kianggeh are given. We should bear in mind, however, that anachronism and mythical elements cannot be easily separated in *SAS*. Indeed, it has no dating system.

Nevertheless, the value of the indigenous sources in illustrating the development of the Brunei towns should be properly

---

Tiadalah payah tempat mencari
Di bawah tangga dawai tengiri

Bisainya itu tiada berbanding
Di darat rumah bukit menyinding
Beratur rumah seberang tambing
Tiadalah jauh mengambil ayeng

Mengambil ayeng pun kanak-kanak
Bukannya ayeng di dalam samak
Tiada terkena angin dan ombak
Ayengnya hampir dapat berlumak...

appreciated. They lack precision in describing details and interrelations of events. They also fail to give us full stories of happenings. But they provide us with original viewpoints about events that took place among Bruneis.

Kampong Ayer in the Eyes of the Early Europeans

In this section the discussion is based primarily on European sources. They are gouped into Pigafetta's core and de Sande's core. Interestingly most of the early descriptions on Brunei by the Europeans were undertaken by the Portuguese and Spaniards. The oft-mentioned description by the Italian Pigafetta, who belonged to the crew of Magellan's expedition, is a salient and basic view about the capital of Brunei in the sixteenth century. His description of Brunei is by far more extensive than three or more earlier travelers such as Friar Odoric about 1322 (Treacher 1889:14), Ludovico Varthema about 1504, the Portuguese Tome Pires about 1515 (Nicholl 1975:3, 7) and Lorenzo de Gomez of Lisbon in 1518 (Treacher 1889:14).

By the time of Pigafetta's visit to Brunei in 1521 (Blair and Robertson 1903–1909, 33:211-235), Brunei was ruled by Muslim sovereign. His detailed account of the socio-religious condition, however, leaves us with an idea that the impact of Islam in Brunei was not quite extensive. Perhaps I am expecting too much from a contemporary Italian observer like Pigafetta to depict the development of Islamic urbanism in Brunei.[1] For example, he claimed that he was provided with plenty of distilled rice wine; he also described the simple attire of the population and the

[1]An interesting note (no.428) provided by Blair and Robertson (1903-1909, 33:354-355), quoting Stanley's comment can further, and perhaps more appropriately, explain this point.

royal aides who were mostly daughters of the chiefs as well as the presence of women in the central hall. Moreover, within the same port area, a non-Muslim ruler continued to pose a threat to Brunei. This last statement is also confirmed by a report made by the Portuguese Jorge de Albuquerque, Captain-General of Malacca, to King Joao III three years later.[1] Despite some negative depiction of the religious life in Brunei, Pigafetta provided information on the application of Islamic teachings and education in Brunei. For example, the Bruneis were strict in having *ḥalāl* flesh meat; they practiced circumcision and adopted prescribed rules of cleanliness. Furthermore, the *Sharī'a*-mindedness, to use the Hodgsonian term, of the Bruneis was also confirmed by de Albuquerque's envoy, Vasco Laurenco, in his visit in 1526. In this occasion, the King of Brunei refused to accept a tapestry of arras which had life size figures of men and women (Nicholl 1975:22-33).[2]

For some time scholars have questioned as to why Brunei failed, or rather was unwilling, to Islamize its interior tribes. Although Pigafetta did not give us an answer to this question, he let us examine the phenomenon through his, and others', accounts of Brunei during the sixteenth century. By 1521 Brunei prospered as a state capital and at the same time a trading center. Since the

[1]". . . another ruler who lives on the island of Burneo, and is a lord by himself: he is a heathen, whereas the King of Burneo is a Mauro [read: Muslim] and the people of his land are Mauros also . . ." Nevertheless, de Albuquerque insisted that the relations between the two realms were cordial as the people from both kingdoms were involved in exchange and trade (Nicholl 1975:21).

[2]The main reason of the refusal, I think, is not the one given by Laorenco, who held that the King was worried of sorcery worked by the Portuguese envoy through the human-depicted tapestry. Rather the reason was based on the contemporary Islamic teaching of not keeping living pictures, especially human ones, at one's house. For further information about the phenomenon see Faruqi and Faruqi (1986:314-316).

state officials preferred to stay in the capital, leaving their territorial domains to be administered by their local representatives, communications and exchanges did not run in two-way traffic. Put differently, the human flow was centripetal, meaning local people who were interested in Islam and urban culture were induced to move to the capital and, in the long run, Bruneianized; and not the other way around. Since Brunei at the time was more interested in pursuing its interinsular and even international role, it could have not stressed its presence locally. By the sixteenth century, Brunei emerged as a very important nodal point of Islamic network in Southeast Asia, particularly following the downfall of Malacca and the rise of new centers such as Aceh, Johor and Banten (see Reid 1988:6). Before making any general statement it is important to look closely at Pigafetta's account.

The formation of states in Southeast Asia predated Islamization, meaning Islam did not found states but inherited them. The Muslim states, however, fostered the emergence of new institutions, including new towns, religious orders (*ṭarīqa*s), the use of a common language, and a political system. The concept is not far from what Lapidus calls "pluralistic social systems, organized on different institutional levels" (Lapidus 1989:150). The information given by Pigafetta will be presented in accordance with the above model.

Pigafetta's description of the capital of Brunei focuses on the court, officials, urban elements and trading activities. The Brunei court was located on semi-*terra firma*, as can be seen in the presence of streets, a courtyard of the palace, elephants, and walls. At the same time it is also clear that the population lived mostly on water settlements, as I shall elaborate below. The court where the palace of the sultan stood had "a large brick wall". Pigafetta's statement was also corroborated by Gonzalo Pereira, who visited Brunei in August 1530 (Nicholl 1975:

26).[1] The palace of the sultan was connected to important places in the capital with streets. During Pigafetta's visit these streets were guarded by men with swords, spears and shields. This was an honor given to him by the sultan. His description about the palace is given in detail and generally leaves us with an impressive picture of the palace buildings. Indeed, the palace had more than sixty canons, facing the river. It is curious though, that Pigafetta failed to mention the presence of a religious center or a mosque in the capital.

Pigafetta notes in passing several higher officials in the capital. He names the governor[2] as the most important official under the sultan. Although he mentions the presence of chiefs, he does not give any detail about their titles or functions. Moreover, when entering the audience hall he encountered many nobles sitting down upon a carpet. Again, Pigafetta avoids providing any details about these nobles. The earliest report which comes to my notice on some titles of the nobles can be found in Matelin Magat Buxa Amat's account of his experience in Brunei during the Spanish attack of 1578 (Blair and Robertson 1903–1909, 4:182). He mentions the presence of *Tumango*, *Bandahala*, the two most important *wazīrs*,[3] and Pengiran Seri Laila (*Panguilan*

---

[1]Pereira even stated that it is "the city of Borneo" which was "surrounded by a brick wall."

In a different account, he was said to report that "The city of Borneo is big, surrounded by a brick wall, with many buildings where the kings live, and has magnificent palaces" (Nicholl 1975:25).

[2]In 1530 Gonzalo Pereira reported that the governor was locally known as Xabandar (*Shahbandar*) who rules the kingdom on his behalf, see Nicholl 1975:25.

[3]It is important to mention here that *SRB* categorically states that prior to the reign of Sultan Muhammad Hassan (early part of the 17th century) only two *wazīrs* were appointed. During his rule two new wazirites, Digadong and Pemancha, were created (Sweeney 1968:A). This information corroborates Buxa Amat's account on the wazirite in Brunei during the 16th century.

Salalila) among the Sultan's forces during the mobilization of defense against the Spanish attack of 1578. The three belonged to the core nobility, the sultan's brother, nephew and uncle respectively.

During his visit to the town proper, Pigafetta was given a state honor. Not only was he applauded by the spectators and well-wishers, but he was given an opportunity to walk through a line of special corps of the sultan's armed forces which consisted of no less than 300 heavily armed men. From his description it is evident that these men were a part of the regular forces.[1] Since Pigafetta first anchored at a sea off Muara, he waited the arrival of the sultan's representatives to permit him proceed to the capital. We are not informed who are those representatives who came six days later in three boats (*praus*) "with great pomp" (Blair and Robertson 1903–1909, 33:211). Earlier eight chiefs consisting of "old men" were sent to present a *prau* and consumption goods to Pigafetta.

Pigafetta leaves us with a picture of a town with strong urban elements. From the variety of gifts which he presented to the king, the governor and other chiefs,[2] it is clear that he highly respected the progress and culture of the country and its people. Even Crawfurd suggests that Pigafetta's is "a faithful representation of a Malay court in the beginning of the sixteenth century, and shows a very considerable advancement in

---

Another account of de Sande's mission (Blair and Robertson 1903-1909,4:197-200) gives more details about the higher officials in Brunei, including Pangiran Salam, Pangiran Maharaja Diraja and other *pangiran*s (princes).

[1]It is interesting to note that many observers during the 19th century insisted that Brunei could no longer maintain a regular army, see for example St. John 1862; Treacher 1889.

[2]Among the presents were dresses, glasses, needles, caps, writing books, cases, and a velvet chair.

civilisation" (Crawfurd 1856:72). Moreover, he was provided with amenities and facilities which showed the cosmopolitan characters of Brunei. For example, during his first night in the house of the governor he slept on cotton mattresses which were decorated with a lining of taffeta and also sheets made in Gujerat. And the next day upon his return to the house of the governor from the palace, he was served drinks and more than thirty varieties of dishes. The spoons and cups were equal to those utilized by the Spaniards. Oil lamps and torch candles were provided in the rooms for lighting. During his audience with the ruler he saw the delicate and grand interior of the palace. The ceremonies were highly developed and refined. More interestingly, the means of communication between the ruler and his audience was arranged as such as to give visual access to the ruler without being too close by providing a sophisticated audio tube. As can be seen in the exchanges of presents and the friendship agreement between the ruler of Brunei and Spain represented by Pigafetta, it is clear that Brunei at that time was highly integrated in international diplomacy.

The prosperity of the Brunei capital depended very much on external trade. Brunei played an important role as a nodal point for the extensive trading networks in the region. Junks from various parts, including Malacca, Patani, China, Java and Luzon (Nicholl 1975:10-20, 29) were seen in the Brunei port. The attraction that Brunei enjoyed had something to do with its access to gold, camphor and jungle produce. The expansion of such international trade could not be achieved without the regional security and support provided by Brunei. During this period, therefore, the problem of piracy in the region could not have arisen.

The internal trade of Brunei was lively. Money in form of bronze was used for payment. Other methods of payment and exchanges, however, continued to be widespread. The oft-mentioned trade on water needs not be repeated here.[1]

The coming of the Spaniards under Dr. de Sande left important new sources for the history of the Brunei capital. From the time of Pigafetta's visit and the coming of de Sande, many European visitors and traders did come and write on the city; however, they only added little to what Pigafetta described. For example, a Portuguese captain, Antonio Galvao received unfriendly treatment by the Bruneis when he anchored at the port in 1536. This act was an expression of their protest against the mistreatment of the Moluccan Muslims by the Portuguese (Nicholl 1975:28). In general, the Portuguese were always on good terms with the Bruneis. In fact, it was reported that shortly following the departure of de Sande from Brunei in July 1578, Brunei made a request to a visiting captain of a Portuguese warship for help against the Spaniards (Blair and Robertson 1903–1909, 4:223).

Since the main concern here is to relate de Sande's account[2] to urbanism in Brunei, it is necessary to be eclectic. De Sande's mission was to "teach [the] natives there the Christian law, and to reduce them to the dominion of his Majesty." He came to Brunei well-prepared for any event, including war. The battles did take place. The Spaniards won; but the ruler had taken a flight upriver. For various reasons[3] the Spaniards fairly soon

---

[1]For further details see Forrest 1969:381; Saunders 1994.

[2]In this paper, de Sande's account is used in order to indicate reports about de Sande's mission in 1578 to Brunei. Thus it is not necessarily reported or written by him. Reports by others on the mission, in fact, is included in his account. The main source for de Sande's mission can be found in Blair and Robertson 1903-1909, 4.

[3]On these points see Saunders 1994. It is reported that the sickness and death occurred among the Spaniards in Brunei were caused by "a herb which the natives put into the food, or which they had thrown into the water. [De Sande] was, therefore, forced to abandon the settlement and return to Manila"

withdrew from Brunei. Yet, as Brown (1970:142) rightly admits, de Sande's mission left "another detailed and first-hand account of the capital and its inhabitants."

From de Sande's accounts it is clear that by 1578 Brunei was as strong and prosperous as during the time of Pigafetta's visit. For instance, it was claimed that de Sande's mission to Brunei was a response to the previous attempted attack by Brunei on Manila with "more than three hundred sails" (Nicholl 1975:34). Again on the arrival of de Sande on the Brunei water he encountered approximately 30 warships, which blockaded the mouth of the Brunei river (Blair and Robertson 1903–1909, 4:156-159, 184). Although de Sande's account dismisses any serious military challenge from the Bruneis,[1] it gives a glance at the might and preparation of the Brunei forces.[2]

The location of the town proper was not different from that described by Pigafetta. It remained in the Brunei river with its "great settlement of houses." Interestingly, he categorically states that he entered a large house belonging to the old king of Brunei, most probably Sultan 'Abdul Qahhar. This does not necessarily mean that the palace and the court were located in the river. Rather the courtiers and other nobles owned houses in the river.

(Nicholl 1975:54). De Sande abandoned Brunei sometime toward the end of July 1578, after approximately 105 days in Brunei, see de Sande's letter to the king of Spain on July 29, 1578, a report of 1586 and an account on the visit of the Portuguese in August 1578 in Nicholl 1975:52-56.

[1]De Sande's entrance to Brunei town, like his exit some time later, leaves many puzzles. His forces are depicted as strong and effective; they achieved what they had planned. For example they entered Brunei town after some time when the Bruneis "retired and fled" upriver (Ibid., pp.160-161). The Bruneis, however, were said to precipitate the fight by firing artillery shots at the Spaniards (Ibid., p.186).

[2]On his letter to the king of Spain in July 1578, de Sande describes the remnants of ships, galleys and artillery left by the Brunei in the town (Nicholl 1975:52-53).

More specifically, the palace of the king and other important houses of the higher nobility and officials, including chiefs and captains, were said to be located in the "village" (Blair and Robertson 1903–1909, 4:166-167; cf. 171). This term, I suggest, should mean a central place separated from the river settlement proper. It was on the *terra firma*.[1] During the negotiation, a messenger sent by de Sande was held prisoner and taken to the prison in chains. The prison, located in the middle of the river,[2] was guarded by an officer called *tuan patih* or *Patimuhaurat*—from *Patih* Muhammad (Ibid., p.183) perhaps. Since the situation was chaotic, the prisoner could have easily paid a ransom with the help of a relative in Brunei, to the guard. Thus, he was set free to rejoin de Sande's forces (Ibid.:161-166).

Furthermore, it is clear that Brunei during the time of the Spanish attack of 1578 was an important international trading network and city. De Sande's account describes in detail the variety and a considerable number of cannons, arms, ammunition, poison, and galleys left by the Bruneis in the river during their flight. One of the guns was a gift from the king of Portugal. In one of the houses, de Sande found a collection of papers within a large gourd. Among them were letters sent by a certain Don Leonis Ferreyras in Malay and another in Portuguese from "the King" of Evora.

De Sande's account gives a more extensive picture about the impact of Islam in Brunei town. For the first time, the existence of a mosque was mentioned.[3] Its building was apparently

---

[1]Indeed, it is also stated that at one time during the inspection of the village, de Sande "went also by land to a house"..., see Blair and Robertson 1903-1909, 4:166-167. Later de Sande decided to build a fort, a house, a hospital and a store, more probably, in the land settlement not on the river, see Ibid., p.172.

[2]It is possible that this prison was originally a house of the previous ruler, see Ibid., p.182.

[3]*SRB* mentions that one of the contributions of Sultan Sharif 'Ali to

magnificent, as even de Sande ordered that valuable materials, including a pulpit, a block of ornamented marble and a trough be taken away (Ibid.:167-168).[1] We do not know why de Sande ordered that the "very sumptuous mosque" be burned before he returned to Manila in the same year (Ibid., p.388; Nicholl 1975:52-53).[2]

Here, as in many other Muslim countries, the *khaṭībs* (preachers) taught Islam to the people. In Brunei, the religious bureaucracy has been highly developed and structured. As can be seen in de Sande's account, the *khaṭībs* were prominent. We may surmise that they were most probably a member of the religious bureaucracy. The bureaucracy of the time was not necessarily elaborate and well structured as found in the later period (see below). Nevertheless, the foundation of the *jāmi'* mosque in the capital required the appointment of religious officials. By the time of the writing of *SRB* sometime before 1735, the mosque in the capital became the central office of the religious establishment. Even the writer of *SRB*, Pehin Datu Imam,

---

development of Islam in Brunei was his founding of a mosque in the capital (Sweeney 1968). Although I hold that this cannot be the first mosque in Brunei, it signifies that the mosque built by Sharif 'Ali was more elaborate and formal.

[1]It should be added that de Sande's decision to take away various articles from the mosque, houses and places in Brunei indicates, *inter alia*, that he was not only curious about, but also impressed by, them. The amount of the collection was so high that a large house was occupied for the purpose before his departure to Manila (Ibid., pp.169, 172).

[2]Nevertheless, consistent with the religious zeal and old antagonism against the Moors among de Sande's contemporaries, it is possible that the burning of the mosque was de Sande's policy to win the support of the local population and destroy the power of the Muslims, see the following for example: when in Mindanao he ordered to "burn the edifice in which the accursed doctrine [of Islam] was read and taught, and . . . none like it shall be built" (Ibid., p.234).

came from this circle (see Sweeney 1968). Again in 1609, during his refuge in Brunei, Father Antonio Pereira (Nicholl 1975:89-90) reported that he was invited to the palace of the ruler of Brunei in the presence of three higher religious officials (*Alfaquies* and *Caciques*)[1] for a discussion on religious issues. We may surmise that by this time[2] religious officials were well organized and bureaucratized. Apparently the religious officials in Brunei were also active, from quite an early period, in spreading and, more importantly, publishing their teachings (Blair and Robertson 1903–1909, 4:151). On the other hand, the court in the capital often welcomed visiting Christian priests for discussion of religious issues. For example, in December 1587, the sultan welcomed a Franciscan priest to the palace, where the latter was given a chance to express his religious ideas, even to the extent of "offending" the host (Nicholl 1975:77).

When taking flight from the Spanish fleet, the Bruneis fled upriver. Since the Brunei river had only a few miles of water which was suitable for larger vessels, they had to walk. The journey to their place of hiding took almost two days (Blair and Robertson 1903–1909, 4:171). For our study about urbanism in Brunei, this information is helpful in explaining the link between Brunei and the interior. The Bruneis indeed felt secured to take refuge among the population in the interior. In another report (Ibid., pp.198-200), it is understood that the king of Brunei took refuge as far as the Melanau area in Sarawak. If this statement is

---

[1]*Alfaquies* is probably derived from Arabic *al-faqīh*; whereas *caciques* from *al-khaṭīb*. They were higher religious officials known as *imāms* in Brunei. Originally they consisted of four higher officials (*pehin manteri*): Datu Imam, Siraja Khatib, Tuan Imam and Udana Khatib. Later a higher official, entitled Pehin Datu Seri Maharaja, was appointed to lead the religious bureaucracy (Pehin Yahya 1988:14).

[2]The ruler of Brunei at the time was no other than the great Sultan Muhammad Hassan, see Saunders 1994.

true, it is indicative of the strong influence Brunei had on the outlying regions at the time.

When the Spaniards left Brunei sometime in late July 1578, the Bruneis under Sultan Saiful Rijal soon rebuilt their capital city. This episode is an interesting reference in looking at urbanism in Brunei. First of all, the sultan ordered the reorganization of the defense and the armed forces. Two forts were quickly erected; one was located upriver and another in the proximity of the old mosque. The first was primarily intended as a temporary lodge for the ruler's household.[1] The second seems to have been erected for purely defense purpose. Its control was entrusted to the Pangiran Bendahara and the Pangiran Temenggong (Blair and Robertson 1903–1909, 4:210). The sultan was able within a short period of time to gather about 200 pieces of artillery, besides restoring many galleys.[2] At this time, the main allies of Sultan Saiful Rijal were the Bisayas and the Moros. Many of the high officials who collaborated with the Spaniards were purged (Nicholl 1975:54); however, those who returned to the capital and joined their ruler in rebuilding the capital were accommodated (cf. Blair and Robertson 1903–1909, 4:211). The mosque was given priority for restoration (Blair and Robertson 1903–1909, 4:198-200; 211).

From the accounts of de Sande's mission to Brunei, it is evident that slaves, especially those who belonged to the ruler and the higher officials, played an important role in the capital. Many of them were trusted even to command galleys supported with pieces of artillery (Blair and Robertson 1903–1909, 4:182, 184, 210). Some slaves were educated. In the capture of five slaves by Spanish Sadornil in 22 March 1579, it was found out

[1]It is also reported that this fort was built in response to the possible second attack by the Spaniard in March 1579 (Ibid., pp.195-196). It is also reported that this fort accommodated other peoples too (Blair and Robertson 1903–1909:210-211).

[2]For example a vessel was sent to Siam for artillery (Nicholl 1975:68).

that two of them were literate (Nicholl 1975:68). Since at times a slave enjoyed close relations with his master, he was generally loyal. He thus became the backbone of his master's supporters.

On the other hand, Islam in the capital of Brunei was not reflected in de Sande's account as a force of resistance or a rallying banner during the occupation.

The influence of the ruler upon the inhabitants was strong. We do not know exactly what networks other than the traditional multiplication-of-four bureaucracy was the ruler able to utilize in mobilizing the population. It is not far-fetched to surmise that the fishermen were put under the jurisdiction of the *shahbandar*. This is especially so since they were involved in the trading and communication with foreign traders around the port. During the second Spaniard mission to Brunei led by Sadornil in 1579, it was assumed that the fishermen did not come to the Spanish fleet because the ruler forbade them to do so for security reasons (Blair and Robertson 1903–1909, 4:208). Moreover, the ruler provided the visitors to the capital with houses to stay (Nicholl 1975:76).

The appointments of many members of the ruling family to key posts in the capital formed an important element in the composition of power structure.[1] Not only did the ruling family dominate key political and administrative positions, they also enjoyed privileges on and access to economic advantages. Indeed, the crucial position of the ruling family *vis-à-vis* the state became clearer in the nineteenth century.

The aquatic life in urban Brunei had its own varied characteristics. Brunei town with its waters had a strategic and geographic advantage. Therefore when making an assessment

[1]For example during the welcome for the Portuguese in August 1578, the ruler was surrounded by his relatives and other *pangirans* in the palace, see Ibid., p.222.

for a colony in 1579, for instance, Sadornil, the commander of the Spanish fleet, recommended that the only way to control Brunei was to settle in Brunei town (Blair and Robertson 1903–1909, 4:215).[1] The oft-mentioned shops on water, streets of water and the structure of houses need no repetition here. A point that the study raises at this point is related to the defense of the city. Brunei, like many other realms of the period, maintained warships and heavy pieces of artillery, in addition to conventional weapons and guns. However, after their defeat at the hands of the Spaniards, the Bruneis resorted to the traditional means of warfare. As stated in many reports by the Spaniards who participated in de Sande's missions of 1578 and 1579, poison was used by the Bruneis in foods and water (Blair and Robertson 1903–1909, 4:217; cf. Nicholl 1975:54)

Following the departure of de Sande, the Bruneis quickly revived their service and trade with visiting foreign ships to the country. Apparently dealings with these ships were organized formally by the authorities in the capital, more probably under the *shahbandar*. But in August 1578, it was the *bandahala tua* who led the negotiations with the visiting Portuguese ship. They brought foodstuff, fruits, fowls, beverages and other items[2] to the ship for sale or barter. On the other hand, the Portuguese sold several hundred pieces of cloth in exchange for wax, camphor, tortoise-shell, and slaves.[3] Previously, they had brought a valuable present to the ruler (Ibid., p.224). In the capital, the dealers for

---

[1]It is implied that to deal effectively with the Bruneis, there was no other choice but to settle among them, and not to establish a rival settlement (Ibid.).

[2]It is reported that cows were raised in Brunei, including Muara and Bengkurong, even though their numbers were not very high. For example, the Spaniards were warned by their commander not to kill any cattle, particularly cow in the country, see Ibid., pp.191, 217.

[3]Interestingly by 1579, the Spaniards in the region made a vow upon themselves not to purchase "native slaves" in Brunei, Ibid., p.191.

second-hand goods and articles seem to have prospered, as indicated by the trade of those articles sourced from the foreign visitors (Nicholl 1975:76).[1]

De Sande's account of Brunei of 1578, which was written in 1586, best illustrates the situation of the period.

> [De Sande] followed up his victory and entered the city, where he pillaged a great part of its wealth. Almost all the people fled to the mountains. That city was very large and rich, and was built over a very broad and deep river and had the appearance of another Venice. The buildings were of wood, but the houses were excellently constructed, many of them being constructed of stone work and gilded, especially the king's palaces, which were of huge size. That city contained a very sumptuous mosque, a very large and interesting building, quite covered with half relief and gilded. When [de Sande] returned to Manila he ordered that the mosque be burned. That the king of Burney was a Moro from Meca, and is the ruler of seaports and rivers of that island, where he has settlements of Moros (Nicholl 1975:54).

The visit to Brunei by Olivier van Noort of Amsterdam provides another important account of the history of Brunei town. His two weeks stay[2] in the town was too short to learn about Brunei in much detail. His information, however, confirms both Pigafetta's and de Sande's accounts. For example, during his visits he saw the Bruneis brought basic necessities to his ship for sale. He asserted that in 1600, the capital was located three miles[3] from the coast; and the houses in the capital *per se* were between 200 and 300, "surrounded by a good stone wall," surprisingly

---

[1]In this episode several members of Spanish mission were robbed, and their belongings were sold publicly in the capital.

[2]From December 1600 to early January 1601 (Nicholl 1975:82-87).

[3]The term "mile" used here does not mean the same as our usage today. For he said that Brunei "lies one hundred and eighty miles from Manila" (Nicholl 1975:82). The distance is in fact more than 700 miles. I am convinced that the capital remained in a place close to Kampong Ayer (cf. Cleary 1990:3).

located in a swampy area. Van Noort also mentioned the active role of the ruler of Brunei in providing security for fishermen and traders along the coast by his maintaining "a large number of vessels."[1] In addition, he noted the active role played by the Chinese in trade. They became an important group among various foreign traders who constantly conducted business in the country. He also found out that the nobility were living in "great luxury... Their palaces could be called beautiful houses, albeit they are made of wood, and built on such light piles that when there is a storm or some other untoward event these houses can be removed from one side of the river to the other" (Nicholl 1975:83).

By the time of van Noort's visit in 1600, the Bruneis seem to have been more committed to Islamic teaching than during Pigafetta's visit in 1521. If previously rice wine had been provided for Pigafetta, no such liquor was made available to van Noort. And according to his report, the Bruneis "would rather die than eat pork" (Ibid., 87). They were also very protective towards women. By the seventeenth century the Brunei court maintained an elaborate religious bureaucracy supported by the *alfaquies* and *caciques* (see above p.187). These were Muslim scholars who were well acquainted with Islamic literature which was widely read in the centers of Islamic learnings in the region. Interestingly, the ruler of Brunei allowed his court to be used as a forum for discussions between Christian priests and his Islamic religious officials. Without firm confidence in the erudition of his officials, the ruler would not have held such a meeting. This gesture of the

---

[1]Even though van Noort added that outside the stone-walled town he saw "several other houses," it is clear that for him the numbers of houses are around 300, see quotation in Nicholl 1975:83, 87. I think van Noort ignored the houses located in the heart of Kampong Ayer. Since he felt that the population and the court were not in favor of having him around, he had little time to go around. Indeed, he also stated that "the inhabitants have more further inland."

ruler confirmed the reports by Spanish missionaries during the seventeenth century that the Bruneis were tolerant Muslims (Nicholl 1975:94-95).

Towards the end of the 17th century, Brunei established closer ties with the Spaniards of Manila. Missions from both countries were exchanged, and agreements on trade and commerce were ratified (Nicholl 1975:95-96).[1]

Brunei continued to enjoy the fortune of commercial and trading activities well towards the end of the 18th century. During a visit to Kampong Ayer in February 1776, Thomas Forrest claimed to have seen two-storey houses "with stages or wharfs before them, for the convenience of trade" (1969:380). The trading position of Brunei was evident in that an average of a China junk of more than 500 tons burden from Amoy and other Chinese ports disembarked at the Brunei harbor every two months. Large junks were also built in Brunei using local timber. Many Bruneis acted as brokers for goods imported from China. They then resold these goods to the people of Kampong Ayer as well as to the interior inhabitants. The much bigger traders moved around the regional trading centers to conduct business (Forrest 1969:383-384). There was also a brisk market, dominated by women vendors who stood on a fleet of boats moving around the river town.[2] The beauty and perhaps the seeming prosperity of Brunei inspired Forrest to compare it with Venice. Its houses were built on water almost schematically "with channels like lanes, between the rows."

---

[1]A similar tone was also noted in *SRB* when describing the cordial relations between Brunei and Manila around this period, Sweeney 1968:A51-52.

[2]According to Low's observation in the 1840s, this fleet consisted of between 150 and 200 boats (1848:153).

Brunei Town Prior to the Residency Period

Before the development of Bandar Brunei proper with the establishment of the municipal board in 1921, Bandar Brunei was synonymous with the Water Village (*Kampong Ayer*). From the early part of the nineteenth century onwards, more and more observers, officials and visitors had provided better information about Brunei. Many European writers even had described Brunei at that time as decadent and unattractive.[1]

With the increasing pressure meted out by the European powers in the region since the 19th century, Brunei suffered politically and economically. More and more local leaders at the peripheries exercised power on their own or in collaboration with outsiders (Mundy 1848,1:189). Accordingly, the elites in Brunei competed more aggressively to secure better political position and access to the limited economic resources available.[2] Not surprisingly, political crises and rivalry among the ruling class became recurrent features during the first half of the 19th century (Brown 1970; Saunders 1994).

Despite the political and economic decline, Brunei Town continued to attract attention. It was in this period that the first

---

[1]Baring-Gould, for example, identifies Brunei with the "nest of murderers and robbers" (1909:327). Crawfurd writing in mid 19th century regards Brunei as in "a more backward state than Malacca was near 350 years ago" (1856:69). James Brooke describes Brunei of 1842 as a town "in distress and difficulty from within: trade ruined, piracy abounding, the mouth of the river unsafe, their forts insulted by the pirates, the communication with their dependencies cut off, food dear . . ." (Keppel 1846/1991,1:321; cf. Mundy 1848,1:179-181). Similar tones have also been voiced by St. John (1862), Low (1848) and Keppel (1846), to mention a few of them. Although their descriptions may be not too far from truth, they fail to explain, other than misrule, oppression and injustice, the factors which brought to the decline.

[2]A good summary of the existing literature on the subject can be found in Cleary and Eaton 1992:47-48.

detailed description of the capital was undertaken by the colonial official-cum-researcher, Spenser St. John. While Kampong Ayer may have lost most of its splendor and opulence, it had retained its structure and livelihood.[1] Using the existing studies of Brunei Town based on St. John's account, Cleary analyzes them under Sjoberg's categorization of pre-industrial cities. Brunei Town is seen as a dominating center, a well-protected entity with spatially segregated units (Cleary and Eaton 1992:37-39). This study is interesting since it describes Brunei Town as a central point of complex networks. However, its superimposed depiction of spatial gradation and occupational specialization is less convincing. Brown's categorizing the roles of two wards, Kampong Saba and Kampong Burung Pingai, pointed to their special position in the state (1970:54-56), even though they were not geographically close to the palace. Indeed, Burung Pingai was located upriver towards the southwest end of Kampong Ayer. During the 19th century it facilitated interinsular trading by the participation of their merchants (*nakhoda*s) and therefore played a major role in the capital's politics through its support for a faction.

In the religious field, the sultan enjoyed a paramount position. Religious officials were appointed and granted titles by him. The control, and perhaps influence, of the palace on religious matters continued to be a crucial factor in making religious ideas uniform and less prone to external pressure. This does not mean that Brunei was free from any religious controversy. In the early 1840s, Brunei experienced the first and, perhaps, the most significant religious schism.[2] The leader of the opposition group

---

[1]Treacher makes interesting comparative notes on Brunei Town according to Pigafetta's account and that of his joint-observation with Stair Dalrymple in 1884 (1889:45-53). According to Treacher "all [workers, artisans and producers] have their own *kampong*s, and are jealous of the honour of each member of their corporation" (1889:53).

[2]For further discussion of this phenomenon see my article "Intellectual

was a non-religious official, Haji Muhammad. His success in mobilizing a large following was due mainly to his close contact with a faction of the ruling class, and the manipulation of the prevailing political rivalry among the elites. He obtained support from an increasingly strong prince at the time, Pengiran Temenggong and even proceeded to found a splinter mosque across the river.[1] The episode of Haji Muhammad illustrated the possibility of religious deviance if the political constellation is splintered and vicissitude exists. The fact, however, remains that the deviance was temporary and ended with the death of Haji Muhammad, including the political settlement that materialized in the early 1850s. Thereafter, the sultan continued to be the paramount symbol of religious establishment in the country.

Nineteenth century Brunei evidenced the weakness of utilizing personal networks as a strategy in governing the state. In the past, it was the source of strength and stability. The central government was more interested in controlling people than territory.[2] Economically, Brunei had enjoyed a monopoly of external trade by controlling trading centers in the river mouths of Northwestern Borneo. Politically, the personal networks of nobles and higher officials resulted in the recognition of the authority of the central government by the people in the river valleys. However, it was the people, regardless of their residence, which eventually accounted for support and obedience. Culturally, the personal allegiance of the subjects resulted in the migration

---

Tradition in A Malay State: '*Ulama*' and Education in Brunei Darussalam," *Jurnal Pendidikan* 1992:35-60.

[1]It is probable, comparable to general cases in other Islamic towns, that only one formal *jāmi'* mosque existed in Brunei Town. Interestingly, Hugh Low reported that in 1845 there were "several [mosques] in the town" even though they were in a "ruinous state" (Low 1848:152).

[2]For more analyses on this point, even with different perspectives, see Treacher (1889:37-39); Brown (1970); and Cleary and Eaton (1992:47-48).

of the Bruneianized citizen to the Brunei proper. This did not much affect Bruneianization at the local level. It was a centripetal and not a centrifugal process as most of the officials remained most of the time in the capital.[1] The increasing encroachment of Europeans into the country, especially in the nineteenth century, posed an additional threat to the existing networks of personal allegiance of local officials (cf. Horton 1987:23-24). Brunei was plagued with internal squabbles and declined in economic resources. It was consequently difficult for the central government to maintain the network and win allegiance from its subjects. The dismemberment of the Brunei territories during the period can therefore be partly explained in this light. Nevertheless, the network remained strong within the core region of Brunei.

Although reports in the second half of the nineteenth century indicated that the sultan was losing control over his key ministers, the sultan as an institution was still crucial in the social formation of the Brunei Town. The town-cum-capital resided in the crown land (*kerajaan*) and was inalienable. The *kerajaan* belonged to the reigning sultan. Thus it had not experienced any reduction nor division, unlike the *kuripan* (appanage) or the *tulin* (hereditary property). Under certain circumstances, the *kerajaan* might have absorbed the *kuripan* and the *tulin*. The ruler, in fact, enjoyed better economic resources and a more strategic location than the others in the capital, not to mention its peripheries. He had the power to initiate many undertakings, including those requiring the support of other higher princes. By the 19th century, unlike during Pigafetta's visit, Brunei no longer had a regular army nor navy (Treacher 1889:42). Thus, the ruler had no direct means to

[1]It should be mentioned here that at times, particularly during a crisis, prominent figures were sent to outlying regions to settle the unrest and at the same time, perhaps, to get rid of these influential figures. A case in point was the sending of Pengiran Muda Hashim to Sarawak during the reign of Sultan 'Umar 'Ali Saifuddin II.

impose his will upon his higher officials, particularly the *wazīrs*. In his report of 1904, McArthur opines that the "curious constitution of the country makes the Sultan only supreme in name, and his position is so much a matter of accommodation with Ministers as strong as himself..." (Horton 1987:121; also 126-127). Yet the ruler had direct access to his large household and traditional supporters for any action. To illustrate his comment about the Brunei court in 1880s, Treacher emphasizes the dependence of the ruler on his "confidential agents" in discussing and arranging important, even difficult, businesses or negotiations with outsiders (1889:63). Moreover, the pressure on Brunei's resources and economy gave a way to *homines novi* in banking, trade and commerce. By 1884 Treacher dared to generalize that "what money there is in the city [of Brunei] is almost entirely in the hands of the Chinese traders" (Treacher 1889:51; cf. Horton 1987:120).

The trade monopoly increased the cost of exchange, together with the prices of goods, in Brunei. In 1904 McArthur reported in a particular instance that the monopoly over a type of imported goods led to sky-rocketing prices as the original owner sold the monopoly to the other traders; the latter repeated the pattern before the goods came to the hand of buyers (Horton 1987:124-125).

In 1904, McArthur also claimed that Brunei had no salaried officers, "no forces, no police, no public institutions, no coinage, no roads, no public buildings except a wooden mosque, and—[the] most crying need of all—no gaol" (Horton 1987:127-128). McArthur was a shrewd and sympathetic observer; but he needed more time and information to understand the workings of the Brunei system.[1] With the population of around 10,000, state

[1]It is important to note in this context that McArthur shares with us his observation of the delicate method of settling dispute. Even the ruler preferred

institutions and public domains could have been neglected and collapsed. The governing and social relations thus required more personal touch and *ad hoc* handling. Accordingly, important institutions came to oblivion, as was witnessed by McArthur. Interestingly, he still found a mosque, however moderate a building it was. This explains much of Brunei's situation in the early 20th century. The affairs of the state were handled or channeled through the palace, the mosque and through many other private houses of various leaders. Despite the informality of the latter, they had definite systems, networks and patterns understood well by the population.

The first British resident in Brunei was quite optimistic and confident about the plan to shift the center from Kampong Ayer to land settlement. Several preliminary studies about the movement to land settlement have been done by a number of contemporary scholars.[1] For this paper it is necessary to pinpoint some salient features of the phenomenon.

The movement to settle on land was initiated by the resident office. Yet the British resident was careful in securing a base for local support. First of all, the first mosque ever built of brick was erected on land after the old one was burnt during the Spanish occupation of 1578. The mosque represented the continuing symbol of the sultan's authority on religious field (see Iik Arifin 1992). The sultan also promoted the movement to settle on land by extending parts of the palace farther inland (cf. Franz 1990:166). Moreover, several higher royal families initiated the resettlement on land. Nevertheless, the movement to settle on land gained little support from the inhabitants of the Water Village.[2] The

to leave some matters to be decided by headmen (Horton 1987:129).

[1]Cleary and Eaton 1992; Enggu 1993; Kaloko 1995.

[2]As noted by Chi *et al.* the most enthusiastic participants in the scheme of land occupation or settlement were shop owners who came mainly from among the Chinese (1991:11).

foundation of various modern facilities on land, including administrative offices, shopping arcades, trading houses, and eating places seem to have little impact on the general population. They shared the new establishments and services on land by remaining in the old water settlement.[1] For them the pattern of relations between the land and the water settlement was nothing new. They had done so before with the Kedayans, who occupied and worked on the land surrounding Kampong Ayer and beyond.

Nevertheless, Kampong Ayer experienced fundamental changes. The foundation of administrative and modern facilities on land shifted the center and capital to new location on land. Moreover, the deliberate policy of undermining the economic and demographic bases of Kampong Ayer slowly eroded the identity and occupational specialization of individual wards (*kampongs*).[2] Nevertheless, it is evident that the "creation of Brunei town on land, although acting as a magnet for at least some of the population of Kampong Ayer did not automatically lead to the depopulation of the settlement" (Chi *et al.* 1991:13). Indeed, in 1971 the population of Kampong Ayer represented 60 percent

---

[1]The statement of the resident in 1916 that the "population in the *kampong* on the water in Brunei is understandably diminishing, while the new town of Brunei on the mainland is growing larger" should be taken cautiously.

[2]For further discussion of the development of Brunei Town, see Cleary and Eaton 1992:124-126; Chi *et al.* 1991; Kaloko 1995. In 1970 Bandar Brunei was renamed Bandar Seri Begawan to honor Sultan Omar Ali Saifuddin, who stepped down from the throne in 1967 in favor of his eldest son, the present ruler of Brunei Darussalam.

"Modernization has undoubtedly destroyed the occupational and social identities of individual *kampongs* although they continue to play a part in communal life" (Chi *et al.* 1991:13). Thus, the change of Kampong Ayer identity from pluralism of *kampongs* to unitarian entity reflects the shift of its characteristics and significance from a center to a mere suburb of the capital (cf. Abdul Latif 1971:56).

of the total population of Bandar Seri Begawan.[1]

Kampong Ayer undoubtedly will survive not only because many inhabitants prefer to remain there, but they have also adapted to the new situation in the town as a whole and have accepted the challenge by improving their living conditions. Moreover, the government has almost made Kampong Ayer self-sufficient by providing it with modern conveniences such as piped water, telephone lines and electricity together with such community facilities as schools, mosques, police stations, clinics and fire service (see Kaloko 1995:12).

The rapid development of the land-based town of Bandar Brunei after the Pacific War, especially since the 1960s, was due to a definite plan, political will, and abundant fund. The increasing accumulation of oil fund by the government enabled its leaders to implement major developments in the town. For example, since the mid 1950s, the inhabitants of Kampong Ayer have been encouraged to move to land settlement, they were provided with funds for building their houses and land for cultivation (*Pelita Brunei* 15.12.1958:2). Interestingly, the early resettlements consisted of the inhabitants of the same wards in Kampong Ayer. It is thus not surprising to find that such wards as Burung Pingai

---

[1]See Franz 1990:166-168. But in 1981 it represented only 53 percent and in 1986 52 percent. The census of 1991 indicates that the population of Kampong Ayer declined from 27,125 in 1981—27,080 in 1986—to 24,745 in 1991. The decline of Kampong Ayer population, relative to the composition of the state population as a whole, will continue to be a future trend as suggested by the 1993 survey (cited in Kaloko 1995:10). For example 43% of the existing population expressed a desire to relocate somewhere outside Kampong Ayer.

With the increasing pressure upon the inhabitants of Kampong Ayer to change, through the impact of education, mass media, or government policy, the physical appearance of Kampong Ayer also has changed significantly. For example, traditional building techniques and styles of stilt, piles and rattan have been replaced, in many instances, today by concrete, corrugated zinc, tile, brick, formica and plywood.

Darat, Berakas, Gadong, Lambak, and Bunut originally harbored inhabitants from the same old wards. These initial schemes and those which followed in the late 1960s until the 1980s had only limited success, and were in the main rejected by the communities in Kampong Ayer.

Since the top-down policy was crucial in the move for settlement on dry land, the role of the policy makers and the rulers was determinant in urbanism of the town. During the residency period, urban centers and institutions expressed the British preference for urbanism. After the transfer of the internal administration to the sultan in 1959, and more particularly after independence in 1984, the sultan has been instrumental in making urbanism in Brunei more consonant with local and Islamic features. Yet the development of the modern town of Bandar Seri Begawan remains basically a modern phenomenon, beset with global impact and ideas.

Summary

Kampong Ayer had developed into a vibrant center and powerful state capital following the spread of Islam. The patronage of the state upon religion, culture, local trade, industry, and other professions led to the rapid growth of the water settlement. It was the ruler who strengthened the centripetal networks of diverse ties. The advantage of enjoying economic prosperity, religious revivalism, and strong political power enabled the ruler to provide a conducive environment for increasing the growth of Kampong Ayer as an urban settlement.

The physical characteristics of Southeast Asian cities under Muslim rule also materialized in Brunei Town. It had elaborate defense of wall and cannons. Brunei Town enjoyed a position of center of power and government. Various nomenclatures of urbanism were found in it. Furthermore, the Islamic character of Brunei Town was emphasized by its attraction of religious scholars and figures from the Middle East. With the ever increasing prosperity of the Islamic trading networks, the ruler participated in the trade. However, the over-emphasis over the external and international link in the long run negated Brunei's interest in the hinterland. Thus no significant expansion of Islam was introduced upriver. More importantly, no comparable "regular mass of wandering" *shaykh*s had mediated between the new religion of the town and that of the interior (cf. Kathirithamby-Wells 1986:345-346).

The rulers of Brunei made the mosque and market, in addition to palace, points of gravity for many state activities. They were directly controlled by them.

The ruler emerged as the head of religious functionaries in an elaborately developed religious bureaucracy. The ruler directly appointed them and became himself the highest authority.

Although Brunei no longer maintained a regular army by the nineteenth century, as early as 1521 it had well-trained soldiers as reported by Pigafetta. The security achieved in the Brunei waters and beyond during the period facilitated the growth of trade, urban growth and economic exchange. At the same time, the Bruneis took full advantage of the opportunity to join in the Islamic, if not international, trading network.

Nevertheless the personal nature of the state power and structure limited the breadth and stability of the networks. For example, the territorial divisions and organization of the country were trusted to higher nobilities who consequently delegated the power and administration to their respective followers. Yet others could have directly contacted the ruler for deals. As a result formal arrangements were often upset by such maneuvers.

Kampong Ayer had its own dynamism in achieving unity and identity. It had separate wards with their concomitant occupational specialization. Rivalry between wards or groups of wards was a common feature in the history of pre-twentieth century Kampong Ayer. Since all of them supported the sultan, their rivalry culminated into achieving glory for the sultan, and consequently for Brunei.

Increasing external pressure since the nineteenth century, however, undermined the economic fiber of Brunei, particularly Kampong Ayer. Occupational specialization slowly gave way to mere economic survival. Not only did the local market fail to patronize its industry, but the industry itself could not compete with foreign goods.

In fact, the introduction of the British Residency in 1906 marked the climax of the external pressure. Old formal networks were thus severely weakened, if not destroyed. The guarantee that Islam remained to be solely the domain of the sultan, of course, saved the religious bureaucracy from being replaced or even eliminated. But even here, reform was unavoidable.

As far as Islamic urbanism is concerned, the biggest change occurred when the plan to move the capital to a land-based settlement was announced in 1908. Despite the major change in the occupation of the inhabitants of Kampong Ayer and the shift of the capital, Kampong Ayer remained a lively suburb with a proud cultural heritage. It continued to be seen as a cradle and an embodiment of Brunei culture.

The new capital on land evidently rivaled the old settlement. Although during the British residency, the town had less Islamic characteristics, the sultans of the period who had full control over Islamic affairs were able to maintain some features of Islamic urbanism. For example, a *jāmi‘* mosque was founded in the heart of the town. Indeed, the farther the period went away from the initiation of the residency, the stronger Islamic urbanism were evident in the town. We have to bear in mind, however, that different and diverse factors also worked in the development of

Brunei town during the period. Thus Islamic urbanism in general no longer formed the ubiquitous and dominant factor, but was only an ingredient in modern urbanism in Brunei Town.

The stable and continuing bastion of Islamic urbanism in Brunei resided with the sultan. Thus, the wealth and the power of the ruler at times also were manifested in the materialization of the facets of Islamic urbanism in Brunei. The political will of the ruler was the primal determinant of Islamic urbanism in Brunei.

References

Abdul Latif Haji Ibrahim. 1971. "Variations and Changes in the Names and Locations of the Wards of Kampong Ayer over the Last Century." *Brunei Museum Journal*, 2,3:56-73.

Abu-Lughod, J. 1989. "What is Islamic about A City? Some Comparative Reflections." In *Proceedings of International Conference on Urbanism in Islam, October 22-28, 1989.* Tokyo: The Middle Eastern Culture Center.

Baring-Gould, S and C.A. Blampfylde. 1909. *A History of Sarawak under Its Two White Rajahs 1839-1908.* London: Henry Sotheran.

Blair, Emma H. and James A. Robertson, eds. 1903-1909. *The Philippine Islands, 1493-1803.* Vols.4 and 33. Cleveland: A.H. Clark Company.

Brown, D.E. 1970. *Brunei: The Structure and History of A Bornean Malay Sultanate.* Brunei: Brunei Museum Monograph No.2.

Chi, S.C, M.C. Cleary, T.S. Kam. 1991. "Kampong Ayer Report: 1." Bandar Seri Begawan: University of Brunei Darussalam, Faculty of Arts and Social Sciences, Working Paper No.6.

Cleary, M.C. and Peter Eaton. 1992. *Borneo: Change and Development.* Singapore: Oxford University Press.

Enggu Rangga. 1993. "Sejarah Pembentukan dan Perkembangan Bandar Brunei 1906-1959." Unpublished Thesis, University of Brunei Darussalam.

al-Faruqi, Isma'il, L.L. al-Faruqi. 1986. *The Cultural Atlas of Islam.* New York: Macmillan.

Forrest, Thomas. 1969. *A Voyage to New Guinea and the Moluccas 1774-1776.* Kuala Lumpur: Oxford University Press.

Franz, Johannes C. 1990. *The Sultanate of Brunei: Oil Wealth and Problems of Development.* Tr. M. Schmitz and A. Sharp. Bandar Seri Begawan:

University of Brunei Darussalam.

Goto, Akira. 1995. "Urbanism in Islam." In *Historical Studies in Japan (VIII) 1988-1992*. pp.223-234. Tokyo: Yamakawa Shuppansha.

Groeneveldt, W.P. 1960. "Notes on the Malay Archipelago and Malacca compiled from Chinese Sources." Reprint. Jakarta: Bhratara.

Horton, Anthony V.M. ed. 1987. *Report on Brunei in 1904 by M.S.H. McArthur*. Athens: Ohio University, Monograph in International Studies, Southeast Asia Series No.74.

Iik Arifin Mansurnoor. 1992. "Intellectual Tradition in A Malay State: *'Ulama'* and Education in Brunei Darussalam." *Jurnal Pendidikan* 3:34-60.

Kaloko, Franklyn R. 1995. The Evolution and Development of Kampong Ayer Water Settlements in Brunei Darussalam. Paper presented in *International Conference of Historical Geography*, July 3-7, 1995, Perth, Australia.

Kathirithamby-Wells, J. 1986. "The Islamic City: Melaka to Jogyakarta, c. 1500-1800." *Modern Asian Studies* 20:333-351.

Keppel, Henry. 1846/1991. *The Expedition to Borneo of HMS Dido*. Two Volumes. Singapore: Oxford University Press.

Lapidus, Ira. 1967. *Muslim Cities in the Later Middle Ages*. Cambridge, Mass: Harvard University Press.

______. 1989. "Muslim Cities as Plural Societies: The Politics of Intermediary Bodies." In *Proceedings of International Conference on Urbanism in Islam, October 22-28, 1989*. Tokyo: The Middle Eastern Culture Center.

Lambton, A.K.S. 1984. *State and Government in Medieval Islam*. Oxford: Oxford University Press.

Low, Hugh. 1848/1990. *Sarawak: Its Inhabitants and Productions*. Kuala Lumpur: Pustaka Delta.

Matassim Haji Jibah. 1980. "Shaer Awang Semaun." *Berita Muzium* 2.

Mundy, Rodney. 1848. *Narrative of Events in Borneo and Celebes down to the Occupation of Labuan*. Two vols. London: Murray.

Nicholl, Robert, ed. 1975. *European Sources for the History of the Sultanate of Brunei in the Sixteenth Century*. Bandar Seri Begawan: Brunei Museum, Special Issue Series No.9.

Pelita Brunei. 1956–. Official Publication, Brunei Government.

Reid, Anthony. 1988. *Southeast Asia in the Age of Commerce 1450-1680. The Land below the Winds*. Vol.1. New Haven: Yale University Press.

Saunders, Graham. 1994. *A History of Brunei*. Kuala Lumpur: Oxford University Press.

St. John, Spenser. 1962. *Life in the Forests of the Far East*. Two vols. Singapore:

Oxford University Press. Reprint.
Sweeney, P.L. Amin. 1968. "Silsilah Raja-Raja Berunai." *JMBRAS* 41,2:1-82.
Treacher, W.H. 1889. "British Borneo: Sketches of Brunai, Sarawak, Labuan and North Borneo. Part One." *JSBRAS* 20:13-74.

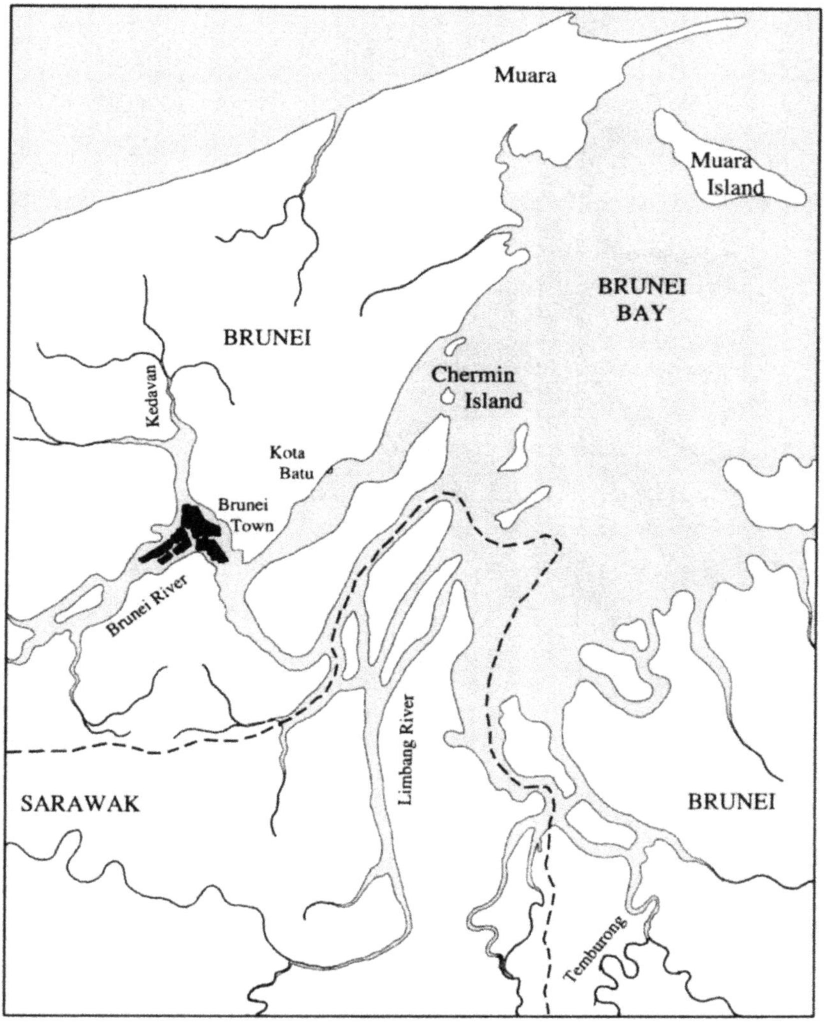

Brunei Bay Area
(Source: Donal E. Brown. 1970. *Brunei: The Structure and History of a Bornean Malay Sultanate*. Bandar Brunei: Brunei Museum.)

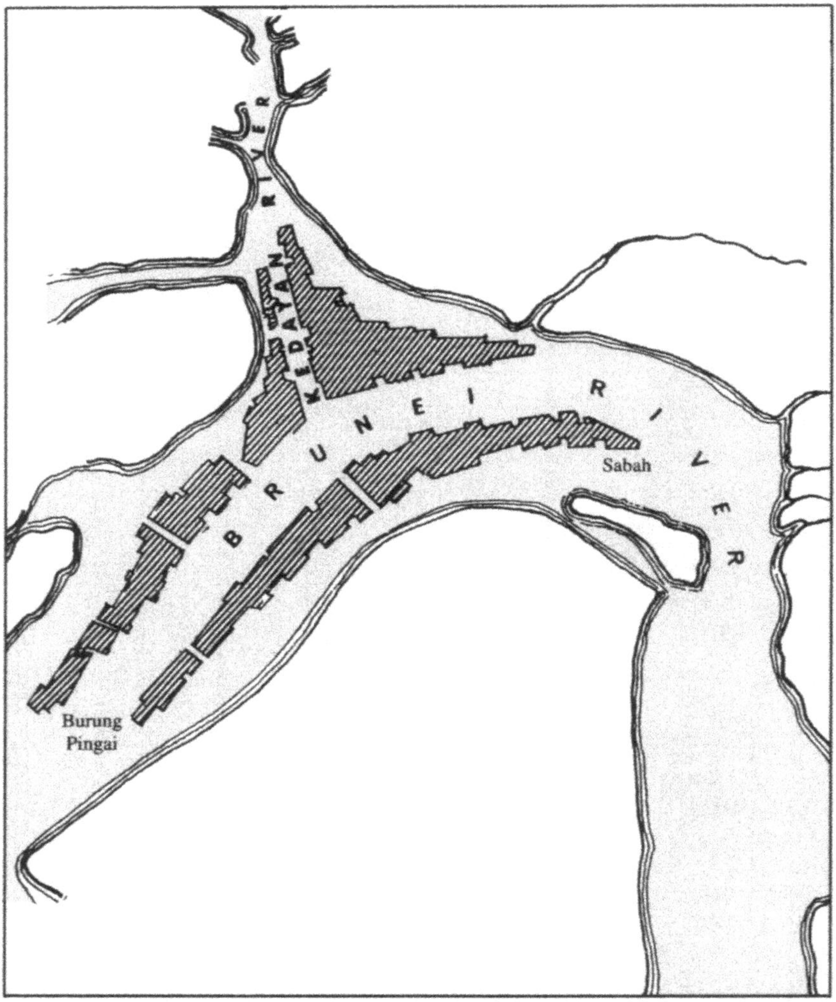

Bruney Town
Mid-Nineteenth Century
(Source: Donal E. Brown. 1970. *Brunei: The Structure and History of a Bornean Malay Sultanate*. Bandar Brunei: Brunei Museum.)

CHAPTER SEVEN

ELITES, NOTABLES AND SOCIAL NETWORKS OF EIGHTEENTH-CENTURY HAMA

James A. REILLY

Historians have associated the concept of "social networks" with that of "Islamic urbanism" to characterize the underlying structures of Middle Eastern towns in the pre-modern or pre-colonial period. Drawn principally from the work of Ira Lapidus, the "network model of Islamic society" consists of "an image of society as a network of relationships between component groups rather than an image of society as an architectural or hierarchical structure."[1] The urban population were divided into various groups defined by residence, occupation, or sect, and—according to the network model—they constantly re-negotiated their relationships with other groups through their *shaykh*s or group headmen.[2] Relationships between imperial rulers and urban populations also were subject to re-negotiation.[3] Though Lapidus's specific urban references were to the Mamluk period in Syria, he considers the network model to be relevant to the wider study of "Islamic society,"[4] including Islamic urbanism.

Leaving for later the question of whether "Islamic urbanism" (manifested in "Islamic cities") is a sound concept, this paper will test the compatibility of the network model against empirical

---

[1]Ira M. Lapidus, "Hierarchies and Networks: A Comparison of Chinese and Islamic Societies," in *Conflict and Control in Late Imperial China*, ed. Frederic Wakeman, Jr. and Carolyn Grant (Berkeley, 1975), 34-35.
[2]Ibid., 37-38.
[3]Ibid., 39.
[4]Ibid., 40-42.

data from one Middle Eastern town—Hama in Syria—in the late eighteenth century. Hama is located on the Orontes river in a fertile agricultural region; its "dependent countryside" included some 51 villages.[1] Hama's importance in the Ottoman period stemmed from its location along intra-Syrian trade routes and the annual pilgrimage route from Anatolia and Aleppo to the Hijaz. From 1724–1725 onward it was administered by a district governor (*mutasallim*) who was appointed by the provincial governor in Damascus.

The primary source for this inquiry is volume 46 of the Islamic law-court registers of Hama covering the years 1786 to 1800.[2] Hama's law-court registers offer a local, urban-based view of selected social, legal, and economic matters. They are to a certain extent normative, in the sense that their presentation and ordering of material is commensurate with the interests, perspectives, and prejudices of the local Ottoman administration and its religio-judicial functionaries. However, the registers also reflect aspects of local society that are not always evident in material generated by and for the central government in Istanbul.[3]

---

[1]'Abd al-Wadūd Muḥammad Yūsuf, "Ta'rīkh Ḥamāh fī al-qarn al-thāmin 'ashar," mimeo, n.d., 48-49. "Dependent countryside" is a phrase borrowed from Abdul-Karim Rafeq, and indicates those villages that fell within the purview of urban-based administrators and judicial officials; see his "Economic Relations between Damascus and the Dependent Countryside, 1743–71," in *The Islamic Middle East, 700–1900: Studies in Economic and Social History,* ed. A. L. Udovitch (Princeton, 1981), 661.

[2]For a discussion of these registers see Vladimir Glasman, "Les documents du tribunal religieux de Hama: leur importance pour la connaissance de la vie quotidienne dans une petite ville de la Syrie centrale à l'époque ottomane," in *Les Villes dans l'Empire ottoman: activités et sociétés,* ed. Daniel Panzac (Paris, 1991), 17-39.

[3]On these points see Amy Singer, *Palestinian Peasants and Ottoman Officials: Rural Administration around Sixteenth-Century Jerusalem* (Cambridge [UK], 1994), 20-21; and Khālid Ziyāda, *Al-Ṣūrat al-taqlīdiyya li-al-mujtama' al-*

This paper identifies the social networks that are evident from the judicial records, and then ask questions of these networks' boundaries and interrelationships.

Families, Notables, and Elites

The family was the fundamental social group in Hama as elsewhere, and it is unnecessary to belabor this point except to point out that the workings of Islamic inheritance laws produced a proliferation of jointly owned family properties: houses, shops and workshops, and farms. Apart from the kinship ties that offered nurture and shelter, families were bound together by property relationships.[1] A group of kin might act as one party in a business relationship[2]; and merchants and tradespeople raised money in part from their spouses and relations.[3] On occasion a husband bought property for his wife, ensuring her ownership of a larger proportion of the property than she would otherwise receive

---

madanī: Qirā'at manhajiyya fī sijillāt maḥkamat Ṭarābulus al-shar'iyya fī al-qarn al-sābi' 'ashar wa-bidāyat al-qarn al-thāmin 'ashar (Tripoli [Lebanon], 1983), 28, 33.

[1]E.g., the disposition of properties belonging to a prosperous farmer, and divided among or jointly owned by his surviving wives and adult and minor children. Law Court Registers of Hama (LCR Hama) vol. 46, pp.205a-207a, documents 467, 494, 495, 10 Rajab 1209/ 31 Jan. 1795.

[2]E.g., LCR Hama 46:208, doc. 458 [pt. 2], end of Dhū al-Qa'da 1211/ 27 May 1797.

[3]E.g., the thread seller 'Alī b. Ma'rūf; the wool dealer 'Abd al-Raḥmān al-Ṣawwāf; the soap, henna and livestock merchant Aḥmad b. Yūsuf 'Uwayda; and the cloth merchant and property owner Ṣāliḥ b. Aḥmad al-'Alwānī. LCR Hama 46:148, 191, 216, 379-380, docs. 306, 426 [pt. 1], 483, 676, 681, 8 Ṣafar 1208/ 15 Sept. 1793, 13 Jumādā I 1208/ 17 Dec. 1793; 17 Shawwāl 1209/ 7 May 1795, 4 Sha'bān 1214/ 2 Jan. 1800.

through inheritance from him.[1] Though property relationships could express mutual support among kin, they also were a source of conflict among heirs.[2] Ironically, however, such disputes underscore the intensity of family relationships and the importance of the family as a fundamental social unit. Wealthy individuals often kept their property intact for designated descendants by putting it into pious trusts (*waqf*s). *Waqf*s helped to preserve the integrity of property held by families at the apex of local society, such as the ʻAlwānī and Kaylānī.

The ʻAlwānī and Kaylānī were "notables" of Hama in the sense used by Julia Clancy-Smith. Writing about Ottoman Algeria, Clancy-Smith has drawn a useful distinction between "elites" and "notables." In her formulation, elites

> drew some, although not all, of their political authority from relationships with the state—either contesting it, or supporting it—or both . . . Religious notables on the other hand, tapped deep into other sources—sharifian descent, special piety, erudition, charity—the attributes demanded of the holy person.[3]

Namely, elites' authority was mainly political and administrative in origin, whilst notables' authority was social and moral. The ʻAlwānī and Kaylānī were sharifian families of long standing in Hama. They held religio-judicial posts, including jurisconsult,[4]

---

[1]E.g., ʻAbd al-Wāḥid b. ʻAbd al-Raḥmān al-Kaylānī's purchase of two shops for his wife Fāṭima. LCR Hama 46:174, doc. 368, 8 Rabīʻ II 1208/ 13 Nov. 1793.

[2]E.g., LCR Hama 46:161, doc. 340 [pt. 2], 1 Jumādā II 1208/ 5 Dec. 1793.

[3]Julia A. Clancy-Smith, *Rebel and Saint: Muslim Notables, Populist Protest, Colonial Encounters (Algeria and Tunisia, 1800–1904)* (Berkeley, 1994), 369, n. 4.

[4]E.g., ʻAlī Efendi al-Kaylānī and his successor Aḥmad Efendi al-ʻAlwānī between 1187 and 1190 (1773–1774 and 1776–1777). Yūsuf, "Ta'rīkh Ḥamāh," 41.

deputy judge,[1] and *naqīb al-ashrāf*.[2] In addition 'Alwānī and Kaylānī were local heads of major Sufi orders, the Shādhiliyya and Qādiriyya respectively.[3] The properties of their family *waqf*s were extensive and not limited to Hama. For instance, the grandchildren of Shaykh 'Abd al-Qādir al-Kaylānī[4] derived income from properties that he had endowed as *waqf* in the villages of Damascus[5] as well as in Hama. Beneficiaries of 'Alwānī family *waqf*s drew incomes from endowed properties in Hama and Tripoli.[6]

The leading "elite" family (as defined by Clancy-Smith) were the 'Aẓms, whose earliest traceable ancestor, Ibrāhīm Bey, was an Ottoman soldier in the region of Ma'arrat al-Nu'mān in the 17th century.[7] After serving as *mutasallim* of Homs, Hama and Ma'arra for seven years, Ibrāhīm's son Ismā'īl Bey al-'Aẓm was promoted to *pasha* and became governor of Damascus in

---

[1]E.g., Ibrāhīm al-Kaylānī in 1799. LCR Hama 46:316, doc. 602, 23 Ṣafar 1214/ 27 July 1799.

[2]E.g., the *naqīb*s 'Abd al-Razzāq Efendi b. Ismā'īl Efendi al-Kaylānī *naqīb* in the early 1790s; and one of his predecessors Muṣṭafā b. Ibrāhīm al-'Alwānī (d. 1779-80). LCR Hama 46:173-174, doc. 364, *awāsiṭ* Rabī' I 1207/ 31 Oct. 1792; Aḥmad al-Ṣābūnī, *Ta'rīkh Ḥamāh* (Hama, 1956), 167.

[3]Ibn Maḥāsin, *Al-Manāzil al-Maḥāsiniyya fī al-Riḥlat al-Ṭarābulusiyya*, ed. Muḥammad 'Adnān al-Bakhīt (Beirut, 1981), 63, n. 2 [note by 'Adnān al-Bakhīt]; LCR Hama 46:140, doc. 286, 15 Dhū al-Qa'da 1207/ 24 June 1793; al-Ṣābūnī, *Ta'rīkh Ḥamāh*, 173-174.

[4]A well-traveled man who was born in Baghdad and spent the last years of his life in Damascus, 'Abd al-Qādir was extremely wealthy though not universally admired. See Muḥammad Khalīl al-Murādī, *Silk al-durar fī a'yān al-qarn al-thānī 'ashar* (Baghdad, 1874), 3:46-48.

[5]LCR Hama 46:257, doc. 544, 25 Dhū al-Qa'da 1211/ 22 May 1797.

[6]LCR Hama 46:381, doc. 682, 6 Sha'bān 1214/ 4 Jan. 1800.

[7]'Abdul-Karim Rafeq, *The Province of Damascus 1723–1783* (Beirut, 1966), 86-92.

1725.[1] Members of the 'Aẓm family were among the wealthiest of all whose fortunes were recorded in vol. 46 of the Hama court registers. For instance, when Fāris Bey al-'Aẓm of Hama died in 1794, he left to his heirs a range of residential, commercial and agricultural properties in Hama, Homs, Tripoli, Jabla and Latakia with a net worth of 7000 piasters.[2] The 'Aẓms had reached the apex of locally rooted elite power in the eighteenth century, and their status endured into the twentieth century. Other elite and notable families of lesser stature included, respectively, the Ḥatāḥit family of military commanders and tax collectors and the Bārūdī and Shārabī families of *shaykhs* and quarter notables.[3]

Consistent with Lapidus's network model, elite and notable families in Hama were identified with particular urban quarters. The Kaylānī, for instance, were associated with al-Ḥāḍir, on the right bank of the Orontes River,[4] whilst the 'Alwānīs were associated with the older 'Alaylāt quarter on the left bank.[5] Fāris Bey al-'Aẓm's palatial mansion was in al-Bārūdiyya quarter,[6] while the Sharābī family of lesser notables were based in al-Ṣafṣāfa quarter.[7] Greater and lesser notable families—i.e., the Kaylānī, 'Alwānī, and Sharābī—owed their geographic bases to religious

---

[1]Ibid., 94; see also Munīr al-Khūrī 'Īsā As'ad, *Ta'rīkh Ḥimṣ,* 2 vols. (Homs, 1984), 2:342-344.

[2]LCR Hama 46:207-208, doc. 457-458, *awāsiṭ* Dhū al-Ḥijja 1208/ July 1794.

[3]LCR Hama 46:126, docs. 260-263, 1 Jumādā II 1206/ 26 Jan. 1792; 46:148, doc. 295, n.d. Muḥarram 1208/ Aug.–Sept. 1793; 46:192, doc. 430, 6 Sha'bān 1208/ 9 March 1794; 46:263, doc. 553, 26 Rabī' I 1213/ 7 Sept. 1798.

[4]LCR Hama 46:253-254, doc. 542, 25 Dhū al-Qa'da 1211/ 22 May 1797.

[5]LCR Hama 46:379-380, doc. 676, 4 Sha'bān 1214/ 2 Jan. 1800.

[6]LCR Hama 46:207-208, docs. 457-458 [pt. 1], *awāsiṭ* Dhū al-Ḥijja 1208/ 13-14 July 1794.

[7]LCR Hama 46:178, doc. 378, 17 Jumādā I 1208/ 21 Dec. 1793; 46:190, doc. 426, 26 Rajab 1208/ 27 Feb. 1794.

edifices supported by their family *waqf*s.[1] The Kaylānīs' imprint on one district of al-Ḥāḍir was such that by the twentieth century the district was known as al-Kaylāniyya.[2]

Urban Neighborhoods

Another type of social network in eighteenth-century Hama was based on the urban quarter (*maḥalla*). A fiscal document of 1800 lists 21 quarters of Hama and their tax assessments.[3] Headmen (*shaykh*s) answered to the authorities on behalf of their quarters.[4] But the quarter was a complex social organism, and within it were other foci of identification and representation as well. For instance, administration of the quarters was vested in local residents identified as "*ahl al-maḥalla*," "the people of the quarter." When someone bought a residential property in Hama, the sales deed frequently specified that a fixed ground-rent (*ḥikr*) should be paid to "*ahl al-maḥalla*,"[5] or alternatively to a *waqf*.[6] In one case[7] the *ḥikr* was owed to an individual (Shaykh 'Abd al-Qādir al-Sharābī) apparently in his capacity as administrator

[1] al-Ṣābūnī, *Ta'rīkh Ḥamāh,* 109-111; LCR Hama 46:148, doc. 295, n.d. Muḥarram 1208/ Aug.–Sept. 1793; 46:253-254, doc. 542, 25 Dhū al-Qa'da 1211/ 22 May 1797.

[2] *Ḥamāh: Ma'sāt al-'Aṣr* ([Lebanon], 1983), 50. This book was published by "a group of researchers in the information office of the Muslim Brotherhood." The longevity of the Kaylānī family's association with the Kaylāniyya district is poignantly illustrated by a list of its "martyrs" who fell during the anti-government uprising of 1982. The overwhelming majority of those named are Kaylānīs. Ibid., 346-348.

[3] LCR Hama 46:376, doc. 672, *awāsiṭ* Ramaḍān 1214/ 10 Feb. 1800.

[4] LCR Hama 46:57, doc. 138, 3 Jumādā II 1202/ 11 March 1788.

[5] E.g., LCR Hama 46:179, doc. 379, 17 Jumādā I 1208/ 21 Dec. 1793.

[6] E.g., LCR Hama 46:184, doc. 405, 5 Jumādā II 1208/ 8 Jan. 1794.

[7] LCR Hama 46:178, doc. 378, 17 Jumādā I 1208/ 21 Dec. 1793.

of his great-grandfather's *waqf*.[1] At other times *ḥikr* was negotiated between home-owners and the "elders" (*ikhtiyāriyya*) of a quarter.[2] The "*ahl al-maḥalla*" and "*ikhtiyāriyyat al-maḥalla*" shared fiscal and administrative functions with the quarter *shaykh*s. Sometimes they were linked to the major *waqf* of the quarter, underscoring the connection between notable families, their *waqf*s and their exercise of local leadership.

As if to make matters more interesting, the law-court registers refer to yet another type of urban leadership or representation: "spokesmen" (*mutakallimīn*) for the population.[3] Because the *mutakallimīn* are referred to in the same breath as "*shaykh*s of the quarters," the *shaykh*s and *mutakallimīn* would appear to have been different people. Therefore various levels of representation and identification were at work in the sphere of urban geography. *Maḥalla*s themselves were referred to by different names in different circumstances. One glaring example is al-Ḥāḍir, a well-known and oft-cited place-name. Typically the documents refer to it as "Maḥallat al-Ḥāḍir,"[4] but sometimes by the name of a sub-section such as "Maḥallat qaṣabat al-Ḥāḍir"[5] or "Maḥallat al-'Āqiba bi-al-Ḥāḍir."[6] Moreover, despite its frequent occurrence in judicial documents, the name al-Ḥāḍir does not appear in the fiscal list of Hama's *maḥalla*s referred to above. To complicate matters further, certain neighborhoods were recognized or known by more than one name, especially when they were connected to ethnic or confessional identities. For

---

[1]LCR Hama 46:192, doc. 430, 6 Sha'bān 1208/ 9 March 1794.
[2]LCR Hama 46:186, doc. 413, 5 Rajab 1208/ 6 Feb. 1794; 46:187, doc. 417 [pt. 1], 17 Jumādā I 1208/ 21 Dec. 1793.
[3]LCR Hama 46:57, doc. 138, 3 Jumādā II 1202/ 11 March 1788.
[4]E.g., LCR Hama 46:253-254, doc. 542, 25 Dhū al-Qa'da 1211/ 22 May 1797.
[5]LCR Hama 46:151, doc. 314, 29 Ṣafar 1208/ 6 Oct. 1793.
[6]LCR Hama 46:178, doc. 375, 20 Jumādā II 1208/ 23 Jan. 1794.

instance, the fiscal list of Hama *maḥalla*s makes no mention of the "districts" (sing. *ḥāra*) of Christians or Sakhkhāna Bedouins, yet both of them are mentioned in other contexts. The "Christian district" (Ḥārat al-Naṣārā) was a part of Ḥārat or Maḥallat al-Madīna, which adjoined the Great Mosque.[1] The Sakhkhāna quarter was named after Bedouins from the oasis settlement of al-Sukhna, who were specialized in the caravan trade and in the provisioning of the annual pilgrimage caravan at the local government's behest.[2]

The above discussion demonstrates that neighborhood-based social networks operated at different levels simultaneously: those of *maḥalla*, of *ḥāra*, of ethnicity. *Shaykh*s and elders had overlapping spheres of authority, and at this historical distance from the eighteenth century one cannot be certain about the respective roles of *shaykh*s, *mutakallimīn*, *ahl al-maḥalla* and local notables in the unfolding of urban political life.

Social Mosaic, Social Tapestry

The Christian and Sakhkhāna districts highlight religion and ethnicity as additional elements of Hama's social networks. These identities mattered according to circumstance; fiscal records designate Christians as a distinct group subject to special taxation, and Turcomans and Bedouin Arabs as tribal and ethnic collectivities with which officials dealt.[3] The Turcomans and Arabs

---

[1]For Ḥārat al-Naṣārā see, e.g., LCR Hama 46:187, doc. 418, 20 Rajab 1208/ 21 Feb. 1794. For the identification of Ḥārat al-Naṣārā with Ḥārat al-Madīna see 46:183, doc. 400, 15 Jumādā II 1208/ 18 Jan. 1794. For a reference to Maḥallat al-Madīna see 46:113, doc. 233, 1 Muḥarram 1206/ 31 Aug. 1791. On the location of the Great Mosque see al-Ṣābūnī, *Ta'rīkh Ḥamāh,* 103.

[2]Yūsuf, *Ta'rīkh Ḥamāh*, 62.

[3]The exact reference to Christians in the fiscal document is *jamā'at al-*

were further subdivided into lineage groups, such as the Būzliyya Turcomans and Mawālī Arabs.[1] Here, if anywhere, Hama and its hinterland would seem to conform to Lapidus's description of Syria as an "incredible mosaic." But the mosaic metaphor has its drawbacks.

Although network theory offers valuable insights into the social organization of pre-modern Middle Eastern life, Lapidus implies that the various networks were discrete and to a large extent mutually exclusive, whose members formed wider inter-relationships on an unstable and opportunistic basis through the mediation of *shaykhs* and headmen. But this perspective understates the overlapping and interwoven characteristics of social networks. Indeed, they more resemble a complex tapestry than a mosaic.[2] The confessionally mixed networks formed by craft corporations[3] and some urban neighborhoods[4] are cases in

---

dhimmiyyīn, "the group of *dhimmīs*," which hypothetically could have included Jews as well as Christians. But there is no evidence of a settled Jewish community in Hama during this period. LCR Hama 46:376, doc. 672, *awāsiṭ* Ramaḍān 1214/ 10 Feb. 1800. The phrase for Bedouins is *'ashāyir* [sic] *al-'Arab*, "Arab tribes," and for Turcomans is *al-Turkumān al-iskān* ("settled Turcomans"?).

[1]LCR Hama 46:105, doc. 206, 1 Rajab 1205/ 6 March 1791; 46:113, doc. 234, 22 Muḥarram 1206/ 21 Sept. 1791.

[2]In recent years Lapidus has characterized social networks in a way that I find congenial, viz.: "Invisible lines of reciprocal obligation ran through the whole of Muslim society, bonding disparate people and families together." See his "Muslim Cities as Plural Societies: The Politics of Intermediary Bodies," in *Urbanism in Islam: The Proceedings of the International Conference on Urbanism in Islam,* vol. 1 (Tokyo, 1989), 144.

[3]E.g., the corporations (sing. *ṭā'ifa*) of merchants, apothecaries, and copper workers. LCR Hama 46:243, doc. 569, 8 Rajab 1211/ 7 Jan. 1797.

[4]E.g., the Muslim Shaykh Ibrāhīm Efendi who lived in Ḥārat al-Naṣārā; and the Christian *ikhtiyāriyya* of al-'Āqiba quarter who reached an agreement on *ḥikr* with two Muslim home-owners. LCR Hama 46:174, doc. 366, 8 Rabī' II 1208/ 13 Nov. 1793; 46:186, doc. 413, 5 Rajab 1208/ 6 Feb. 1794.

point, as are the unmediated commercial dealings between individual townspeople and Bedouins.[1] The tapestry metaphor serves as a reminder that Hamawis, like other people, had a multiplicity of identities. They belonged to clusters of networks that placed demands on their loyalties and behavior depending on particular pressures and circumstances. Partha Chatterjee's discussion of the pre-colonial Bengali *jātī* (caste, community, nation) is relevant here:

> One could, obviously and without any contradictions, belong to several jātī, not simultaneously but contextually, invoking in each context a collectivity in which membership is not a matter of self-interested individual choice or contractual agreement but an immediate inclusion, originally, as it is by birth. We should not be surprised therefore when political discourse permits the imagining of collective solidarities to slide from one particular form to another, each activated contextually but proclaiming each time a bond of kinship, a natural bond that unites all who share the same origin and who therefore must share the same destiny.[2]

Chatterjee's treatment of Bengal suggests an analogy with the Middle East: the "mosaic" conceptualization of "Islamic society" is linked to a modern, state-oriented world-view that is anachronistic to eighteenth-century Syria:

---

[1]E.g., Muḥammad al-Ḥamad, "the Bedouin from the Iskandar Arabs," who was a creditor to two beys and to an 'Alwānī; the urbanite 'Izz al-Dīn b. al-Hājj A'rābī who was a creditor to a Banī Khālid Bedouin; the wool dealer 'Abd al-Raḥmān al-Ṣawwāf who was a creditor to one Muḥammad the Bedouin; and the existence of a partnership between a Bedouin and a man apparently linked to Hama's dye trade. LCR Hama 46:154, doc. 321, 14 Rabī' I 1208/ 20 Oct. 1793; 46:165, doc. 348, 18 Jumādā I 1208/ 22 Dec. 1793; 46:191, doc. 426 [pt. 1], 13 Jumādā I 1208/ 17 Dec. 1793; 46:445-446, doc. 533 [pt. 1], 27 Rajab 1211/ 26 Jan. 1797.

[2]Partha Chatterjee, *The Nation and its Fragments: Colonial and Postcolonial Histories* (Princeton, 1993), 221-222.

> . . . [A] fundamental change effected in the discursive domain of modern politics in the colonial period was the impoverishment of the earlier "fuzzy" sense of the community and an insistence upon the identification of community in the "enumerable" sense. Earlier, communities were fuzzy, in the sense that, first, a community did not claim to represent or exhaust all the layers of selfhood of its members, and second, the community, though definable with precision for all practical purposes of social interaction, did not require its members to ask how many of them there were in the world. The colonial regime, once firmly in place in the second half of the nineteenth century, sought to fashion the conceptual instruments of its control over an alien population precisely by enumerating the diverse communities that, in the colonial imagination, constituted the society over which it had been destined by History to rule.[1]

The assumption that eighteenth-century Hama was a society of interwoven social networks whose boundaries could be overlapping and "fuzzy" raises questions about social networks and politics. How did Hamawis define and understand their interests? What forms did political relationships take, and how were they tied to the social tapestry? Such questions bring the discussion back to Clancy-Smith's concept of "elites" and "notables," the leaders of local society who were recognized and dealt with as such by Ottoman authorities. How were elites and notables linked to Hama's various social networks, and vice-versa? The judicial records offer some clues in terms of material and property relationships, and it is to these issues that the discussion now turns.

Elites, Notables, and Social Networks

In Hama and its dependent countryside, elites were of two general

[1]Ibid., 223.

types: those whose authority was derived from the state almost exclusively, and those whose clan, kinship or tribal connections gave them some leverage *vis-à-vis* the state. For the latter, temporary loss of state patronage did not mean the end of their social authority. State-dependent elites included the frequently rotated *mutasallims* or district governors appointed to Hama by the *pasha* of Damascus. Few *mutasallims* enjoyed long tenures,[1] and some were dismissed in disgrace amidst accusations of administrative or legal transgressions.[2] These included forced loans, intimidation, and arbitrary taxation,[3] all behaviors endemic to the provincial administration of the day.[4] Although governors of Damascus denounced these practices,[5] their reproaches were directed against subordinates who had fallen out of favor for other reasons. As if to illustrate this point, the position of Hama's *mutasallim* was occasionally filled on a revolving-door basis: a *mutasallim* who had been denounced for his transgressions and dismissed would nevertheless be reappointed to office after only a short interval.[6]

---

[1]Yūsuf, *Ta'rīkh Ḥamāh,* 22-23.

[2]E.g., 'Abdallāh Āghā, dismissed in 1793. LCR Hama 46:138-139, doc. 283, 23 Shawwāl 1207/ 3 June 1793.

[3]LCR Hama 46:74-77, doc. 170, 15 Rabī' I 1203/ 14 Dec. 1788; 46:210, doc. 459 (pt. 2), 29 Dhū al-Ḥijja 1209/ 17 July 1795; 46:259, doc. 546, 13 Sha'bān 1213/ 20 Jan. 1799.

[4]James A. Reilly, "Ottoman Authority and Local Society in Late Eighteenth-Century Hama," *Proceedings of the VIth International Symposium of Ottoman Studies* (Tunis, in press).

[5]E.g., LCR Hama 46:74-77, doc. 170, 15 Rabī' I 1203/ 14 Dec. 1788; 46:259, doc. 546, 13 Sha'bān 1213/ 20 Jan. 1799.

[6]E.g., Wafā Āghā, replaced by 'Abdallāh Āghā, followed again by Wafā Āghā, replaced again by 'Abdallāh Āghā, all in the course of 15 months! LCR Hama 46:131-132, docs. 272-273, 24 Muḥarram 1207/ 11 Sept. 1792; 46:138-139, doc. 283, 23 Shawwāl 1207/ 3 June 1793; 46:168, doc. 355, 14 Jumādā I 1208/ 18 Dec. 1793.

Craft corporations were the most extensive type of urban social network with which elites in Hama were linked. The corporations were fiscal and regulatory units which, *inter alia*, served the elite[1] who simultaneously patronized the corporations through their purchases of goods and services. The largest single patron of the craft corporations was the *mutasallim*'s headquarters, the serail.[2] On occasion *mutasallims* mustered the craft corporations for marches and celebrations, such as the one marking the victory of Ottoman governor al-Jazzār over Napoleon Bonaparte at Acre in 1799.[3]

Elites also were patrons and associates of merchants and traders. In part this relationship grew out of elites' (particularly *mutasallims*') official responsibilities, notably overseeing and protecting the annual pilgrimage caravan to and from Mecca when it passed through Hama district.[4] The caravan had considerable commercial significance,[5] and supplying its needs enmeshed elites in the camel trade.[6] Hama's *mutasallims* were also involved in the silk trade between Tripoli and Hama, and helped to recover looted merchandise such as silks that Bedouins looted from a caravan traveling between Hama and Aleppo.[7]

---

[1]See, e.g., the organization of the butchers' tax farm in LCR Hama 46:237, doc. 519, n.d. Sha'bān 1210/ Feb.–Mar. 1796. Taxes owed by the corporations generally were collected by the *muḥtasib*. Yūsuf, *Ta'rīkh Ḥamāh*, 27.

[2]See, e.g., LCR Hama 46:52, doc. 123, 8 Muḥarram 1202/ 20 Oct. 1787; 46:177, doc. 373, n.d. Rajab 1208/ Feb.–Mar. 1794; 46:243, doc. 569, 8 Rajab 1211/ 7 Jan. 1797.

[3]LCR Hama 46:276, doc. 567, n.d. 1213/ 1799.

[4]LCR Hama 46:79-80, doc. 173, 5 Jumādā II 1203/ 3 March 1789.

[5]Yūsuf, *Ta'rīkh Ḥamāh*, 62-63; Abdul-Karim Rafeq, "Maẓāhir iqtiṣādiyya wa-ijtimā'iyya min liwā' Ḥamāh 942–943/ 1535–1536," *Dirāsāt Ta'rīkhiyya* no. 31-32 (March–June 1989), 38.

[6]LCR Hama 46:247, doc. 535, 2 Ramaḍān 1211/ 1 March 1797.

[7]LCR Hama 46:117, doc. 241, 12 Ṣafar 1206/ 11 Oct. 1791; 46:118, doc. 244, 15 Ṣafar 1206/ 14 Oct. 1791.

Indeed, merchants' prosperity depended to a degree on the kind of relationship that they had with the *mutasallim* and the local elites,[1] who were associated with local as well as inter-regional trade. At one point the governor of Damascus owned a *qayṣariyya* (covered market or caravanserai[2]) at Jisr al-Qāḍī, a market that he had purchased from a local *āghā* (a title denoting military rank and status).[3] A member of the local administrative elite, A'rābī Āghā al-Ḥatāḥit, bought six shops in Sūq al-Manṣūriyya in 1792, and was promised ownership of any dwellings he might build in an adjoining vacant enclosure.[4] A'rābī Āghā's possession of shops had the potential to create a patronage relationship between him and any craft workers who might rent the shops from him. At the same time, shop possession made him responsible to the administrators of the Kaylānī *waqf* to which the land and shops ultimately belonged.

In addition to their patronage of and association with craft corporations, trade and commerce, elites also extended their influence into the countryside where they were tax collectors and enforcers of government authority. *Mutasallims* and *āghās* were responsible for provisioning troops and towns with grain,[5] and as such they acted as grain merchants.[6] Their associates in Hama's countryside included urban-based moneylenders (especially Christians), tax farmers and lower-ranking officials—*muqaddams*—who served as relays between the

---

[1]LCR Hama 46:259, doc. 546, 13 Sha'bān 1213/ 20 Jan. 1799.

[2]On *qaysariyya* see André Raymond, *Artisans et commerçants au Caire au XVIIIe siècle* (Damascus, 1973), 1:252-253.

[3]LCR Hama 46:96-97, doc. 196, 3 Rabī' I 1204/ 21 Nov. 1789.

[4]LCR Hama 46:126, docs. 260-263, 1 Jumādā II 1206/ 26 Jan. 1792.

[5]LCR Hama 46:56, doc. 136, 9 Jumādā II 1202/ 17 March 1788; 46:226, doc. 502, 11 Muḥarram 1210/ 28 July 1795; 46:360, doc. 652, 28 Ṣafar 1214/ 1 Aug. 1799.

[6]As'ad, *Ta'rīkh Ḥimṣ*, 2:342.

governor and *mutasallim*, on the one hand, and villagers and their *shaykh*s on the other.[1] Elites' fiscal privileges were sublet; in 1793, for instance, an *āghā* and a Christian moneylender sublet from Turcoman *ikhtiyāriyya* the latter's right to the taxes of certain Turcoman villages outside of Hama.[2] Elites' fiscal authority could resemble a *de facto* form of ownership, whereby a village was designated as being "dependent upon" (*tābi'a ilā*) a given *āghā*.[3] Individuals of the elite amassed considerable fortunes in agriculture through ownership of cultivation rights and speculative advance purchases of crops (*ḍamān*).[4] Some also owned significant herds of livestock, especially sheep.[5] Trade in livestock was particularly identified with elites of Kurdish or Turcoman origin.[6]

In addition to relying on military and administrative elites, the Ottomans also depended on local notables to solidify their rule. To the degree that notables, including those of the 'Alwānī and Kaylānī families, ameliorated the misdeeds of venal or unjust *mutasallim*s, they defended the interests of the community and added to their own professional and familial luster.[7] Unlike most of the military-administrative elite their authority was moral and did not depend exclusively on their appointment to posts. Highly regarded religious notables retained their moral authority even after dismissal or retirement from appointed positions, and some

---

[1]LCR Hama 46:160, doc. 339, 28 Rabī' II 1208/ 3 Dec. 1793.
[2]LCR Hama 46:155, doc. 325, 21 Rabī' I 1208/ 27 Oct. 1793.
[3]E.g., LCR Hama 46:144, doc. 292, 15 Muḥarram 1208/ 23 Aug. 1793.
[4]E.g., the receipts of Fāris Bey al-'Aẓm in LCR Hama 46:164, doc. 346, n.d. 1207–1208/ 1792–1794.
[5]E.g., LCR Hama 46:66-68, doc. 161, 19 Dhū al-Qa'da 1202/ 21 Aug. 1788.
[6]Rafeq, "Maẓāhir iqtiṣādiyya," 18; As'ad, *Ta'rīkh Ḥimṣ*, 2:332, 343.
[7]For analogous cases see Muḥammad al-Makkī, *Ta'rīkh Ḥimṣ*, ed. and introduced by 'Umar Najīb al-'Umar (Damascus, 1987), e.g., 20, 27-28, 52, 54, 60-61, 67.

enjoyed reputations that extended beyond their home towns.[1] They used their cultural capital and religio-judicial positions to amass and consolidate material affluence, undergirding their position as local notables and "natural" leaders of urban society. As Sufi *shaykh*s, jurisconsults, deputy judges and preachers, the leading lights of the Kaylānī and 'Alwānī families represented both popular religious devotion and the legal-scholarly vocation.

'Alwānīs, Kaylānīs, and lesser notables were administrators of charitable *waqf*s including mosques and hospices.[2] Administration of charitable *waqf*s gave notables supervisory powers over substantial commercial and some agricultural properties in Hama and its countryside.[3] In addition, the personal wealth of notables and their families also was significant. In 1791, for instance, two children and a grandson of the prominent *'ālim* al-Shaykh Isḥāq al-Kaylānī (d. 1185/1771-2)[4] endowed as a family *waqf* a coffee house which they owned in Maḥallat al-Madīna.[5] Another coffee house in al-'Alaylāt was owned (at least in part) by members of the 'Alwānī family.[6] Kaylānīs owned shops in Sūq al-Manṣūriyya and al-Ḥāḍir,[7] plus luxurious houses

---

[1]E.g., Muṣṭafā b. Ibrāhīm al-'Alwānī (d. 1779-80), who was born in Hama, studied in Damascus with the noted Shaykh 'Abd al-Ghanī al-Nābulsī, served as *naqīb al-ashrāf* of Hama, and after his dismissal from that post was in great demand as a teacher in Damascus. al-Ṣābūnī, *Ta'rīkh Ḥamāh*, 167.

[2]E.g., the mosque of al-Shaykh 'Alwān and of Bīmāristān al-Nūrī. LCR Hama 46:127-128, doc. 265, 13 Jumādā II 1206/ 7 Feb. 1792; al-Ṣābūnī, *Ta'rīkh Ḥamāh*, 113.

[3]al-Ṣābūnī, *Ta'rīkh Ḥamāh*, 108-109.

[4]Ibid., 166.

[5]LCR Hama 46:113, doc. 233, 1 Muḥarram 1206/ 31 Aug. 1791.

[6]LCR Hama 46:205a, doc. 466 [pt. 2], *awākhir* Jumādā II 1209/ 21 Jan. 1795.

[7]E.g., 'Abd al-Wāḥid b. 'Abd al-Raḥmān al-Kaylānī's purchase of four shops in al-Ḥāḍir for himself and his wife; and al-Shaykh 'Abd al-Razzāq b. al-Shaykh Ismā'īl al-Kaylānī's ownership of a carpenter's shop in Sūq al-Manṣūriyya in

in al-Ḥāḍir,[1] shops, gardens, the 'Ādiliyya coffee house, an artisanal workshop, water mills, a public bath, and residential compounds (*aḥwāsh*).[2] Individuals of notable status often had diverse property interests; Ṣāliḥ b. Aḥmad al-'Alwānī left an estate that included a large house; a bakery; half an orchard, half a shop, and two groves (sing. *karm*) in al-Ribāḥ village; and a share of the 'Alaylāt coffee house.[3] Aḥmad b. Ḥijāzī al-'Alwānī left houses and shares of an oven, a shop and the coffee house in al-'Alaylāt, and lands and orchards in al-Ribāḥ and Zawr al-Khamsa.[4] Notables also possessed mills; in 1792, for instance, the *muftī* and the *naqīb* of Hama (both Kaylānīs) jointly purchased a mill at Amnūn near Homs from villagers, local elites, and the *muftī* of Homs, all of whom owned shares.[5] In addition to owning mills (or possessing them via long-term *ḥikr* contracts), notables administered *waqf*s such as that of 'Abd al-Qādir al-Kaylānī whose properties included mills.[6]

Ultimately, the interests of elites and religious notables were intertwined. In some cases, such as the domain of the alimentary economy (food production and processing), elites and notables formed partnerships. For instance, the *muftī* Ibrāhīm al-Kaylānī and the "*āghā* of the *shaykhs*" (*āghāsi shaykhūn*) had a farming and livestock partnership in the village of Kafr 'Ayn for a period

---

1794. LCR Hama 46:174, docs. 367-368, 8 Rabī' II 1208/ 13 Nov. 1793; 46:186, doc. 412 [pt. 1], 4 Rajab 1208/ 5 Feb. 1794.

[1]LCR Hama 46:253-254, doc. 542, 25 Dhū al-Qa'da 1211/ 22 May 1797.

[2]LCR Hama 46:251-253, doc. 541, 13 Dhū al-Qa'da 1209/ 1 June 1795.

[3]LCR Hama 46:380, doc. 681, 4 Sha'bān 1214/ 2 Jan. 1800.

[4]LCR Hama 46:349-350, doc. 636, 21 Jumādā II 1213/ 5 Dec. 1798.

[5]LCR Hama 46:172, doc. 362, 10 Rabī' I 1267/ 26 Oct. 1792; 46:173, doc. 363, 10 Rabī' I 1207/ 26 Oct. 1792; 46:173-174, doc. 364, *awāsiṭ* Rabī' I 1207/ 31 Oct. 1792.

[6]LCR Hama 46:134-135, doc. 278, 22 Ṣafar 1207/ 9 Oct. 1792.

of time until 1793.[1]

In the absence of local chronicles, it is difficult to know how these various social networks interacted in eighteenth-century Hama. Unfortunately the picture that has been depicted here is static and does not portray the society in motion. Arguing from analogy with Hama's better known and better documented cousins (Damascus and Aleppo), one can hypothesize that clientage ties and factional politics were characteristic of the social order, with different groups of elites and notables jockeying for political and material advantage under the watchful eye of a less-than-omnipotent state. It would be helpful to know more about the revolt of 1788, during which Hamawis rose up against an unpopular *mutasallim* and caused the governor of Damascus to appeal to local notables for support and cooperation in helping to disarm the populace.[2] Linda Schilcher has shown for Damascus that such revolts offer glimpses into factional networks defined by geography, occupation, social status, and links to the urban and regional economy.[3] Unfortunately, the politics of eighteenth-century Hama remain something of a mystery at this point.

Conclusion: Social Networks and Islamic Urbanism

Nevertheless, the available Hama data are useful for considering the subject of social networks in Islamic urbanism. The concept of social networks—*de jure* and *de facto* groupings of people according to religion, ethnicity, occupation, and residence—reflects the way in which eighteenth-century Hama was organized.

[1]LCR Hama 46:152, doc. 316, 5 Rabīʻ I 1208/ 11 Oct. 1793.

[2]LCR Hama 46:57, doc. 138, 3 Jumādā II 1202/ 11 March 1788; Yūsuf, *Ta'rīkh Ḥamāh*, 33.

[3]Linda Schatkowski Schilcher, *Families in Politics: Damascene Factions and Estates in the 18th and 19th Centuries* (Stuttgart, 1985), 40-43.

However, the Hama case does not lend itself particularly well to an interpretation of social networks as discrete and mutually exclusive entities. Christians and a Muslims lived in the same neighborhoods and worked in the same crafts. Networks based on religion, quarter, and craft were sources of identity and set parameters of behavior and of action, but the predominance of one identification over another varied according to context. On this basis one should not automatically assume that political factionalism and ethnic-sectarian hostility were endemic or rampant in societies organized according to the social networks model.[1] To be sure, Lapidus's network model does not automatically assume that urban societies are fragmented to such a high degree, and he writes of the role of "notables" as intermediaries between the various networks. But while Lapidus implies that the networks are discrete, and their respective "notables" mediate the differences and conflicts of interest between and among them, the Hama evidence paints a different picture. Elites and notables had complex, parallel, and interlocking interests expressed via different social networks. In certain contexts a Kaylānī *shaykh*, for instance, might act as a Sufi leader, or as a judicial official, or a *waqf* administrator, or a quarter notable, or a landowner. His elite counterpart (an ʿAẓm, for instance) might be a power broker, a landowner, the representative of a given urban quarter, or a patron of the craft corporations, a partner of the Kaylānī in a mill, or all of these things concurrently. People of different social networks struck deals and made agreements between each other without recourse to intermediaries, e.g., urban traders and merchants with Bedouins. A complex and

---

[1]An example of this kind of assumption is the characterization of "traditional Damascene society" in Yūsuf Jamīl Nuʿaysa, *Mujtamaʿ madīnat Dimashq fī al-fatra mā bayn 1186–1256 hijrī 1772–1840 milādī*, 2 vols. (Damascus, 1986), 1:203, 264-265.

interwoven tapestry is a more evocative metaphor than a mosaic. Since tapestries are stretched and sometimes torn, the tapestry metaphor does not rule out the existence of factional struggles and conflicts. But it does suggest a greater degree of durability and flexibility than a mosaic, which shatters into small fragments if dropped from too great a height.

Finally, to what extent is this model rightly called "Islamic" urbanism? Many of the characteristics of pre-modern Middle Eastern towns that have been associated with "Islamic" society are characteristic of pre-industrial towns generally. These include the importance of family networks, the existence of distinct quarters, and the organization of craftworkers into corporate groups.[1] The "Islamic" character of eighteenth-century Hama is related to the special role played by local notables who were linked to religious law and institutions, which gave a distinct "Islamic" cast to urban high culture.[2] But it is important to distinguish between this cultural manifestation of "Islamic urbanism" and other aspects of pre-modern urbanism that depended on factors not determined or conditioned by religion, such as geography, climate, technology, and administration.[3] Social networks may be a phenomenon of Middle Eastern urbanism, but we should be cautious about identifying them with "Islamic" urbanism, a concept that simultaneously implies too much and says too little about a town like Hama.

---

[1]Gideon Sjoberg, *The Preindustrial City: Past and Present* (New York, 1960), 323-326.

[2]Cf. Lapidus, "Muslim Cities as Plural Societies," 134.

[3]Janet L. Abu-Lughod, "The Islamic City—Historic Myth, Islamic Essence, and Contemporary Relevance," *IJMES* 19 (1987), 155-176.

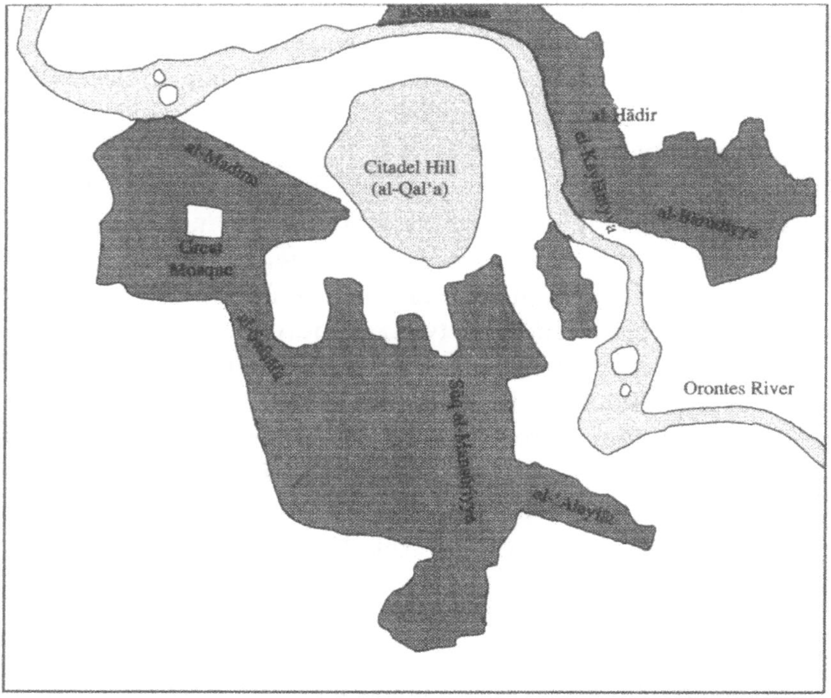

Ottoman Hama ca. 1840

INDEX

W

Y

Z

CONTRIBUTORS

SATO Tsugitaka, the volume author, is Professor of West Asian History at the University of Tokyo. He is the author of *State and Rural Society in Medieval Islam: Sultans, Muqta's and Fallahun*.

Abdul-Karim RAFEQ is Professor of History at Damascus University. He is the author of *The Province of Damascus 1723–1783*.

MIURA Toru is Associate Professor of History at Ochanomizu University. He is the co-editor of *Islamic Urban Studies: Historical Review and Perspectives*.

Diane SINGERMAN is Assistant Professor of Political Science at Department of Government, the American University. She is the author of *Avenues of Participation: Family, Politics, and Networks in Urban Quarters of Cairo*.

Mohamed MEZZINE is Professor of History at Facultè des Lettres & Sciences Humaines Sais, Université Sidi Mohamed Ben Abdellah. His published books include *Fās wa-Bādiyathā 1549–1637*.

HANEDA Masashi is Associate Professor of History at Institute of Oriental Culture, the University of Tokyo. He is the co-editor of *Islamic Urban Studies: Historical Review and Perspectives*.

Iik A. MANSURNOOR is Professor of History at Universiti Brunei Darssalam. His recent study concerns with the history of urban settlement in Brunei.

James A. REILLY is Associate Professor of Middle East and Islamic Studies at University of Toronto. His most recent article is “Prosperity, Status, and Class in Ottoman Damascus.”

www.ingramcontent.com/pod-product-compliance
Ingram Content Group UK Ltd.
Pitfield, Milton Keynes, MK11 3LW, UK
UKHW020355010325
455677UK00021B/468

9 780415 760140